Language and Education in Multilingual Settings

To the Hebrew teachers of the USSR and all others who struggle for the linguistic rights of minorities.

Multilingual Matters

Books available from College-Hill Press are marked ●

● Bilingualism: Basic Principles (second edition)
  HUGO BAETENS BEARDSMORE
Evaluating Bilingual Education: A Canadian Case Study
  MERRILL SWAIN AND SHARON LAPKIN
Bilingual Children: Guidance for the Family
  GEORGE SAUNDERS
Language Attitudes Among Arabic-French Bilinguals in Morocco
  ABDELÂLI BENTAHILA
Conflict and Language Planning in Quebec
  RICHARD Y. BOURHIS (ed.)
● Bilingualism and Special Education
  JIM CUMMINS
Bilingualism or Not: The Education of Minorities
  TOVE SKUTNABB-KANGAS
An Ethnographic/Sociolinguistic Approach to Language Proficiency Assessment
  CHARLENE RIVERA (ed.)
Communicative Competence Approaches to Language Proficiency Assessment: Research and Application
  CHARLENE RIVERA (ed.)
Language Proficiency and Academic Achievement
  CHARLENE RIVERA (ed.)
Pluralism: Cultural Maintenance and Evolution
  BRIAN BULLIVANT
Placement Procedures in Bilingual Education: Education and Policy Issues
  CHARLENE RIVERA (ed.)
● The Education of Linguistic and Cultural Minorities in the OECD Countries
  STACY CHURCHILL
Learner Language and Language Learning
  CLAUS FAERCH, KIRSTEN HAASTRUP AND ROBERT PHILLIPSON
Bilingual and Multicultural Education: Canadian Perspectives
  STAN SHAPSON AND VINCENT D'OYLEY (eds.)
Multiculturalism: The Changing Paradigm
  LOIS FOSTER AND DAVID STOCKLEY
● Language Acquisition of a Bilingual Child
  ALVINO FANTINI
● Modelling and Assessing Second Language Acquisition
  KENNETH HYLTENSTAM AND MANFRED PIENEMANN (eds.)
Aspects of Bilingualism in Wales
  COLIN BAKER
Minority Education and Ethnic Survival
  MICHAEL BYRAM
● Age in Second Language Acquisition
  BIRGIT HARLEY
● Language in a Black Community
  VIV EDWARDS
● Language and Education in Multilingual Settings
  BERNARD SPOLSKY (ed.)
Code-Mixing and Code Choice: A Hong Kong Case Study
  JOHN GIBBONS

Please contact us for the latest information on recent and forthcoming books in the series.
Derrick Sharp, General Editor, Multilingual Matters,
Bank House, 8a Hill Road, Clevedon, Avon BS21 7HH, England.

Language and Education in Multilingual Settings

Edited by
Bernard Spolsky

COLLEGE-HILL PRESS, San Diego, California

First published by
Multilingual Matters Ltd.
Bank House, 8a Hill Road,
Clevedon, Avon BS21 7HH
England.

as part of a series of books edited by
Derrick Sharp under the heading
Multilingual Matters. Full details of
the other books and related journals are
available from the address above.

Library of Congress Cataloging-in-Publication Data

Language and education in multilingual settings.
    Includes Index.
    1. Language and education.   2. Multilingualism.
    3. Language policy.   4. Language planning
    I. Spolsky, Bernard.

P40.8.L34   1986   401'.9   86–8319

ISBN 0–88744–286–2 Pbk

College-Hill Press Inc.,
4284 41st Street,
San Diego, CA 92105, U.S.A.

Copyright © 1986 B. Spolsky,
D. P. Pattanayak, M. Mikes, M. N. Guboglo,
B. McLaughlin, R. A. Benton, R. Phillipson,
T. Skutnabb-Kangas, H. Africa, J. J. Smolicz,
and C. Bratt Paulston.

Typeset by Wayside Books, Clevedon, Avon.
Printed and bound in Great Britain by
The Bath Press, Bath BA2 3BL.

Contents

Acknowledgements

Six of the papers in this volume — those by Benton, Guboglo, McLaughlin, Mikes, Phillipson and others, and Skutnabb-Kangas — were originally written for and presented at the Symposium organized by the AILA Scientific Commission on Language and Education in Multilingual Settings as part of the 1984 Applied Linguistics Congress held in Brussels.

The paper by M. N. Guboglo was translated from Russian by Dr. Stephanie Hoffman.

The paper by D. P. Pattanayak was specially written for this volume.

The paper by C. B. Paulston was written for a Conference on "Education and Cultural and Linguistics Pluralism" organized by the Centre for Educational Research and Innovation of the Organization for Economic Co-operation and Development, Paris, from 16th to 18th January, 1985, and is reprinted with permission.

The papers by Phillipson, Skutnabb-Kangas and Africa and by Skutnabb-Kangas appeared as working papers in ROLIG-papir 35, and the former is also to appear in *Linguistic liberation and unity of Africa*, edited by Kahombo Mateene and to be published by the OAU Bureau of Languages in English and French.

The paper by J. J. Smolicz is reprinted by permission from the *Southeast Journal of Social Science*, Vol. 12 (2) 1984.

The paper by Bernard Spolsky is a revised version of one written for a Symposium on Education to mark the 75th anniversary of the city of Tel Aviv.

1 Introduction

BERNARD SPOLSKY

The difference between languages that children learn in the home (their mother tongues) and the languages valued by society and established therefore as the medium of instruction at the various levels of schools is an almost universal problem in educational systems, although one that is often made worse because it is not always clearly recognized. Proposals for mother tongue education, for bilingual programmes of various kinds, or for more effective teaching of literary or standard languages all alike depend on an understanding of the underlying problem of language education in multilingual settings and represent various analyses of the best way to resolve it.

It is not the purpose of this volume to propose solutions but rather to explore some of the methods of recognizing and analysing the problem; only if this difficult first step of agreeing on the dimensions of the problem is carried out successfully can there be any chance of finding acceptable and workable solutions. The writers of this volume do not have a single view of the issues, for they are international in background and experience, and interdisciplinary in training and approach; moreover, as will be clear, they differ in political and philosophical beliefs, in scholarly rhetoric, in research paradigms and in personal circumstances. By inviting some of them to participate in its first Symposium, the AILA Scientific Commission on Language and Education in Multilingual Settings hoped to encourage a free exchange of ideas among scholars from different countries; by publishing in this volume some of the papers from the Symposium together with others selected to complement their coverage, we hope to widen the debate and work towards the development of a common effort at understanding. Researchers in the 1980s do not need to be reminded of the example of the blind scholars describing an elephant; only by making a real effort to understand our colleague's point of view can we hope to work together to a common understanding of a phenomenon.

Opening this collection and written especially for it, we have a clear and eloquent argument for the fundamental value of the mother tongue for all pupils by D. P. Pattanayak. Pattanayak goes beyond asserting that mother tongue education is a fundamental human right by setting out a number of pragmatic reasons for its usefulness and economic value.

In an interesting sketch based on her experience not just in a classically multilingual middle European country, but also in post-colonial Africa, Melanie Mikes first argues with those who would take a purely pragmatic view of the central problem and then suggests a simple but powerful model to investigate the congruence of language instruction policy to children's home situation and to social policy. Her model is less complex than others (cf. Mackey or Spolsky) but its simplicity suggests power and the opportunity to go beyond description to empirical testing.

The Soviet Union is a special case not only in the complexity of its linguistic situation but in the weight of authority that has been made available for centralized planning. Guboglo analyses the next stages in the continuing tension between the centrifugal trends towards Russian and the centripetal forces maintaining the National Languages, to use terms from Glyn Lewis's (1972) brilliant analysis. He makes clear that alongside the firm intention to maintain the strength of designated National Languages, the Russian language is now firmly established not just as a language of communication among the various nationalities but also as the language of the new culture; difficulties of implementation of course remain.

In keeping with the comparative approaches of the Symposium, McLaughlin argues for the need for Western scholars to be aware of work in the field in the Soviet Union. From Cummins and debates over initial instruction, he concludes that mother tongue instruction is necessary, but that it must be combined with second language learning in contact with speakers of the standard language. He compares the Natural and Communicative approaches to foreign language teaching currently fashionable in the West with Soviet theory, with its emphasis on conscious learning. His view of Soviet language policy is an interesting complement to Guboglo's, and his final point is a plea both for learning from Russian practice and for greater amounts of scholarly exchange.

To provide perspective on the similarities and differences between different parts of the world, the organizers of the Symposium planned some comparative papers. The chapter by Benton is such a comparative study, looking at issues of language revival as they affect the attempts to revive Irish as a national language and the more recent efforts in New Zealand to reverse the trend of Maori language loss. Both are often held to be no more than futile attempts to recapture a lost past; they show nevertheless the way in which claims for ethnolinguistic identity can transcend pragmatic concerns.

Africa is often cited as a special example of the problems of post-colonial language policy, and the paper by Phillipson, Skutnabb-Kangas and Africa analyses the implications of the adoption by the South West Africa People's Organization of English as official language for Namibia once it is independent. Before looking at the Namibian case, they sketch a model of bilingual programmes and consider their relative success in various cases. They then apply these principles to argue that the decision to use English as the official language must be balanced by a policy of extensive use of mother tongues.

If a language expresses its culture, is it possible for a new nation to give up on the "one nation, one language" policy without risking disunity? Looking in particular at the case of the Philippines, Smolicz argues that attempts to impose one language on all groups is destructive and divisive; that the adoption of a lingua franca or official language need not involve rejection of other minority languages. He argues then for pluralism.

Language policy is a field where theory and practice are often in close even if not necessarily happy connection. In a chapter written for the OECD, Paulston first sets studies of language choice and language planning against their theoretical background, and then shows the relation between language shift and bilingualism. She considers the influence of religion and the importance of ethnicity and nationalism. From this perspective, she argues for the need to base language policy decisions on the best possible under-standing of the social and economic context. Her chapter is another import-ant contribution to the theory of the field.

One of the principal aims of the Symposium, and one of the obvious tasks of the Scientific Commission, is not just to report research but to consider the basis on which research is done. The chapter by Skuttnab-Kangas is an (admittedly not disinterested) attempt to look at the conflicting views not just of opponents and supporters of mother tongue maintenance programmes but also of those who do research in the area; the debates between politicians and educators are reflected in and supported by the debates between scholars. The chapter tries to show the nature of the resulting biases; it will encourage, we may hope, a process of what Haj Ross has labelled "elephanting" — a genuine attempt by any scholar to try first to understand what part of the elephant (or other object of study) his potential opponent is describing.

In the closing chapter, written originally for a meeting on the educa-tional problems of the city in the modern world, I attempt to sketch a sociolinguist's analysis of an educational problem: while recognizing that the underlying issues are not just linguistic nor even just educational, but are at the heart of the definition of the values of a society, I try to show how sociological pressures have sociolinguistic consequences that produce special problems for linguistic minorities, and to conclude with my own draft of a statement of linguistic rights that I believe to be basic to language education policy in multilingual settings.

2 Educational use of the mother tongue

D. P. PATTANAYAK

Language has been the object of intense passions, prejudice and patronage, but seldom has it been a concern for those working in the area of development planning. And yet as a factor providing or withholding access to education and therefore to human resource development, as a key to knowledge, information and communication, as an indicator of appropriateness of technology, as a major element in elite formation and alienation, as a barrier to or equalizer of social, political and economic opportunities, language plays a central role in the modernization and development of the country.

The so-called neutral mediation of colonial languages in Third World education as a substitute for many mother tongues has created a chasm between the elite and the masses. It has resulted in stunted cognitive growth and lack of creativity and innovativeness in children and the atrophy of indigenous cultures. As the medium of education such languages do not only impede the growth of indigenous languages but they also inhibit the interaction of science with society, generate inappropriate technology and create an educated elite committed to pursuing the life style of the developed world.

The education system in any country of the First World is a public response to private demands and aspirations. In the Second World, education is controlled by a public policy for the mobilization of human resources that aims to achieve an even higher First World life style within a strictly monitored political system. When such educational systems are transplanted to the Third World, they not only serve to perpetuate the generation,

5

sustenance and socialization of the life styles for which they were originally intended but also result in the creation of a developed mini-sector within the country and lead to skill migration to developed countries. Restrictive language use policy in a plural society is thus an ally of elitist education.

The term mother tongue has been a subject of debate and dissension among scholars and layman alike. Pattanayak (1981) discussing in detail the confusion and equivocation relating to the term mother tongue points out the different meanings in which the term is used by various people. Ivan Illich (1981) makes a distinction between a taught mother language and a vernacular tongue and demonstrates how "the radical monopoly of taught mother tongue over speech" has resulted in the "class-biased intensity of this vernacular paralysis". Fishman (1981) points out on the other hand how "the transethnifying and translinguifying forces of large scale, modern, urban, industrial society" have rendered the school as a social institution powerless to resist the pressure of dominance. Fishman, pleading for this urban modernism says that the schools which use "the child's weaker language as a major medium of instruction may actually be questionable from the point of view of objective achievement". Having reduced the child's mother tongue to a "weaker language" it is not at all surprising that its use in the school would be judged questionable. It is interesting that while Illich stands up for the users of the vernacular, Fishman seems here to be pleading for the usurpers of the vernacular.

Theories constructed by scholars in the developed world on the basis of their predominantly monolingual experiences have damaging effects on millions of people all over the world who co-operate with one another entirely through the mother tongue. It has been contended that (a) countries which are economically backward are also linguistically backward (Ferguson, 1962), (b) in countries where the GNP is low, the languages are diverse and the countries are underdeveloped (Fishman, 1968), (c) a common language would obviously make for a more unified and cohesive society (Kelman, 1971), (d) monolingualism is a necessary condition for modernization (Neustupny, 1974) and (e) complete equality of status seems possible only in countries that have two or at least three languages. No country could conduct its affairs in four or more languages without becoming hopelessly muddled (Kloss, 1967). With such negative approaches to multilingualism, there is no wonder that a make-believe world has been created in which the majority has no mother tongue; only the minorities, the immigrants and the guest workers have mother tongues. The majority has no ethnicity, for "ethnic group" refers only to the minority and immigrant groups. The major and majority languages have no dialects, have a uniform standard and have no educational problems. The minority and migrant mother-tongue speakers have dialects, and all kinds of socio-politically divisive potentials and their existence is a threat to the majority privileges.

Since in their chosen ignorance planners in multilingual countries have adopted measures which have resulted in the denial of language and culture to large number of minority groups all over the world, it is necessary to understand the role of many languages in plural societies and the role of mother-tongue in the socialization process. Srivastava (1981) has examined the early socialization function, the identity function and the psychic function of the mother tongue and has concluded that these functions are often shared by two or three languages in a multilingual setting. Pattanayak (1981) suggested that when one language is confined to the intimate domain and another language is used in all other domains, the latter may be called the *Culture Language*. This relationship between a home language and a culture language may involve a dialect and a standard or a vernacular and the taught mother tongue or two mother tongues. What is important is to note that the early socialization of the child may take place through one, two or more mother tongues.

A mother tongue is the expression of the primary identity of a human being. It is the language through which a person perceives the surrounding world and through which initial concept formation takes place. The child is acclimatized to its environment through naming each object, phenomenon and mood of changing nature. Thus the flora, fauna, the colours of the sky, the rhythm of the rainfall and everything that excites the child and encourages exploration of the mysteries of nature assume a name and a habitat in the child's mind. The mother tongue is the medium through which the child also establishes kinship with other children and with the adults around. This assures the child that outside his or her limited ego there is a society from which help can come at a time of stress. In societies where joint families exist, such naming captures the complex three dimensional relationship which binds the society together. Terms expressive of relation such as mother's brother's son, father's sister's daughter, bind the ego not only with the peer group but also with the generation above and the generation below.

The role of the mother tongue in anchoring the child to its culture can also be seen from the point of myth. Whether the myth is transmitted through grandparent's tales, feasts and fasts at home, the ancestral tomb-stones or the portrayal of Gods and demons in sophisticated temple architecture, the child is slowly socialized into a system of beliefs and practices through the mother tongue. The performing arts which have a typical mythic base in any culture help cultivate the child's mind. The mother tongue is that language, the loss of which results in the loss of rootedness in traditions and

mythology of the speech community and leads to intellectual improverish-
ment and emotional sterility. While tests are devised to measure the effect of
teaching in the mother tongue on scholastic attainment in schools, there is
no test to measure the cultural perception blind spot of otherwise "successful" persons who have been deprived of the mother tongue in their early
socialization.

In multilingual countries there is enough evidence of a child growing up
with two or more languages. Even in dominant monolingual countries such
instances are not rare. In such cases the child usually has a greater emotional
pull towards one of the languages which is identified as the mother tongue.
Even if the child does not "know" the mother tongue, it becomes a group
solidarity symbol for which sacrifices can be made. There are no indices to
measure the extent to which out-of-school mother tongue education aids
school education and lack of it hinders the growth of the child.

Just as the accentuated poverty in the Third World is the result of
resources capitalism in the developed world so ignorance and illiteracy are
due to knowledge capitalism. Even within the developing world the same
capitalist principles have divided the populace into a small minority elite
appropriating to themselves rank, status and wealth and a vast mass of
people deprived of the very means of subsistence. There has been no
attempt to measure the money and human resources that have been invested
to build the privilege base through the imposition of a dominant language.
Education should be treated not as expenditure but as investment. But if
investment results in run-away capital, then it is a greater loss than slow
growth due to investment in poverty sectors. The UNCTAD study which
revealed that in 1971 the developing countries exported 2,960 crores of
rupees (about three hundred billion US dollars) of trained manpower to the
United States alone is one proof of educational wastage of systems which
neglect native interests and mother tongue education. It must be made clear
here that the argument is neither against other tongue education nor against
educated persons going abroad, but against neglect of mother tongue education. Emphasis on the mother tongue dictates an education which relates it
to languages of intercommunication at various levels and thus imparts
education relevant to the societal needs. Replacement of the mother
tongues by another language which is the ally of an empire, deprives many
people of their subsistence and makes a few privileged.

It is important to note the formal and functional difference between the
vernacular mother tongue and the taught mother tongue. It is an irony that
teaching Mandarin to Hokkien speakers in Singapore, French to Tahitians,
Italian to Venetian speakers, Dutch to Flemish speakers and Hindi to

Maithili speakers is presumed to be mother tongue teaching. The standard English taught as a mother tongue in different parts of the world is not the same as the mother tongue Black English in the USA, as Anglo-Indian English in India, or as the Fijian, Australian or Welsh varieties of English. The teaching of classical Arabic to speakers of a vernacular Arabic mother tongue or of standard literary Tamil to the many vernacular mother tongue speakers of Tamil is also argued to be mother tongue teaching by its protagonists. In the absence of clear strategy for linking the vernacular with the systematized and standardized variety, the poor performance of children in the taught mother tongue is immediately publicized as the failure of mother tongue instruction. In any case, the distance between the vernacular mother tongue and taught mother tongue has been reflected as a major variable in the measurement of scholastic attainment of school age children.

Another source of confusion about the desirability of mother tongue teaching has arisen from research in Bilingual Education in the developed countries. Swain & Lapkin (1982) have claimed that anglophone students do as well as the French students in regular French classes after time in a French immersion programme. The detractors of mother tongue teaching and those having vested interest in the colonial languages use this argument in their favour and cry that any expenditure for mother tongue education is a waste of scarce resources. Without going into the details of arguments in this score, suffice it to point out that European schools which accept the mother tongue principles as their point of departure have demonstrated that their results are comparable, if not superior to the Canadian immersion programmes (Baetens Beardsmore & Swain, 1985). The question then is, if scholastic attainment is comparable both with and without mother tongue mediation as would appear from the contentions of both group of researchers, should the economic advantages of cultural genocide, if sustained, be arguments against instruction in the mother tongue?

Mother tongue education is a matter of right as well as a need for every child. If academic opinion favours teaching reading and writing in the mother tongue before teaching reading and writing in a foreign language, it is based on the sound educational principles of step-incremental learning and progression from the familiar to the foreign. The special problems of migrants and of highly mobile children and the colonial interests of the world languages lead to attacks on the possibility of mother tongue education of small groups and in plurilingual communities. In raising political and economic questions about the *raison d'être* of mother tongues, the national-ism of the rich and powerful seeks the complete annihilation of the national identity of small and defenceless groups.

Plurality of interests of mother tongues have made a single solution impossible for the entire world. In Latin America an intolerable situation is created in which the mother tongues of millions are not used even for literacy campaigns, and whole communities are wiped out in "wars of pacification". In Africa and Asia, while the mother tongues are considered by some as barriers against upward mobility, they are for others the only key to equality of opportunity. In Asia, where either multiple mother tongues are crushed under a deliberate policy of dominant monolingualism or neglected because the small numbers speaking the language lack cohesive political mobilization, a different context is created. Only when a child grows up with two mother tongues one of which is the culture language or acquires early bilingualism are alternate educational choices available to make a significant projection for the future.

Positive attitudes towards one's own language and culture have maintained languages in India for thousands of years even under extremely adverse situations. There is evidence in Africa and Latin America that negative attitudes towards one's own language has led to the extinction of languages. Experiments in Canada with French Canadians and Anglo Canadians (Lambert, 1983) have shown that negative attitudes provide justification to the minority for inequality as much as they lead to a change of values. It is important that their educational consequences are studied carefully.

The experience of immersion programmes in Canada (Lambert & Tucker, 1972) has demonstrated that when children speaking the socially dominant language, which speaking children are required to study through the medium of the minority tongue, they not only do better in comparison to independent Foreign Language Teaching programmes involving that language, but also enrich their mother tongue (Lambert, 1981) in the process so that they do not lag behind their monolingual counterparts. Secured in the assurance of their identity, the children of the dominant language community in a pluricultural society gain advantage whether they study through their mother tongue or through one of the minority languages. Recent studies in America show that given a chance in mother tongue education, the minority French-speaking child not only excels in language skills in both the dominant language and the mother tongue, but also in content subjects in comparison with their peers studying through the dominant language. Similar studies with Spanish American children show that initial mother tongue education not only gives greater coping ability but also leads to better conceptual development of the child and that the language of the dominant culture develops in meaningful dimensions in a child anchored in education in the mother tongue. It is not at all surprising that some scholars in the West concerned about the additive value of bilingualism have appropriated to themselves the values of mother tongue instruction.

The study of Srivastava & Khatoon (1980) of the different effects of using a mother tongue and another language as the medium of instruction on achievement, mental ability and creativity of the 8th standard children in selected Indian schools has pointed out that the socio-economic status of the children, school climate, methods, materials and media of teaching all have significant influence on achievement. It is evident from this study that the mother tongue schools are invariably inferior to the English medium schools in the country both in terms of the conditions of teaching and the calibre of students. It is further demonstrated that when improved conditions of teaching are provided, mother tongue medium students do as well as English medium students. It is well known that better schools attract better students and children from families with greater achievement orientation. When the mother tongue is seldom the instrument of achievement of wealth and status in the society, it is natural that the basis of comparison between the mother tongue medium and other tongue medium will remain unequal. This is seldom recognized by those engaged in comparisons.

It is possible to take this argument one step further and seek a parallel between colonial language medium and major language medium schools in India on the one hand and major language medium and minority and minor language medium schools on the other in terms of investment and achievement. In the latter, the education is so irrelevant and the language problem so acute that enrolment is low and the dropout rate is high. Thus it will be seen that in the primary, junior basic and pre-primary schools in the Indian state of Assam, out of a total enrolment of 1,575,938 in 1978–79, the total reported school enrolment of children from scheduled tribes and castes (who make up the lowest social class) enrolment is only 151,035, whereas these two groups constitute 17.22% of the state's population. It should be noted that the reporting of this enrolment is likely to be overstated to claim better performance in goals for educational equality.

A study by Srivastava & Ramasamy (1983) on the effect of medium of instruction, socio-economic status and sex on academic achievement and intelligence of VIII and IX standard students in trilingual media schools is an advance on the Srivastava & Khatoon (1980) study cited above. Two major conclusions have been reached from studying three groups of students, one where the mother tongue and the medium of instruction are the same language, one where they are different but both cognate languages, and one where they are not cognate (*viz.*, English as medium of instruction for speakers of Dravidian as a mother tongue). The first conclusion is that the effect of medium of instruction is not the same for all subjects. The effect of medium of instruction and academic achievement was significant in the study of language, second language and mathematics. While the students taught in English scored better than the other two groups in these subjects, the mother tongue or cognate medium groups appear to have scored marginally better in sciences and social science. Among the three fields where English medium students scored better, the highest advantage was in English as a second language. The English medium students scored decisively better in non-verbal intelligence over the other two groups. The second conclusion is in some sense related to this. The authors conclude on the basis of ANCOVA partialling out intelligence that:

> "it appears that except second language English the difference among the three groups is not so much in quality and content of attainment as in form, expression and technique of writing the examinations."

In view of this, in spite of socio-economic status, school conditions, etc., it is not possible to say that education in the colonial language education is superior to education through the mother tongue.

All the above show an edge for using the mother tongue rather than other languages as medium of instruction. Those who advance arguments against mother tongue education by saying that scarce resources should not be spent on inessential applications are practising bad economics. The mother tongue is an essential sector because:

(a) it offers equal opportunity to large majority of people to participate in national reconstruction;

(b) it gives greater access to education and personal development to a greater number of people;

(c) it frees knowledge from the preserves of limited elites and by enabling greater number of people to interact with science lays the foundation for appropriate technology;

(d) it demands decentralization of information and ensures free as opposed to controlled media; and

(e) it provides greater opportunity for the political involvement of greater number of groups and thus is a greater defence of democracy.

If the aim of economics is not mere growth to be measured in terms of GNP but achieving all round social well being, then the educational use of mother tongue is more likely to contribute. More economic assets are wasted because of neglect of mother tongues in education as evident from drop out, wastage, stagnation, educated unemployment, and people opting out from their own milieu and own country.

The Physical Index of Quality of Life (PIQL) developed by UNESCO uses illiteracy as one of its three criterion measures. The Third World countries house most of the illiterate population of the world. Growing poverty and growing illiteracy in the Third World and the lingering poverty and literacy among immigrants in the developed countries appear to be connected. The fond hope that economic development of a small sector could percolate to the lower levels has been belied the same way as there was hope that the development of higher education would automatically take care of education at the lower stages. A higher education system that is impervious to the educational use of the mother tongue not only bypasses the majority and creates widespread deprivation, but resulting as it does in saturation of a few, it also creates a larger body of educated unemployed and a socially discontented population.

Apart from the doubt expressed that many languages cannot unite the many ethnolinguistic subgroups in a pluralistic society, an objection is raised about the ability of the school to cope with many languages. As Lambert & Sidoti (1981) point out,

"Educational planners tend to argue that in such cases one could never satisfy all pupils and parents, and thus a choice of one among the many is both logical and practical. Reasoning in this way starts a search for rationales for the best choice among the alternatives, but it is a mistake to assume that 'one among many' solution is the only or the best solution. Choosing a subset of languages in particular multilingual setting — 'the some among many' option — is an intriguing alternative."

This suggests that given the will to cope with many mother tongues the school can not only act as a policy instrument for maintaining multilingualism, but can create a milieu where use of many languages will lead to the fullest co-ordinated and balanced development of human personality.

The above discussion might give an impression that the focus is minority mother tongue rather than the educational use of a mother tongue whether minor or major. Since the dominant language is often the medium of instruction in the school, those privileged to have the same language at home, in the school, in the work place and in the mass media get reinforcement from different sources. Even dialectal and diglossic differences, if they exist, act as resources for creative exploration of their inner and outer world.

It is only when difference between the vernacular speech and the cultivated taught language or the mother tongue and the culture languages results in inequal opportunities and arrests the growth of individuals and groups, that the mother tongue debate assumes importance. Whatever principle is good for the majority is also good for the minority. Educational use of mother tongue is validated for the majority mother tongues in the world and its denial to the minority is discrimination against them and a violation of a fundamental human right.

Bibliography

BAETENS BEARDSMORE, H. 1979, Bilingual Education for highly mobile children. *Language Problems and Language Planning*, Vol. 3.3, 9, 38–152.

BAETENS BEARDSMORE, H. & SWAIN, M. 1985, Designing bilingual education: Aspects of immersion and "European school" models. *Journal of Multilingual and Multicultural Development*, 6:1, 1–16.

DUBE, N. C. & HERBERT, G. 1975, St. John Valley Bilingual Education Project. Report prepared for the US Department of Health, Education and Welfare under contract No. OEC-0-74-9331.

FERGUSON, C. A. 1962, The language factor in national development. *Anthropological Linguistics*, 4.1, 23–27.

FISHMAN, J. A. 1968, Some contrasts between linguistically homogenous and linguistically heterogenous politics. In: J. A. FISHMAN *et al.* (eds), *Language Problems of Developing Nations*. New York: John Wiley & Sons, pp. 53–68.

— 1981, Mother Tongue as Medium of Instruction in the USA. Paper presented in the UNESCO expert meeting relating to the use of the mother tongue as medium of instruction, Paris.

ILLICH, I. 1981, Taught Mother Language and Vernacular Tongue. In: D. P. PATTANAYAK (ed.), *Multilingualism and Mother Tongue Education*. Oxford: Oxford University Press, pp. 31–48.

KELMAN, H. 1971, Language as an aid and barrier to involvement in the national system. In J. RUBIN & B. H. JERNUDD (eds), *Can Language be Planned?* Honolulu: University of Hawaii Press.

KLOSS, H. 1979, Bilingualism and Nationalism. *Journal of Social Issues*, 23.2, 39–47.

LAMBERT, W. E. 1981, Bilingualism and Language Acquisition. In: H. WINTZ (ed.), *Native Language and Foreign Language Acquisition*. The New York Academy of Sciences, Vol. 379.

— 1983, Language as a factor in personal identity and inter-group Relations. Paper presented at the Desert Language and Linguistics Society Meeting in Provo, Utah, March 21, 1983; and at UNESCO, Venice on May 4, 1983.

LAMBERT, W. E., GILES, H. & PICARD, D. 1975, Language Attitudes in a French-American Community. *International Journal of the Sociology of Language*, 4, 127–52.

LAMBERT, W. E. & TUCKER, G. R. 1972, *Bilingual Education for Children*. Rowley, Mass.: Newbury House.

LAMBERT, W. E. & SIDOTI, N. 1981, Choosing instructional languages for educational radio broadcasts in less developed countries. Chapter V, The Educational Use of Mass Media, World Bank Staff Working Paper No. 491.

NEUSTUPNY, J. 1974, The modernization of the Japanese system of communication, *Language in Society*, 3.1, 33–50.

PATTANAYAK, D. P. 1977, Language planning and language development. In: P. SHARMA GOPAL & SURESH KUMAR (eds), *Indian Bilingualism*. Agra: Kendriya Hindi Sansthan.

— 1981, *Multilingualism and mother tongue education*. Oxford: Oxford University Press.

SRIVASTAVA, R. N. 1981, The "out group" languages of India. Paper presented at the International Conference on Language and City held at Baku, USSR.

SRIVASTAVA, A. K. & KHATOON, R. 1980, Effect of difference between mother tongue and another tongue as medium of instruction on achievement, mental ability and creativity of the VIII standard children. In: E. ANNAMALAI (ed.), *Bilingualism and achievement in school*. Mysore: CIIL. Pp. 31–48.

SRIVASTAVA, A. K. & RAMASAMY, K. 1983, 'Effect of medium of instruction, socio-economic status and intelligence of VIII and IX standard students. Paper read at the 20th Annual Conference of Indian Academy of Applied Psychologists, Hyderabad.

SWAIN, M. & LAPKIN, S. 1982, *Evaluating Bilingual Education: A Canadian Case Study*. Clevedon: Multilingual Matters.

SZAMOSI, M. & LAPKIN, S. 1979, Do early immersion pupils know French? *Orbit*, 49.

TUCKER, G. R. 1980, Comments on proposed rules for non-discrimination under programs receiving federal financial assistance through the Education Department, Center for Applied Linguistics, Washington, D.C.

3 Towards a typology of languages of instruction in multilingual societies

MELANIE MIKES

In a recent paper on the relation of mother tongue use to educational attainment, Mackey (1984) identifies a number of apparent dilemmas which follow from his assumption that a person's mother tongue is an alienable possession and no more than a tool of socialization. As Mackey sees it, it is only under the influence or even presure of an ethnic collectivity that an individual is prevented from discarding a mother tongue of minor functional value and replacing it with a more useful one. Following an analogy taken from Saussure who compared language to a currency whose values are both arbitrary and conventional, Mackey is led to conclude that if

> "languages were independent of nation-states and of their boundaries, the languages of mankind would be in a sort of free-market situation whereby people no matter where they might live could opt for education in the language or languages of their choice, according to the needs and availability of these languages."
> (p. 44)

In Mackey's opinion, the native language can not only be given up freely, but it can lose its vitality: "Each culture has the language it needs to function. If needs change, so must language." If this meant that the structure of an individual language changes in accordance to changing circumstances and needs, it would be understandable, but it is rather a claim that one language can be replaced by another. In Mackey's view, then, a child who is taught a language of minor functional value is at a disadvantage. The dilemma is whether to save the child or the language:

"It is true of course that some parents may opt for the language and are willing to pay the price. A few years of 'retardation' in their child's level of arithmetic may not be too high a price for patriotic parents to pay for the preservation of their ancestral tongue." (p. 44)

True, such extreme situations sometimes occur, but when they do, the fault is not in the desire to preserve the language but in an educational policy that has created a conflicting situation.

Mackey seems to wonder if there is any purpose in arguing for mother tongue education, given the impossibility of making a credible and consistent case for the thousands of languages involved. He argues the case for international languages:

"Many nations thoughout the world are today faced with the unpleasant dilemma. If, for ethnic or nationalistic reasons, they promote an unproductive tongue, they may to that extent, diminish the potential of their people for economic and scientific development. On the other hand, if they fail to develop their national languages, these will always remain secondary instruments of communication." (p. 45)

Is this a real dilemma, or just a complex problem? In a paper dealing with the issue of choice of language of instruction in the process of decolonization and national emancipation of African countries (Mikes, 1984), I have pointed out the existence of two contradictory tendencies: one, towards technological and economic progress, encouraging use of an international and developed language, and the other, towards the affirmation of the autochthonous values and cultural heritage of the people, encouraging the promotion of languages which bear these values. There are models that attempt to deal with this complexity (e.g. Tadadjeu, 1980; Brann, 1981).

Mackey is posing another false dilemma when he sets the culture of an ethnic collectivity in confrontation with that of its members:

"To force an adult member of any group to conform to the group's objectives is to deprive that person of his cultural freedom. This opposition has become one of the saddest dilemmas of our century: the conflict between the right of an ethnic group to cultural survival as opposed to the right of an individual to cultural freedom." (p. 49)

In postulating this as a dilemma, Mackey misses the point that the individual belongs to the culture or cultures of the society in which he has been brought up, and that the individual acquires this culture (including the mother tongue or other language) from earliest childhood. The conflict is not at the level of ethnic freedom, but belongs rather to the socio-political sphere. It may develop within an ethnic collectivity (as happens in Quebec or Wales or among the elites of developing African countries) as a result of former or present political or economic domination by another ethnic collectivity, and may be provoked by conflicting class interests inside the ethnic collectivity itself. But the solution of these conflicts is not a matter of cultural freedom.

In another paper in the same volume, Szépe (1984: 69) argues for the right to a child to be educated in his or her mother tongue whatever its status.

"The right to use one's mother tongue happens to be a funda-mental, socially expressed human right applying equally to children."

For Szépe, the question is not whether but how mother tongue education should be promoted. Nor does he see any conflict between the interests of the community and the individual. He mentions but does not analyse cases where the state's interests might not coincide with those of its citizens.

These issues are more insightfully treated by Fishman (1984: 52), who argues

"that education is a socializing institution and must never be ex-amined without concentrating on the social processes that it serves and the social pressures to which it responds."

Advocates of mother tongue education sometimes say that it serves as a useful first step preparing for later successful learning of the socially dominant language, or that it leads to better academic education. Fishman points out that these reasons are not enough. The promotion of minority mother tongues in education is motivated by the intricate ties between a language and the culture with which it is associated. Every language indexes, symbolizes, and enacts its culture better than any other language does. Minority populations depend on school to enable their children to index as much of their culture as possible. They know that the presence of a minority language in the educational system of a community symbolizes the existence of its culture. They know that the maintenance of culture is impossible without the maintenance of its language, and they therefore focus on the school in their quest for assuring the continuity of their culture through the teaching of and in their language. But, Fishman points out, school alone cannot guarantee the continuity of culture, which requires community support, and this is often missing.

To this point, I agree with Fishman, but I am less happy with his analysis of bilingualism and diglossia and of multi-ethnic states; here, he seems to concentrate too much on the extremes, on situations that divide the community into an advantaged majority and a disadvantaged minority. Considering the phenomena which occur in the large range of the continuum between disadvantage and advantage would lead, I believe, to a much richer model.

To make clear how this can work, I set out in the rest of this paper a sketch for a model based on a typology of languages of instruction. The situation of a language in the educational system is determined in part by institutional factors, such as its past and present legal status (its use as official, national, state, or regional language) and its use by public authorities and the mass media. It is also, in part, dependent on various sociolinguistic factors among which are its use among the population, the socio-economic stratification of its native speakers, the circumstances of its use and its cultural and linguistic proximity to any other language or languages spoken in the region.

All these factors play an essential part in determining the parameters for a possible typology of languages of instruction in multilingual societies. In a model based on such a typology, the pupil may be seen as at the centre of a network of factors, the outer segment of which are the community bound factors: the type of language use in the educational system forms a middle layer, intervening between the child's microenvironment (mostly his family) and the community bound factors.

FIGURE 1

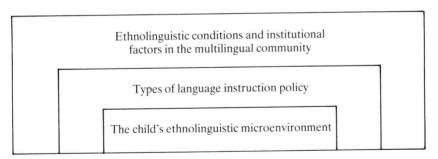

Ethnolinguistic conditions and institutional
factors in the multilingual community

Types of language instruction policy

The child's ethnolinguistic microenvironment

What are the essential tasks of typology? It seems to me that the most useful typology will be one that will permit us to determine whether language policy and use in a given educational system at a given point in time and space are congruent with the microenvironmental and macroenvironmental factors identified by the model.

The typology I have described assumes three sections: the child and his or her microenvironment, the language education policy, and the socio-linguistic situation or macroenvironment within which the programme operates. Each of these three sections is further divisible into three, and so it is possible to represent the intricate network of interaction with which I am concerned.

Because of its centrality to our interest, I shall start with the middle section, the types of language use in educational systems. I propose here the recognition of three types:

Type A. The use of the mother tongue until the child has mastered the second language (the language of the state, the language of the ethnic majority, the language of wider communication, etc.), which will later be used as the language of instruction (a transitional programme).
Type B. The use of the mother tongue as long as possible, potentially until the end of schooling (language-shelter programme).
Type C. The use of the second language from the beginning of education, in order to teach it as well as possible, with or without some teaching in the mother tongue (immersion programme).

Programmes of these three major types have emerged under various conditions, in accordance with the language policy of the socio-political community and with various rationales, and such programmes sometimes reflect but sometimes neglect the ethnolinguistic features of the micro-environment of the children of the various ethnic collectivities.

The child's microenvironment may be grouped into three main types:

Type A1. Monolingual.
Type B1. Bilingual and fostering early bilingualism.
Type C1. Bilingual but directed towards monolingualism.

Of course, one must also take into account variation within each of these three types of microenvironment that may originate in the status relations of the languages (minority, majority, equal), the cultural and linguistic dis-tances, the sociolinguistic type (literary, standard, vernacular, dialect, etc.). All these differences can be important in the working of the full model.

For heuristic reasons, we ignore many peculiarities of diverse multi-national and multilingual communities, and propose to divide the outer segment, the social macroenvironment, also into three major types:

Type A2. The socio-political community of the type "one language, one nation".

Type B2. The pluralistic type of socio-political community with tendencies towards the realization of equal rights for all ethnic collectivities and their languages and alphabets.

Type C2. The type of socio-political community that tends to be selective and maintains the language and culture of some ethnic collectivities but not others.

FIGURE 2

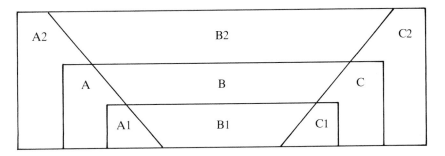

The distribution of the various types inside the three segments of our model (as shown in the diagrams) set up three sectionings which are convergent:

Section A. Monolingual microenvironment, transitional programme, one language, one nation socio-political community.

Section B. Bilingual microenvironment favouring early bilingualism, language shelter programme, pluralistic equal rights socio-political community.

Section C. Bilingual microenvironment favouring monolingualism, immersion programme, selectively pluralistic socio-economic community.

In each of these sections, there is congruence between the type of instruction, the type of community, and the type of environment of the child. In the third case, however, it must be pointed out that the effect will be different depending on whether the child's language and ethnic collectivity is one favoured by the socio-political community or not.

The three types of instructional policy, A, B and C, do not represent homogeneous entities: there is a great deal of variation, in part as a result of differences of duration in compulsory education, the diffusion of the educational system in a community, and the number of children reached, and in part because of differences in school programmes, methods of instruction, and use of modern language teaching techniques. The heterogeneity inside the three types of socio-political community, A2, B2 and C2, is a result of the cultural tradition and the ethno-demographic structure of the population, its political past, and its present socio-political system. The variation inside the microenvironment, types A1, B1, C1, arises from differences originating in socio-economic conditions and cultural and educational level.

It is these internal variations that make the interactions dynamic and upset the stability of the relations between the segments. For this reason, there may be tendencies from the convergent solutions to a divergent solution: for example, when the educational system offers only a few years of education, there will be insufficient mother tongue education for children of type B1 in a type B2 community.

Divergent relations may, however, themselves develop into new convergent relations because of feedback. Thus, type B (mother tongue instruction) applied to the end of secondary school may transform a type C2 (selective) community into type B2 (pluralistic, equal rights), and afterwards this may itself influence the microenvironment to change from C1 (bilingual towards monolingual) into B1 (bilingual favouring early bilingualism).

The typology and model should make it possible to classify and analyse various cases of selection of language of instruction in multilingual societies, and contribute to the solution of problems associated with these communities.

References

BRANN, C. M. B. 1981, Trilingualism in language planning for education in Sub-Saharan Africa. Paris: Unesco.

FISHMAN, J. A. 1984, Minority mother tongues in education. *Prospects*, No. 1.

MACKEY, W. F. 1984, Mother tongue education: Problems and prospects. *Prospects*, No. 1.

MIKEŠ, M. 1984, Pitanje nastavnog jezika u procesima dekolonizacije i nacionalne emancipacije africkih zemalja. Paper presented at the conference on Language and National Relations, Sarajevo, 1984.

SZÉPE, G. 1984, Mother tongue, language policy, and education, *Prospects*, No. 1.

TADADJEU, M. 1980, A model for functional trilingual education planning in Africa. Paris: Unesco.

4 Factors affecting bilingualism in national languages and Russian in a developed socialist society

M. N. GUBOGLO

The Soviet Union is a multinational country whose nations, peoples, national and ethnic groups speak over 130 languages. National literatures are written in 78 languages, plays are performed in 42, journals are published in 46, school textbooks are printed in 56, and radio programmes are broadcast in 67 languages. We can therefore see why Soviet and foreign scholars have concluded that the development and interaction of the languages and cultures of the peoples of the USSR is a unique phenomenon, prescribed in the programme of the Communist Party of the Soviet Union (CPSU) and reinforced by the USSR Constitution of 1977, and with no parallel in the history of mankind. There have of course been, in many parts of the world and at various periods, regions with nationally mixed populations that have used one language in the role of lingua franca. However the Soviet ethnolinguistic experience is unique so that it is expedient to consider it from broad historico-sociological perspectives.

The basic course followed by ethnolinguistic processes in the USSR is the development of the native languages of the nationalities along with the simultaneous diffusion among them of the Russian language. As a result, bilingualism in the National Languages and Russian is being developed on a large scale. This bilingualism is currently accepted as the linguistic model appropriate for the stage of developed socialism. It is manifested in a variety of forms and aspects: from the personal to the national level, from the economic to the psychological sphere, from production to family life, in oral and written form, etc. The exceptional multiplicity of combinations of national languages with the Russian language, which for the USSR is the language of international communication, imposes particular obligations on Russian society with regard to the purposeful supervision of ethnolinguistic processes as a whole and of their most important component — the formation and functioning of bilingualism in the National Languages and Russian. Solving the problems involved in this issue of genuine statewide importance naturally requires a thorough knowledge of the concrete conditions, factors, causes and situations which predetermine the fact of bilingualism in Russian and the various National Languages.

The emergence and development of bilingual processes as a mass social phenomenon is determined by the sum total of objective and subjective factors, chief among them by the broad communication among the people of the USSR. In the age of the scientific and technological revolution and of social progress, contacts between the nations making up the USSR grow stronger and the need increases for more than a language of international communication: a deeper and multifaceted need arises for the Russian language as an important means of access to the cultures of all the peoples of the USSR and to the achievement of world culture. A group of objective factors exerts a basic influence on the development of contemporary ethnolinguistic processes along with these global factors. Prominent among these are the influences of primary, eight-year and secondary general education schools, of army service, and of direct ethnic contacts. For example, census data indicate that by the early 1970s, the proportion of bilingual individuals among the indigenous nationalities of the Union Republics was four times higher among those who had completed eight-year schools and among those who had only completed primary schools; more than a third of all children from 11–15 were bilingual. Among those who had graduated from high school, those who were bilingual made up half of the group between the ages of 16 and 19.[1]

A comparative analysis of the two tendencies in the 1970s — the diffusion of bilingualism in Russian and various National Languages and the raising of the level of education — among those indigenous nationalities with their own Union Republics shows that the two tendencies developed in the same direction: there was a steady increase in educational level and an expansion in the use of Russian. At the same time, a certain complexity was revealed. According to the data from the 1970 census, among half of the indigenous nationalities of the Union Republics (including Ukrainians, Belorussians, Kazakhs, Lithuanians, Moldavians, Letts, and Estonians), the percentage of individuals with a fluent command of the Russian language exceeded the percentage with secondary and higher education. Among the Kirghiz and the Tadzhik, the two indices were practically equal. Among the remaining five nationalities of the Union Republics (Uzbeks,

Georgians, Azerbaidzhanis, Armenians and Turkmens), the percentage of the population with a secondary and higher education exceeded the percentage with fluent command of the Russian language.[2]

No basic change took place in this situation in the next decade. For example, in 1979, in seven Union Republics the percentage of bilinguals among the indigenous nationality was higher than the percentage of educated, but in the seven other republics, the percentage was, on the contrary, lower.

There is no simple explanation for this phenomenon of the existence of a higher percentage of people with a secondary and higher education than of those with a fluent command of the Russian language. Its primary cause is the beneficial results of the implementation of the nationalities policy of the CPSU, a policy which afforded every possibility for the development of the social functioning of the native languages of the peoples of the USSR in the most varied spheres of life: in labour, culture and daily life. But in accordance with the dialectic of ethnolinguistic life, this functional development of native languages parallels the growth of the socio-cultural level of the peoples. This in turn engendered and then deepened the need to know well and to use widely a language of international communication on the same level as the native languages. Apparently, in certain republics in the 1960s, as has already been emphasized in the literature, the study of the Russian language was at times not yet organized satisfactorily; there existed at the secondary and higher levels a shortage in the number of qualified Russian language teachers. Consequently, some of the graduates, even after they had completed secondary or higher education, were insufficiently proficient in Russian to cope with their growing needs for a solid knowledge of the language. Ethnosociological studies provided a basis for the conclusion that in several Union Republics there still exists significant room for further improvement in meeting satisfactorily the needs of the indigenous nationality for fluent command of the Russian language, including segments of the population with a relatively high level of education. K. U. Chernenko, General Secretary of the Central Committee of the CPSU, Chairman of the Presidium of the Supreme Soviet of the USSR, spoke about this particular topic at the June 1983 Plenum of the Central Committee:

> "There are still several instances when a weak knowledge of the Russian language limits a person's access to the riches of international culture, narrows his circle of activity and communication. The Central Committee of the CPSU and the Council of Ministers of the USSR recently adopted a resolution on creating conditions facilitating instruction in the Russian language for the population of the national republics. It must be actively implemented."[3]

The Communist Party and the Soviet State are continually concerned with guaranteeing favourable conditions for the development of the native languages of the peoples of the USSR and at the same time for access to the Russian language. This is shown by a whole series of resolutions adopted by the Central Committee of the CPSU, the Council of Ministers of the USSR, and by party organizations in the republics in the 1970s and 1980s. One might cite as an example that in May 1983 the Politburo of the Central Committee gave special consideration to measures to improve the teaching of the Russian language in general education schools and in other educational institutions in the Union Republics (*Pravda*, May 27, 1983). The urgency recognized for problems in the development and functioning of bilingualism in Russian and the various National Languages and the widespread public interest in the topic was graphically demonstrated in the course of nationwide discussion of the draft prepared by the Central Committee for the reform of the general education school. As was to be expected, the "Basic Directions for the Reform of General Education and Professional Schools", approved by the Plenum of the Central Committee of the CPSU on April 10, 1984 and by the Supreme Soviet of the USSR on April 12, 1984, formulated tasks for improving each of the component parts of bilingualism in Russian and the National Languages. The document contains proposals on the one hand

> "to expand the printing capacity and manufacture of high quality material for publishing textbooks in the languages of the peoples of the USSR," (*Sovetskaia Kultura*, April 14, 1984)

and, on the other hand, it states that

> "the fluent command of the Russian language ought to become the norm for youth who graduate from secondary educational institutions."

Thus, the essence of the national language policy of the CPSU, which is the most important subjective factor in the development of bilingualism in Russian and the National Languages in the Soviet Union, consists of working to secure a universal possibility for the development of the native languages of the peoples of the USSR, while at the same time making it possible for these peoples to have access to the achievements of world culture through the Russian language. From the methodological point of view, a necessary condition for realizing the correlation between language policy and the socio-cultural development of the nationalities is intelligent, purposeful influence, co-ordinated with the needs of the speakers of the languages themselves, on the linguistic aspect of the work of all links in the system of public education, the means of mass communication, the publishing activities of the work of state and social organizations, departments, and institutions.

Let us return to the role of the school as a factor in contemporary ethnolinguistic processes. The multiplicity of languages of the peoples of our country which function in the education system of the USSR as languages of instruction or are taught as a school subject testifies to the care which Soviet society takes of the interests of each nation and people and of the interests of the entire Soviet people as a new historical community of people.

In their efforts to create conditions for the more effective teaching of the Russian language and its literature in national schools, the party organizations in the republics are working on the premise that the study of the Russian language must also mean the study of Russian literature and of Russian history in their interrelationship with the literature and history of the peoples of the USSR.

Analysis of statistical data and of party documents supports the claim for the gradual equalization in providing highly qualified specialists for national language schools and for schools with instruction in Russian. Thus, for example, differences in educational level between teachers of Russian language and literature in schools with instruction in Russian and schools with instruction in other languages decreased from 8.3% in 1969 to 6.3% in 1981.[4]

It is difficult to overestimate the significance of this trend if one considers the level of proficiency in Russian of school children of non-Russian nationalities, and in the final analysis, the fate of the development of bilingualism in Russian and the National Languages depends to a great extent on the professional level of Russian language teachers.

Therefore, one of the social tasks of the 1980s is to solve the pressing problem of improving the training for teachers for schools using different languages of instruction. This includes the problem of equalizing the educational level of Russian philology specialists in schools using national languages and in schools using Russian and also equalizing the educational level of Russian language teachers with teachers of other specialities, including teachers of the native language.

A significant contribution to the spread of the Russian language is made by special schools with parallel classes in Russian and in the National Languages. These schools provide an important channel for increasing the effectiveness of Russian language teaching and at the same time for educating pupils in the spirit of socialist internationalism. Experience has shown that a favourable ethnolinguistic milieu is formed naturally in such schools:

as a result of the environment created, children of non-Russian nationalities are enabled to master the Russian language more quickly and thoroughly.

A great deal is thus being done in Soviet schools to stimulate and raise the level of linguistic competence. At the same time, in contrast to the years immediately after the war, considerable attention is being given both to improving students' linguistic competence and to improving the quality of their oral activity. However, as this work emphasizes, factors in the development of bilingualism in Russian and National Languages do not operate in isolation and autonomously: their influence is complex. Therefore, stimulation of both linguistic competence and of oral activity in both languages should not be limited to the educational sphere, but should be expanded to encompass all the other subsystems in the ecology of languages, first among them the spheres of production and of socio-political and cultural activity.

The language policy of the CPSU and the Soviet State encompasses all spheres of social functioning and interaction of languages. In the conditions of developed socialism, all peoples of the USSR, for example, benefit from in the record-breaking rates in the growth of Russian-language book production, since it serves both national and international interests in the new historical community. At the same time, the needs of non-Russian peoples for books in their native language and in Russian change dynamically in accordance with the varying extent of the spread of the Russian language. The movement of peoples towards nation-wide bilingualism in Russian and in the National Languages accompanied, as analysis of the data has shown, by the increase in readers able to read in two languages, presents publishers in the Union Republics with the task of taking into account the specific interests of the various groups in the population in a planned and complex manner.

In addition to school as a factor, the factor of residence and the related factor of interethnic contrast play an important role in the development and functioning of bilingualism in Russian and the National Languages. The consolidation of mono-ethnicity in several Union Republics in the 1970s led to a decline in the stimulating role of the ethnic milieu, that is interethnic contacts, in the spread and particularly in the functioning of the Russian language. As a result, a dialectically complex position developed. On the one hand, there were mass efforts by the country's non-Russian population to study the Russian language which in the conditions of developed socialism became a truly new, nation-wide phenomenon. On the other hand, there was a decline in the influence of interethnic contacts which have a positive effect on the course of the ethnolinguistic processes and on the further spread of bilingualism in Russian and National Languages.

Like the factor of school, the factor of residence requires careful attention because its influence on the course of ethnolinguistic processes is universal, appearing to one degree or another in the various regions of the country and at various levels and scales. In fact, the more multi-ethnic is the make-up of the republics, oblasts (provinces), territories and districts, the more multinational is the make-up of workers' collectives, the more broadly are ethnolinguistic processes developed, and the more thoroughly accustomed is the non-Russian population to bilingualism in Russian and the National Language.

A typology of ethnic milieux that has worked out in the course of ethnosociological research has made it possible to refine notions about the contact and other ways in which unilateral and bilateral bilingualism emerge among nationalities living together in various types of ethnic milieux. Thus, for example, the scale of Russian-Moldavian bilingualism amongst Russians living in a Moldavian type of ethnic milieu (i.e. in regions of the Moldavian SSR with a predominance of Moldavians) was much greater than the scale of Moldavian–Russian bilingualism among Moldavians (see Guboglo, 1979).

The same factors act on various types and forms of bilingualism with varying force. In a single system of factors which determine the course of ethnolingustic development as a whole, one and the same factor influences the dynamics of each component part of bilingualism with varying intensity. For example, the influence of school as the most universal factor in the formation of bilingualism in Russian and National Language is felt in different ways, on the one hand, on the raising of the level of linguistic competence, and on the other hand, on the extent to which each of the languages is used in oral practice at work, in the cultural or family and daily spheres. There are, in contrast to this, situations in which two or more factors act more or less in concert on both the further mastery of a second language and on the expansion of its sphere of application and the perfecting of the population's linguistic orientation, in particular on the development of an intelligently thought-out attitude toward the need for one, two, or more languages. The entire system of the Soviet general education school, army service, mass media and several other factors, particularly when they all operate in a complementary fashion, produces a deeply thought-out international position — the recognition of the need for the Russian language as a language for communication between the nationalities. At the same time, several difficulties remain in the study of extra-ethnic factors. These appear both on the level of measuring their influence on the development of ethnosocial processes and the development of bilingualism and also in the evaluation of their concrete role in the development of contemporary ethnolinguistic processes.

It would be a mistake to lump together factors and motives in ethno-linguistic processes that are better differentiated according to the direction of their influence on the development of the various components of bi-lingualism. An essential conclusion is that factors of an extroverted nature and motives with an introverted tendency are closely related. The external milieu creates various linguistic needs, and these in turn permit the individual to strive consciously to adapt to the surrounding ethnolinguistic situation and to a certain degree determine its condition.

It is already quite clear that in an exposition of the complex character of the factors in the development of bilingualism in Russian and National Languages we must be careful not to exaggerate or interpret in a one-sided manner the influence of any one factor, such as school and its language of instruction. It is methodologically more accurate to state that a given factor simply occurs among many other phenomena which each to some degree facilitate the development of the basic parameters of bilingualism.

The complex nature of the influence of the external environment on the formation of linguistic indices of bilingualism is to be seen in the fact that the effect of one factor increases significantly when it works in parallel with one or more other active stimuli. The complex influence of the non-linguistic factors on the course of the ethnolinguistic processes increases in extreme conditions, for example, at a time of significant historical events, in particular during the years of the Second World War, during the carrying out of large scale building projects of nationwide importance, the development of the virgin land areas, and of areas of the country which were sparsely inhabited in the past.

The Soviet Union has accumulated substantial experience in achieving conditions that are favourable to the study of the other National Languages and primarily of the Russian language. The work of many organizations in the republics shows an understanding of the multifactored dependence of the linguistic life of peoples, and of the complex nature of factors which determine the course of ethnolinguistic development and the fact of bi-lingualism in Russian and National Languages.

Notes to Chapter 4

1. Cited figures from *Itogi Vsesoiuznoi perepisi naseleniia 1970 g.* Volume 4, Moscow: Statistika, 1973, pp. 360–82.
2. Cited figures from *Itogi Vsesoiuznoi perepisi naseleniia 1970 g.* Volume 4: Moscow: Statistika, 1973, pp. 475–566.

3. *Materialy Plenum TsK KPSS 14–15 iunia 1983 g.* Moscow, Politizdat, 1983, pp. 59–60.
4. *Narodnoe khoziaistvo SSSR v 1969 g.* Moscow, 1970, p. 670; *Narodnoe khoziaistvo SSSR, 1922–1982.* Moscow, 1982, p. 504.

Reference

GUBOGLO, M. N. 1979, Razvitie dvuiazychiia v Moldavskoi SSR. Kishinev, pp. 71–84.

5 Multilingual education: Theory East and West

BARRY McLAUGHLIN

In this chapter I would like to discuss theory as it relates to multilingual education. Specifically, I will look briefly at the writings of two Western authors, James Cummins and Stephen Krashen. Then I will examine some aspects of Soviet theory. In the final section of this Chapter, I will attempt to look at the implications for instructional practice and language teaching that follow from Eastern and Western theories. It is my belief that here, as in other areas, we in the West know too little of the Soviet experience. After all, there is no modern industrial country for which multilingual education has been as central a concern as it has in the Soviet Union.

Theory West

Cummins

Let me begin, then, with a few comments on the theoretical writings of James Cummins. I would like to concern myself principally with the "linguistic interdependence hypothesis" by which, Cummins (1979, 1981) argued that the literacy-related aspects of a bilingual's proficiency in the first and second language are seen as common or interdependent across languages. That is, the skills involved in reading (e.g. inferring and predicting meaning based on sampling from the text) and writing (e.g. planning large chunks of discourse) are thought to transfer across languages. Cummins argued that "experience with either language is capable of promoting the proficiency that underlies the development of academic skills in both languages" (1981: 33).

Cummins advanced his theory as a way of accounting for the marked difference between the outcome of immersion programmes for majority-language children in Canada and "submersion" programmes for minority-language children in the United States. He proposed that:

"When the usage of certain functions of a language and the development of L1 vocabulary and concepts are strongly promoted by the child's linguistic environment outside of school, as in the case of most middle-class children in immersion programs, then intensive exposure to L2 is likely to result in high levels of L2 competence at no cost to L1 competence. The initially high level of L1 development makes possible the development of similar levels of competence in L2. However, for children whose L1 skills are less well developed in certain respects, intensive exposure to L2 in the initial grades is likely to impede the continued development of L1. This will, in turn, exert a limiting effect on the development of L2." (1979: 233).

The key to this argument is understanding what Cummins means by "certain functions of language". In his classic 1979 article he spelled out three general aspects of children's knowledge of language that he felt were critical to school success. They related specifically to the reading process, because, Cummins argued, the primary academic task for the child is learning how to extract information efficiently from printed text and subsequent educational progress depends on how well this task is accomplished. The three aspects were vocabulary-concept knowledge, by which Cummins referred to the child's understanding of the concepts or meanings embodied in words; meta-linguistic insights, such as the insight that print is meaningful and that written language is different from speech; and the ability to deal with language that is decontextualized, that is, taken out of the context of the immediate interpersonal situation. In Cummins' view the problems of many minority-language children in submersion settings stem from their not having been exposed to a literate first language environment prior to school. As Cummins put it:

"Such a child's L1 vocabulary-concept knowledge may be limited, there may be difficulty assimilating decontextualized knowledge, and little insight into the fact that print is meaningful and that written language is different from speech." (1979: 239).

A number of authors have argued that Cummins' thesis constitutes a deficit theory and ignores social variables that can adequately account for the poor academic performance of minority-language children. For example, Rudolph Troike (1981) argued that the linguistic competencies thought by

Cummins to be necessary for success in literacy-related school tasks do not reflect any underlying general ability, but rather degree of acculturation to a culture-specific set of norms, the culture being that of the dominant middle class as reflected in the school. Troike maintained

> ". . . that reading and text-processing skills play a major role in determining school achievement, and that the development of these skills is affected in little-understood ways by home background, including SES, but may be interactionally stimulated or retarded both by pedagogical practices and by sociolinguistic/ cultural attitudes, expectations, and behaviors manifested by the teacher and others (including peers and school administrators) in the school setting." (1981: 10)

Troike concluded that the competencies posited by Cummins are largely an artifact of test results that reveal acculturative approximations to middle-class Western cultural norms and behaviours.

A similar argument was made by Carole Edelsky and her colleagues (Edelsky, Hudelson, Flores, Barkin, Altwerger & Jilbert, 1983). These authors maintained that Cummins accepted current school definitions of reading skill as the ability to perform well on a standardized reading achievement test. Rather than measuring general linguistic competencies, these authors argued, the data on which the theory is based measure test-wiseness, or the ability to do well on an artificial and culturally biased test.

It seems to me that the arguments of these authors are off the point. Cummins in no way denied the importance of social factors, nor did he endorse current forms of literacy instruction. His point was simply that the general linguistic competencies of the minority-language child are one important determinant of the outcome of educational treatments. If certain competencies have not been developed in the first language, Cummins maintained, this will have an effect on their acquisition in a second language.

I think that the strongest support for this point of view comes from recent research by the German linguist, Jochen Rehbein. Rehbein (1982) has shown that the degree of development of conceptual knowledge in Turkish children living in Germany is closely related to the degree of co-ordination achieved in the development of both languages. In other research Rehbein (1984) found that the ability of Turkish children to deal with complex texts in German was affected by their ability to understand these texts in their first language. Rehbein's investigations suggest that there is a strong developmental interrelationship between the bilingual child's two languages and that conceptual information and discourse strategies acquired in the first language transfer to the second.

This research supports Cummins' argument that minority-language children learn a second language best when their first language is maintained and developed. The interesting question from the practitioners' point of view is what bearing these theoretical considerations and empirical findings should have on decisions concerning instructional practice. Cummins (1981) recommended that instruction in the early grades take place primarily through the first language so that children develop the conceptual apparatus to deal with context-reduced input in a second language. Specifically, he proposed that school districts provide at least 50% instruction in the early grades through the first language.

Here it is important not to lose sight of how linguistic and pedagogical arguments can be pre-empted for political purposes. For example, Cummins' theoretical arguments provide an opportune justification for the implementation of home language and national schools in Bavaria, in which minority-language children receive instruction primarily through their first language, but in the process are cut off from contact with their German peers and are effectively deprived of equal educational opportunities. Paradoxically, it is through these home language schools that Bavaria is "reproducing the caste of assembly-line workers" (Skutnabb-Kangas, 1978).

For this reason a number of German authors (Glück, 1984; Graf, 1984) have warned that calls for instruction in and through the home language in the German context are likely to perpetuate the segregation of individuals from minority-language backgrounds and produce two totally separate social and educational systems. There is considerable evidence that daily contact between minority-language children and their majority-language peers is crucial to the success of any bilingual programme. No amount of special training in a second language is as beneficial to the learner as frequent, meaningful interaction with speakers of that language (Wong Fillmore, 1982a). Furthermore, such contact is important for the socialization of both minority and majority groups. The segregation of minority-language children in national or home language schools does not prepare these children — or the majority-language children — to live in harmony with one another.

One way of achieving this integration is through the "reverse immersion" approach, in which majority- and minority-language children are instructed together in the early grades primarily in the minority language, with increasing amounts of instruction in the majority language in the later grades. Such an approach has been used effectively in the San Diego school system with Spanish- and English-speaking children. In such a programme the Spanish-speaking are essentially receiving home language instruction and the English-speaking are in an immersion Spanish programme. Other attempts to integrate minority- and majority-language children, while providing home language instruction, are the "Krefeld Modell" in West Germany (Dickoff, 1982) and "composite" classrooms in Sweden (Lofgren & Ouvinen-Birgerstam, 1980).

I believe that these approaches represent the best direction for bilingual education. It seems to me critical that the first language be used as the prime medium of instruction in the early grades and that minority-language children be allowed to build up literacy-related skills in their first language before reading and writing are introduced in the second. At the same time I would argue that it is critical that these children have daily contact with native speakers from the beginning of their school experience so that oral language skills can develop in the second language.

Krashen

I would like to turn now to the theoretical writings of Stephen Krashen and, specifically, to pedagogical developments on the American scene that developed from Krashen's theory. As is well known, Krashen (1981b) distinguished between "acquisition" and "learning". Acquisition refers to a process similar to the process whereby children acquire languages. It requires meaningful interaction in the target language, in which speakers are concerned not with the form of their utterances, but with the messages they are conveying and understanding. Learning, on the other hand, is a conscious process that involves rule isolation and error correction intended to help individuals obtain a correct mental representation of the target language.

Krashen claimed that conscious learning is available to performers only as a Monitor. In general, he argued, utterances are initiated by the acquired system and conscious learning may be used — through the Monitor — to alter the output of the acquired system, sometimes before and sometimes after utterances are produced. According to Krashen, formal instruction in a second language is effective only as a source of input for some learners, but that there is little transfer from formal, conscious learning to communicative performance. For Krashen and his followers, the only way to develop competence in a second language is through extensive communicative experience.

The implications of the theory for second language teaching have been developed by Krashen (1981a) and Tracy Terrell (1981) in what they call the

Natural Approach. In this approach the emphasis in language teaching is on meaningful interaction, where errors are tolerated as a natural product of the acquisition process, and where the teacher's role is to furnish learners with "comprehensible input" that is understandable to the learner and yet provides new structures or other language materials that the learner has not yet acquired.

The following are some principles of the Natural Approach:

1. The learner must receive "comprehensible input" in Krashen's (1981b) sense. That is, the child must be able to understand the essential meaning of the communication, even though individual words and morphemes may not be understood.
2. Speech must contain a message and there must be a need to communicate that message. Sentences that are taught to children in order to demonstrate a rule of grammar will not help the child to use the rule in speech.
3. The language learning environment should be free of tension. Children will only learn if they feel secure affectively. Related to this is the notion that error correction is ineffectual and tension-creating. Children should feel free to experiment creatively with the new language.
4. No attempt should be made to force production before children are ready. A period of three to six months is necessary for children learning a second language to develop enough competence in understanding to allow them to begin speaking (based on Terrell, 1981).

Although I believe that there are many commendable aspects of the "Natural Approach", there are a number of problems. One problem for the teacher attempting to use this method is to determine what is "comprehensible input" for the children in her class, especially when they vary in ability in the second language. What input is easy enough to be understood and yet sufficiently in advance of what the child knows to provide new material for learning? It is also difficult for teachers to avoid the temptation to correct students' errors. Teachers are likely to feel that unless students receive feedback about their mistakes, they will continue to make them. It is one thing to accept, in theory, the notion that non-native speaking children should be allowed to experiment creatively with the second language; it is another thing to deal with this "creativity" in practice. Indeed, some authors (e.g. Canale & Swain, 1980) have argued that if grammatical accuracy is not emphasized from the beginning, certain grammatical inaccuracies will "fossilize" — that is, will persist over time in spite of further language training. The result can be a classroom "interlanguage" — a language that satisfies communicative needs in the classroom, but does not correspond entirely to the language system used by native speakers of the language (Selinker, Swain & Dumas, 1975).

Another problem with the Natural Approach is that, by stressing Krashen's (1981b) notion of "acquisition" (as distinct from "learning"), this method runs the risk of making it appear that learners will "catch" a second language by exposure, much as children catch the measles or chicken pox (Saville-Troike, 1978). The experience of children in submersion, all-English classes has shown that it is possible for children to have had years of exposure to English without acquiring fluency in comprehension or use.

There is also the question of the role of formal language instruction. According to the Natural Approach, the best form of instruction in a second language is one in which emphasis is given to providing appropriate input to the learners and encouraging them to use the language in meaningful interpersonal communication. This may be an effective method with young children, but older children may also profit from instruction that involves rule-isolation and attention to grammatical usage (Canale & Swain, 1980; Gadalla, 1981). In fact, there is evidence that older children do benefit from being exposed to explicit grammatical instruction (Long, 1983).

Finally, the Natural Approach places its emphasis entirely on language as used in oral, interpersonal interactions. Recently, a number of authors have argued that the kind of language skills children need in the classroom include interpersonal communicative competencies, but also academic communicative competencies. According to the promoters of this approach — which has been called the Functional Approach — what matters for the minority-language child learning a second language in a classroom setting is not just oral interpersonal skills, but also the literacy-related skills that the child needs in the classroom (Chamot, 1983).

The theoretical basis for the Functional Approach can be found in the notional/functional syllabus designed by the Council of Europe (van Ek, 1977) and in Cummins (1979, 1981) model of language proficiency. The Council of Europe's notional/functional syllabus derived from an examination of the linguistic needs of foreign language learners in different European countries. These needs were matched with what could be done in a classroom in a limited time and the syllabus designed accordingly. Thus, if the need of the learner is to develop oral proficiency to survive in a foreign country, language instruction focuses on this survival objective.

Cummins' position is that there are two aspects of language proficiency: (a) those skills needed for context-embedded, face-to-face communication, and (b) those skills needed for context-reduced, academic communicative proficiency. Granted that context-embedded language is present and needed in the classroom, the type of language used in academic instruction and on achievement tests is substantially different (Wong Fillmore, 1982a). The intent of the Functional Approach is to help children learn those functions and uses of language that are part of the decontextualized language proficiency they need to succeed in the classroom.

The limitation of the Functional Approach at the present time is that not enough is known about the functions that characterize normal instruction in schools. There have been some attempts to describe context-reduced academic language (especially Graf, 1984; Wong Fillmore, 1982b), but more careful observational research is needed of the language used in instruction in different subject matter at different grade levels. Furthermore, there is the question of how to teach functional language to minority-language children. Again, there are some beginnings (especially the work of De Avila, Duncan & Cohen, 1981 on discovery learning), but much more experimentation and research is needed.

I do not mean to imply that either the Natural Approach or the Functional Approach are entirely new. In the field of language pedagogy we are continually re-inventing the wheel. The point I wish to make is that these approaches are the most popular current fads or "bandwagons" on the American scene. I find it interesting to compare these developments with theory and pedagogy in the Soviet Union.

Theory East

In the Soviet Union an estimated 150 different languages are spoken, of which Russian is by far the most widely used. Russian is the first language of almost half of the population and has close linguistic affinity to Ukrainian and Byelorussian, languages spoken by another 25% of the population. Nonetheless, in many areas in the Soviet Union only a minority of the population speaks Russian. This is partly due to geographic isolation and partly to an official policy that allows children to be educated in their home language during the early years of schooling. Even in the Russian Federal Republic there are 100 different "nationalities" and 48 minority languages (Baskakov, 1979). In the 14 non-Russian republics there are a total of 169 nationalities and 50 ethnic groups with more than 20,000 members. About 35% of all Soviet children are taught in a language other than Russian (in Central Asian republics about 80% of all children are taught in non-Russian elementary and secondary schools). Throughout the Soviet Union 59 different languages are used as media of instruction (Ferguson, Houghton & Wells, 1977).

This linguistic heterogeneity has been a troublesome issue for Soviet authorities since the October Revolution. Should the peoples of the various republics be allowed to retain their own national languages or should Russian be forcefully introduced as the language of all people of the Soviet Union? There have been various ways of responding to this question that I would like to discuss briefly before turning to Soviet educational practices in teaching Russian as the "first second language" for non-Russian speakers.

Soviet policy toward national languages

There has been a certain ambivalence in Soviet policy towards the preservation of ethnic national languages. The aim of universal literacy in a multilingual state necessitates the use of the national languages in the educational system, yet the goal of creating a single Soviet nation implies a linguistically homogeneous society.

Historically, Soviet policy has swung from one extreme to the other with some attempts to reach a middle ground. In the years after the Revolution the goal of universal literacy held priority. Both Lenin and Stalin supported the use of the national languages in education. Lenin sharply opposed the supremacy of any one language in the Soviet state:

> "If nations are to get along freely and peacefully with one another (or if they wish), go their separate ways and form different states, it is necessary to have a complete democracy, such as the working class stands for. No privilege for any nation, for any language! Not the slightest restriction, not the least injustice toward any national minority! These are the principles of a workers' democracy."
> (1913, cited in Glück, 1984)

Stalin argued that "It is necessary that not only the schools but also all institutions should operate in the languages understood by the masses" (1921, cited in Lewis, 1978: 227).

In time, however, Stalin's view changed. The period from the middle of the 1930s to Stalin's death in 1953 was marked by emphasis on centralism and linguistic homogeneity. Stalin condemned "exaggerated" respect for national languages, and the teaching of Russian was made compulsory throughout the Soviet Union. There was some relaxation of this pressure towards uniformity in the Khruschev era, but there continues to be an emphasis on the central position of the Russian language as a means of co-ordination between the peoples of the 15 republics. In fact, some authors (e.g. Kreindler, 1982) argue that there is a steady movement away from

Lenin's position to a tsarist concept of Russian as "the cement of the Empire".

The central position of Russian is furthered by its international status and by the pre-eminent position of Russian as the language of higher education. Furthermore, Russian is the language of the Communist Party, which has an influence on all aspects of social life in every part of the country. Advancement in education and in the Party requires mastery of the Russian language. In addition, the Soviet Union's position as a modern technological society requires a single language for scientific communication.

Soviet apologists for the Russian language do not limit their case to these arguments, however. There is also the ideological vision of a Soviet state in which all nations are merged into a single people capable of communicating in a single language:

> "Instead of the dominance of the language of the ruling class, as occurs in imperialist countries, the process runs in just the opposite direction in the Socialist State — in the direction of a free adoption of one of the languages by millions of workers, because this language is widely used throughout the many nations of the country." (Chanazarov, 1977, cited in Glück, 1984).

The Soviet state has at its disposal enormous resources for social engineering — especially through education — and one of the principal goals of bilingual education is the realization of this vision of all of the peoples of the Soviet Union united through a single language.

But there are limits to what social engineering can achieve in a country as large and as complex as the Soviet Union. Language and culture are part of the expression of selfhood and to deprive people of their language and culture is to strike at the essence of their personal being. Through experience the leaders of the Soviet state have come to realize the force of emotional attachment to a national language. Even Stalin admitted that it was useless to attempt to suppress national languages. He regarded language as the "opiate of the nations", and adopted the cynical view that it was the right of the people of a non-Russian nation to say what the Kremlin wanted in their own language (Lewis, 1972).

Another consideration that has led to tolerance for the use of non-Russian languages is the awareness that it is only through these languages that non-Russian speakers can become literate. The Soviet state was able to achieve universal literacy only by educating its people in their own languages. It is doubtful whether universal literacy would be maintained if all education were to be in Russian.

Furthermore, recent attempts to introduce all-Russian education at the expense of national languages has met with vigorous resistance from the native intelligentsia of the various republics. This new generation has replaced the intelligentsia eliminated by Stalin and, while likely to be competent in Russian, is at the same time proud of their native language and culture. As one author put it, describing the situation in Uzbekistan:

> "In recent years there has been a growing pride in Uzbek culture and history as Uzbeks begin to search for their 'roots'. Unlike most of the 1930s and 1940s, when expressions of non-Russian ethnic pride were severely repressed, today Uzbek music, art, and literature (even if in their Soviet form) are enjoying something of a renaissance. In everyday life Uzbeks encounter situations in which they are constantly reminded that their own culture is of great antiquity and value." (Fierman, 1982: 76).

The attempt to eliminate the reference to Georgian as the "state language" of that republic led to a language riot on April 14, 1978, which lasted five hours and involved a young crowd variously estimated at several hundreds, as a minimum, or up to 50,000. In the face of that demonstration the authorities had second thoughts and reference to the indigenous language being the "state language" was restored in the state constitutions of Georgia, Armenia, and Azerbadzhan (Bilinsky, 1982).

Thus the official policy of the Soviet Union supports national languages and cultures, while at the same time promoting Russian as the basis for the development of a single "all-embracing" Soviet nationality (*Pravda*, December 19, 1983). Soviet officials are resentful of accusations of "Russification", and argue that they do not merely tolerate, but actively encourage minority languages and cultures. Whether this is simply a rationalization for being unable to eliminate national languages is difficult to say. In any event, it is likely that linguistic issues will continue to be a cause of tension in the Soviet Union both because of minority groups' resentment of Russian predominance and because of Russian prejudice, especially scorn for such groups as the Moslems of Central Asia, the fastest growing sector of the population.

Educational practices

Soviet educational practice is largely determined by ideological principles. The ideology derives from Marxist–Leninist theory, which stresses the identity of language and thought and their dependence on the "objective" conditions of existence. According to Lenin, learning takes place through the action of the human organism on society and through active manipulation of the environment. Learning is essentially a public, social, and active process (Talyzina, 1978; Vygotsky, 1962).

The Soviet approach to language learning is based upon a belief in the primary importance of social experience and on the possibility of manipulating the social environment to accelerate language development. Soviet educators argue that language development — even first language development — can be stimulated and accelerated by instruction. This instruction, however, cannot be left to the teacher's intuition. Soviet pedagogy demands uniformity in order to achieve its results in a limited time with limited resources. A mass system of teaching languages cannot rely upon the inborn talents of the individual teacher. Instead the Soviet system of language instruction depends on standardized procedures, teaching techniques, equipment, and materials. Precise techniques are to be devised on the basis of analysis and research that dictate what it is that the language instructor is to do in the classroom.

Language teaching is based on the notion that language is a rule-governed behaviour. The teacher's function is to bring these rules to the consciousness of the student, to make the student aware of the theory that ties rules together. Linguistic pedagogy involves a progression to an intuitive or unconscious awareness of language through an explicit and conscious appreciation of its characteristics. Various techniques of pattern practice are utilized, not to instill habits through repetition, but to lead to the student's awareness of the structural significance of what is drilled. In recent years more emphasis has been put on drills that can be used actively in communicative tasks (Chernikov, 1979).

With younger children the process of bringing rules to the consciousness of the student is an inductive one. Formal grammatical terminology is introduced gradually to facilitate the students' internal schematization of linguistic experience. Older children, who are aware of the rule-governed nature of language, are taught deductively in systematic fashion (Chernikov, 1979).

Because second-language learning is based upon conscious employment of linguistic rules and strategies, Soviet pedagogues see it to be the reverse of the process that occurs in first-language development. Vygotsky (1962) argued that second-language learning does not repeat the course of first-language learning, but is an analogous system developing in a reverse direction. Each system complements the other and the two languages interact to the advantage of each. By heightening the student's consciousness of rule-governed processes, the learning of a second language benefits and refines control of the first.

Soviet educators stress the importance of the first language in learning a second. They argue that there is a single language competence, or "set", that underlies both languages of a bilingual. This general competence refers to some unconscious "feel" for language that permits its practical use in communicative settings. It is this competence in the first language that provides the basis for second-language learning.

Thus second-language education in the Soviet Union stresses the priority of conscious understanding of the rule-governed characteristics of the language. The ultimate goal is the development of linguistic competence or an unconscious feeling for the language. Because the child has developed linguistic competence in a first language, the home language is given a prominent place in second-language learning. Indeed, comparision and translation from the first language is one means of achieving a conscious understanding of the second.

It should be noted that there is a close bond between Soviet pedagogy and psychological research. In the Soviet Union, leading psychologists, such as Vygotsky, Leont'ev, and Markova, have concerned themselves with the process of second-language learning. There have been numerous experiments involving the application of psycholinguistic principles to school practice.

In all Soviet schools, no matter what the medium of instruction, Russian is taught as the compulsory state language. In many cases instruction in Russian — at least basic sounds and vocabulary — begins in pre-school or kindergarten. Textbooks and materials are standardized and considerable attention has been given to teacher education.

Many of the textbooks used for teaching Russian as a second language are specifically designed for particular non-Russian language groups. Acceptance of the possibility of using translation as a means of understanding the rule system of a second language has led Soviet linguists to develop a form of contrastive analysis (Desheriev & Protchenko, 1979). Soviet authors have given considerable attention to the causes of interference between languages and have attempted to incorporate their findings in language textbooks designed for speakers of specific languages (e.g. Uzbek or Azerbaydzhani) learning Russian as a second language.

There is some question as to how effective Russian instruction is in non-Russian-speaking areas. Lewis (1972) has argued that in spite of the standardization of Russian language instruction in the Soviet Union and the strong motivation of large sectors of the population to acquire Russian, most students in non-Russian areas leave the elementary school with a very deficient knowledge of the language:

> "It is not unlikely that the situation of Russian in the USSR, outside Russia itself, is similar to that of the English language in India on the eve of independence — the perpetration of the same methodological and administrative mistakes, wide diffusion and considerable acquaintance with the language among the intelligentsia, but few and parched roots for the language among the vast majority of the population, even among school children who are instructed in it." (Lewis, 1972: 203)

This view is at odds with the more optimistic Soviet position, according to which there has been — and will continue to be — a steady increase in the proportion of people in the Soviet Union who know Russian (currently estimated at 82%).

East and West compared

Although I certainly do not consider myself an authority on Soviet pedagogy, and I do not think that we know enough to say with certainty how effective Soviet second-language instruction is, I think there are some things we can learn from the Soviet experience with multilingual education. The points I wish to make come under three headings: (1) instructional models, (2) teaching practices, and (3) research strategies.

Instructional models

I find it interesting that Soviet educators stress the notion that there is a single language competence, or "set", that underlies both languages of a bilingual. This is quite consistent with Cummins' "linguistic interdependence hypothesis", according to which he argued that certain aspects of a bilingual's proficiency in the first and second language are common or interdependent across languages. In fact, Cummins is familiar with Soviet writings and his own theory was influenced by the notion of set advanced by Soviet authors.

Both Cummins and Soviet educators draw similar implications with respect to multilingual instruction. For Cummins emphasis in the early grades should be on first-language instruction so that the minority-language child can build up literacy-related skills that will transfer to the second language. This does not preclude early oral exposure to the second language. Cummins' theory does not imply that minority-language children should be segregated and taught exclusively in their first language. In fact, he pointed out that:

"The more context-embedded the initial L2 input, the more comprehensible it will be and, paradoxically, the more successful in ultimately developing L2 skills in context-reduced situations." (Cummins, 1981: 14)

Thus Cummins holds that literacy skills in a second language develop from proficiency in oral skills in that language, as well as from literacy skills in the child's first language.

Soviet educators also believe that it is competence in the first language that provides the basis for second-language learning. Although there are some schools in which minority-language children are taught through Russian in immersion-like programmes, such programmes are predominately found in areas where there are many nationalities living together. In other areas where instruction in the home language is practical, children in the early grades are taught in this language throughout their years in school, with Russian taught as a second language from kindergarten. These schools are either national language schools or schools for large minority-language groups in non-Russian republics.

There has been some experimentation in the Soviet Union with parallel-medium instruction, in which children from different language backgrounds attend the same school and mix socially. In these schools children from different language backgrounds receive instruction in their own language, with Russian used as the language of play and of extracurricular activities. Soviet educators argue that children in such schools learn more Russian than in national or minority-language schools and that such schools avoid the undesirable consequences of segregation inherent in national or minority-language schools.

It should be noted that in such parallel-medium schools, children are taught the same curriculum in their own home languages. There is no mixing of languages in instruction. Dual medium instruction, involving the use of two languages at different times — the practice in most transitional bilingual programmes in the United States — has been forbidden in the Soviet Union since the 1930s (Lewis, 1972).

I think that this is an important point. In many American bilingual programmes minority-language children learn to read and write in both languages simultaneously. A common complaint of teachers is that such an approach does not leave enough time for the practice, review, and repetition needed to learn two writing systems, two spelling systems, and two systems of punctuation (Thonis, 1981). In the early grades, in particular, it may be difficult for minority-language children to use two languages at different times in literacy-related instruction. This is one reason why a number of authors — including Cummins — have advocated that schools adopt an instructional model in which minority-language children learn to read and write in their first language before they receive such instruction in a second language.

Teaching practices

Soviet second-language pedagogy stresses, as we have seen, the notion that language is a rule-governed behaviour. As A. K. Markova, head of the Institute for General and Educational Psychology of the Academy of Pedagogical Sciences, put it in her book, *The Teaching and Mastery of Language*:

> "The period of school age differs fundamentally from other stages in life because during this period language and the system of linguistic devices and tools are the object of special study for the child. In school, children learn socially elaborated means of operating with language as laid down in the rules of grammar. Pupils must acquire a conscious awareness of linguist tools if speech activity is to be cultivated." (Markova, 1979: 26–27)

To achieve this conscious awareness of linguistic structures and tools, Soviet teachers stress rule isolation and error correction. In Krashen's terms, the focus is on "learning" rather than "acquisition" — even with children in the early grades.

Such an approach is antithetical to recent pedagogical developments in the West, particularly the Natural Approach. The Natural Approach deliberately de-emphasizes rule isolation and error correction. According to Krashen and Terrell, the only way to develop competence in a second language is through extensive communicative experience. Focusing on linguistic structures and rule systems is, for these writers, counter-productive.

At this point, it is impossible to say which approach is likely to produce the best results. The Soviet method appears to be quite successful with adult learners in special language schools, many of whom achieve native-like levels of proficiency. But this evidence is more anecdotal than hard, and one would have to have more precise information about how foreign languages are taught in such schools. Hard evidence is also lacking on how successful emphasis on conscious awareness of linguistic structures is as a method of instruction with young children, because there has not been longitudinal research on the Soviet scene comparing this technique with other methods.

Nonetheless, it seems to me that some attention to the formal properties of language can be a healthy antidote to a rigorous and dogmatic
application of the Natural Approach. Especially with older children, conscious awareness of linguistic structures can help second-language learners
to consolidate their knowledge of the language and its application. Any
method of language instruction can become insipid to learners if applied
dogmatically — witness the use of audio-lingual methods in FLES programmes. The doctrinaire application of the Natural Approach faces the same
danger, and some eclecticism in this respect may be a good thing.

Secondly, Soviet educators are aware to a greater extent than are
advocates of the Natural Approach that language learning in the classroom
is a different process than language learning in the "natural" context. As
Leont'ev (1970) pointed out, the school child learning a second language
already possesses a great deal of knowledge about language and its functional uses from experience with the first language. Moreover, the use of
language in the school setting is quite different from its use in everyday
face-to-face interaction. This is the insight of advocates of the Functional
Approach (Chamot, 1983), which seems quite consistent with Soviet
writings about the role of language in the classroom.

Research strategies

The final point I wish to make has to do with Soviet research strategies.
It is here that I think that we can learn most from Soviet practices. There is a
close bond between Soviet psycholinguistic research and second-language
pedagogy. Theory is closely related to practice — much more so than in the
West where theory tends to be *ad hoc* and much research and practice is
carried out in a theoretical vacuum.

Soviet psycholinguistic research has been dominated by the work of
Vygotsky, Luria, and their followers, principally Leont'ev and Markova.
According to this school, speech is one of many human acts that are gov-
erned by the same set of principles. Acts have goals, are composed of
component parts that are hierarchically organized to optimize the realization of the goal, and are learned through initially conscious control until they
eventually become automatic. Psychological research has been concerned
with the internal structure of acts through componential analysis directed at
determining the simplest parts that do not lend themselves to further
analysis.

This way of looking at things is in many respects similar to what we in
the West would call an information processing perspective, although such

terms as "acts", "goals", and "componential analysis" may have a different meaning to Soviet writers because of how these terms have been used in their research tradition. Nonetheless, the theoretical orientation and the mode of analysis used by these influential Soviet authors corresponds closely to those characteristic of contemporary Western cognitive psychology.

I have argued elsewhere (McLaughlin, 1978; McLaughlin, Rossman & McLeod, 1983) for an information-processing approach to second-language pedagogy and research that stresses the limited cognitive capacities of human learners, the use of various information-handling techniques to overcome these limitations, and the need for integration of subskills in mastering complex tasks. In this view, the acquisition of a complex skill, such as learning a second language, is thought to involve the gradual integration of lower-level skills and their accumulation as automatic processes in long-term storage. As automaticity develops, more time-consuming controlled processing is bypassed and attentional limitations are overcome.

I believe that the long-term goal for research on second-language learning should be a "components skill analysis" in which the first step would be to specify the component information-processing skills that make up the task of learning a second language. The next step is to determine which specified skills potentially are involved in determining individual variation in overall success on the task. Finally, one needs to determine the relative contribution to variation in overall success made by each skill or skill group. This research agenda seems to me quite similar to the thrust of recent Soviet research, especially as represented by the writings of Leont'ev and Markova.

The next decade is likely to see an increasing amount of research in the field of second-language learning that uses the concepts and modes of analysis of cognitive psychology. It would be ideal if we in the West could take advantage of Soviet work in this area as well — if more Soviet work were translated and if there were greater opportunities for scholarly exchange. Both sides could benefit from such exchange — Soviet authors rarely cite non-Soviet work.

My argument has been that we would do well to emulate the Soviet practice of using psychology as a feeder discipline for second-language research and pedagogy. This is no substitute for linguistic analysis. But second-language research has been largely concerned with linguistic — and more specifically, syntactic — issues, and there is a definite need to go beyond the product of learning and to examine the process of learning from an information-processing perspective. Both approaches are needed if we are to understand second-language learning.

References

BASKAKOV, N. A. (ed.) 1979, *Puti razvitiia natsional'nogo russkogo dvuiazychiia v nerusskikh shkolakh SSSR*. Moscow: Nauka.

BILINSKY, Y. 1982, Haste makes waste, or the political dangers of accelerated Russification. *International Journal of the Sociology of Language*, 33, 63–69.

CANALE, M. & SWAIN, M. 1980, Theoretical bases of communicative approaches to second language teaching and testing. *Applied Linguistics*, 1, 1–47.

CHAMOT, A. U. 1983, Toward a functional ESL curriculum in the elementary school. *TESOL Quarterly*, 17, 459–72.

CHANAZAROV, K. CH. 1977, Reshenie natsional' no-jazykovoi problemy v SSSR. Moscow: Nauka.

CHERNIKOV, P. K. 1979, Osnovnye problemy formirovaniia in razvitiia dvuiazychiia u uchashchikhsia natsional'noi shkoly. In N. A. BASKAKOV (ed.), *Puti razvitiia natsional'nogo russkogo dvuiazychiia v nerusskikh shkolakh SSSR*. Moscow: Nauka.

CUMMINS, J. 1979, Linguistic interdependence and the educational development of bilingual children. *Review of Educational Research*, 49, 222–51.

— 1980, The cross-lingual dimensions of language proficiency: Implications for bilingual education and the optimal age issue. *TESOL Quarterly*, 14, 175–87.

— 1981, The role of primary language development in promoting educational success for language minority students. *Schooling and language minority students: A theoretical framework*. Los Angeles: Evaluation, Dissemination and Assessment Center. California State University, Los Angeles.

DE AVILA, E. A., DUNCAN, S. E. & COHEN, E. G. 1981, *Improving cognition: A multicultural approach*. Final report. MICA Project: Multi-cultural improvement of cognitive abilities. Rosslyn, VA: National Clearinghouse for Bilingual Education.

DESHERIEV, I. D. & PROTCHENKO, I. F. 1979, Natsional'nye otnosheniia v zrelom sotsialisticheskom obshchestve i razvitie dvuiazychiia v natsional'nykh shkolakh. In: N. A. BASKAKOV (ed.), *Puti razvitiia natsional'nogo russkogo dvuiazychiia v nerusskikh shkolokh SSSR*. Moscow: Nauka.

DICKOFF, K.-H. 1982, *Erziehung ausländischer Kinder als pädagogische Herausforderung: Das Krefelder Modell*. Düsseldorf: Schwann.

EDELSKY, C., HUDELSON, S., FLORES, B., BARKIN, F., ALTWERGER, B. & JILBERT, K. 1983, Semilingualism and language deficit. *Applied Linguistics*, 4, 1–22.

FERGUSON, C. A., HOUGHTON, C. & WELLS, M. H. 1977, Bilingual education: An international perspective. In B. SPOLSKY & R. COOPER (eds), *Frontiers of bilingual education*. Rowley, MA: Newbury House.

FIERMAN, B. 1982, The view from Uzbekistan. *International Journal of the Sociology of Language*, 33, 71–78.

GADALLA, B. J. 1981, Language acquisition research and the language teacher. *Studies in Second Language Acquisition*, 4, 60–69.

GLÜCK, H. 1984, *Der muttersprachliche Unterricht für die Kinder der Immigranten als sprachen- und bildungspolitisches Problem*. Paper given at the Colloquium of the Societa Linguistica Italiana, Cosenza, Italy, March 1984.

GRAF, P. 1984, *Frühe Zweisprachigkeit und schulisches Lernen: Empirische Grundlagen zur Erziehung von Kindern ethnischer Minderheiten*. Munich: University of Munich.

KRASHEN, S. 1981a, Bilingual education and second language acquisition theory.

Schooling and language minority students: A theoretical framework. Los Angeles: Evaluation, Dessemination and Assessment Center. California State University, Los Angeles.

— 1981b, *Second language acquisition and second language learning.* Oxford: Pergamon.

KREINDLER, I. 1982, The changing status of Russian in the Soviet Union. *International Journal of the Sociology of Language,* 33, 7–39.

LEONT'EV, A. A. 1970, *Psycholinguistik und Sprachunterricht.* Stuttgart: Kohlhammer, 1974 (original Russian, 1970).

LEWIS, E. G. 1972, *Multilingualism in the Soviet Union.* The Hague: Mouton.

— 1978, Bilingual education and social change in the Soviet Union. In: B. SPOLSKY & R. L. COOPER (eds), *Case Studies in bilingual education.* Rowley, MA.: Newbury House.

LOFGREN, H. & OUVINEN-BIRGERSTAM, P. 1980, *Model for the bilingual instruction of migrant children.* Stockholm: National Swedish Board of Education.

LONG, M. 1981, Input, interaction, and second-language acquisition. In H. WINITZ (ed.), *Native language and foreign language acquisition.* New York: New York Academy of Science.

MARKOVA, A. K. 1979, *The teaching and mastery of language.* White Plains, N.Y.: Sharpe.

MCLAUGHLIN, B. 1978, The Monitor Model: Some methodological considerations. *Language Learning,* 28, 309–32.

MCLAUGHLIN, B., ROSSMAN, T. & MCLEOD, B. 1983, Second language learning: An information-processing perspective. *Language Learning,* 33, 135–58.

REHBEIN, J. 1982, Wörterklarungen türkischer Kinder. *Osnabrücker Beiträge zur Sprachtheorie,* 22, 122–58.

— 1984, *Diskurs und Verstehen: Zur Role der Muttersprache bei der Textverarbeitung in der Zweitsprache.* University of Hamburg.

SAVILLE-TROIKE, M. 1978, Implications of research on adult second-language acquisition for teaching foreign languages to children. In R. C. GINGRAS (ed.), *Secondlanguage acquisition and foreign language teaching.* Arlington, VA.: Center for Applied Linguistics.

SELINKER, L., SWAIN, M. & DUMAS, G. 1975, The interlanguage hypothesis extended to children. *Language Learning,* 25, 139–52.

SKUTNABB-KANGAS, T. 1978, Semilingualism and the education of migrant children as a means of reproducing the caste of assembly line workers. In N. DITTMAR, H. HABERLAND, T. SKUTNABB-KANGAS & U. TELEMAN (eds), *Papers for the first Scandinavian–German symposium on the language of immigrant workers and their children.* Roskilde, Denmark: Universetscenter.

TALYZINA, N. F. 1978, Odin iz putei razvitiia sovetskoi teorii ucheniia. *Voprosy psikhologii,* 1, 16–27.

TERRELL, T. D. 1981, The natural approach in bilingual education. *Schooling and language minority students: A theoretical framework.* Los Angeles: Evaluation. Dissemination and Assessment Center. California State University, Los Angeles.

THONIS, E. W. 1981, Reading instruction for language minority students. *Schooling and language minority students: A theoretical framework.* Los Angeles: Evaluation, Dissemination and Assessment Center. California State University, Los Angeles.

TROIKE, R. 1981, *SCALP: Social and cultural aspects of language proficiency.* Paper read at Conference on Language Proficiency Assessment, Warrenton, VA.

VAN EK, J. A. 1977, *The threshold level for modern language learning in schools*. The Council of Europe: London, Longman.

VYGOTSKY, L. S. 1962, *Thought and language*. Cambridge, MA: MIT Press.

WONG FILLMORE, L. 1982a, Instructional language as linguistic input: Second language learning in classrooms. In L. C. WILKINSON (ed.), *Communicating in the classroom*. New York: Academic Press.

— 1982b, Language minority students and school participation: What kind of English is needed? *Journal of Education*, 164, 143–56.

6 Schools as agents for language revival in Ireland and New Zealand

RICHARD A. BENTON

New Zealand and the Republic of Ireland share a number of chracteristics: both have populations of just over three million, and a high degree of urbanization with one urban area (Auckland and Dublin respectively) containing a quarter or more of the country's people. Both have a British colonial past (although New Zealand's has perhaps more in common with Northern Ireland than with the Republic, and was of much briefer duration with a considerably less turbulent road to independence). Both have been agricultural countries, although Irish exports are now predominantly of manufactured goods, whereas, despite rapid industrial growth, New Zealand is still heavily dependent on agriculture for earning foreign exchange.

There are other important differences. When measured by criteria like the ownership of cars, telephones, radios, and television sets, New Zealand is a much more affluent country than Ireland. Its gross national product is about double that of the Republic, and government expenditure somewhat lower. More importantly, New Zealand's population is much less ethnically and culturally homogeneous than that of Ireland. Over the centuries, Ireland has been able to absorb a succession of invaders, so that, in the Republic at least, the vast majority of the population has a common ethnic identity, and also shares a common religion (94% of the population of the Republic of Ireland in 1981 were Roman Catholic). New Zealand is a much younger country, having been settled first from Polynesia only about a millenium ago. The first European contact with New Zealand was in 1642, when Abel Tasman sighted the islands and named them after his native province. Two centuries later, European colonization began in earnest.

Today, about 85% of the New Zealand population is entirely of European origin (predominantly English, but with most other European nationalities also well represented), 12% of Maori ancestry (the original "New Zealanders"), 2% from other parts of Polynesia, and a small but growing number of Asians. Both the Maori and Polynesian populations are young (a characteristic they share with the people of the Irish Republic). Because of this, and because of continued intermarriage with the European majority, the proportion of children of Maori ancestry in primary schools is close to 20% of the school population, and the proportion of New Zealanders of Maori and Polynesian origin in the total population has increased steadily over the past few decades, and is likely to continue to do so.

In the area of language policy in education, New Zealand and the Irish Republic have enough in common to make a comparison of the current situation, together with some of its antecedents, and possible future developments a valuable exercise for anyone interested in the effectiveness of using schools as agents for language revival. Such an examination is also instructive for those interested in schools as instruments for accelerating language change, and in the degree to which officially stated policies can be efficiently negated by officially sanctioned practices.

The special relevance of the Irish experience for New Zealand

As W. F. Mackey (1982: 2) has pointed out: ". . . in a world which is returning to its ethnic and regional roots, speakers of other ancient but stateless tongues are looking to Ireland to supply the model for language revival". The Irish model is important in two ways. Firstly, it is an attempt to reverse a well established process of language replacement when that process has almost reached completion. Secondly, the school has been the main instrument through which the attempts to revive Irish as an everyday spoken language have been effected.

English has been the lingua franca in Ireland since the end of the eighteenth century. In the twentieth century, the language has been spoken natively in three areas in the west of Ireland — relatively isolated from each other and the rest of the country — and most native-speakers of Irish have also learned English as children. New Zealand was overwhelmingly a Maori-speaking country until the proclamation of British sovereignty in 1840. Within a decade, English-speaking settlers had outnumbered the Maori population in the country as a whole, and by the turn of the century, little more than 5% of New Zealanders were of Maori origin. As this population was concentrated in the far north, central, and eastern portions of the North

Island, the situation of Maori speakers in New Zealand paralleled that of their counterparts in the Gaeltacht (Irish-speaking districts) in Ireland.

Since the 1920s, Ireland has relied on the education system, and especially upon primary schools, to carry the major part of the burden of language revival. John Harris (1982a: 19) has pointed out that the teaching of Irish in Ireland differs from second language teaching elsewhere in Europe through a unique combination of four factors:

(a) the second language is taught to all pupils from the beginning of primary school;
(b) it is taught mainly as a subject;
(c) there is no significant naturally-occurring pressure to use the language outside the school; and
(d) the aim is to produce spoken proficiency (as against an academic knowledge of the language or an emphasis on reading and writing).[1]

At the same time, there has been a strong movement (pre-dating the establishment of the modern Irish state) for the development of bilingualism through the exclusive use of Irish in the primary schools. For a time, this was also the goal of state policy, but such "all-Irish" schools now represent simply an alternative to the mainly English-medium system for an enthusiastic minority.

There are some striking parallels here to the situation in New Zealand in 1984. Since 1974, all New Zealand primary schools have been officially asked to include "elements of the Maori language" in their curricula, although the manner and timing of doing so has been left to individual school principals. Nevertheless official figures indicate that over 10% of primary school children throughout the country have been formally studying Maori since the late 1970s, and the Department of Education has formed a corps of itinerant teachers to assist schools to develop their own programmes.[2] There is a heavy emphasis on the development of proficiency in spoken Maori, despite the fact that, under current conditions, comparatively few children would be able to use the language at home or in the neighbourhood. It is also generally accepted that children should begin learning Maori (if they are to learn it at all) as soon as possible after they start school, and considerable pressure has been brought to bear on the education system to make the teaching of Maori at primary school level either compulsory or available as of right to any pupil.[3] At the same time, interest in Maori as a classroom language, either alone or in partnership with English, has been growing rapidly, and between 1976 and 1980 the first four Maori/English bilingual primary schools were approved by the Minister of Education.

FIGURE 1 *Maori-speaking Areas of New Zealand (North Island) and Irish-speaking Districts of Ireland*

New Zealand
- ♦ Districts where more than half the *total* population is Maori-speaking
- ▓ Areas where there is widespread bilingualism among the *Maori* population

Ireland
- ■ Areas where Irish is spoken by most of population

Language ecology

Mention has already been made of the Gaeltacht areas in the West of Ireland. In 1971, about 56,000 of the 70,000 residents of these areas were said to be able to speak Irish, so although Irish was widely used in these communities, it had by no means vanquished English (Tovey, 1978: 8). Up until the 1950s, the Maori language possessed similar strongholds in New Zealand (although they did not possess the official status of their Irish counterparts). In 1979, it was estimated that there were about 70,000 native-speakers of Maori in New Zealand (Benton, 1979a: 11). However, comparatively few of these were now living in Maori-speaking districts — the effects of emigration, modernization, and an all-English education system had taken a heavy toll. A glance at the accompanying maps will show both the isolation of the Irish-speaking and Maori-speaking districts in the two countries, and the comparative disadvantage suffered by Maori-speakers through the more rapid anglicization of formerly Maori-speaking areas over the last 20 to 30 years.

Irish-speakers are only slightly more advantaged than Maori-speakers when it comes to the use of their language on radio and television: only about 8% of television time is in the Irish language[4] (less, if one takes into account programmes originating in Northern Ireland as well), and radio broadcasting is also dominated by English. However, since the early 1970s a special Irish-language radio programme has been broadcast to the Gaeltacht areas for several hours daily, and is now relayed to listeners in other parts of the country. Maori-speakers in New Zealand have to be content with a five-minute daily news broadcast on television (begun in 1983), occasional use of the language in programmes of special interest to Maori viewers, and a total of about two hours weekly (including two five-minute news broadcasts daily) on the one national radio network.

Colman O'Huallachain has argued very convincingly that the fate of the Irish language in any part of Ireland, including the Gaeltacht, depends very much on what action is taken in the country as a whole (1977: 147–48). The same is true for Maori in New Zealand. The remaining Maori-speaking communities are currently being given priority in the provision of bilingual primary schools, for example, in the belief that this will assist them to remain Maori-speaking. But in Ireland and New Zealand alike the competition from English undermines the indigenous language everywhere; if it is to be countered effectively, it must also be countered everywhere.

Language policy

According to Article 8 of the Irish Constitution, "the Irish language as the national language is the first official language", and "the English language is recognized as the second official language". Although several attempts have been made to have Maori declared an official or national language of New Zealand,[5] it is at present without any meaningful legal status. An amendment to the Maori Affairs Act, passed in 1974, states that "official recognition is hereby given to the Maori language of New Zealand in its various dialects and idioms as the ancestral language of that portion of the population of New Zealand of Maori descent" (Maori Affairs Amendment Act 1974, Section 51). A series of court cases in 1978–79 has established, however, that these words have no practical import.[6]

Despite the much stronger wording of the Irish Constitution, however, language policy as deduced from actual practice in both countries has been remarkably similar over the last decade. In each case the schools have been given the task of maintaining or reviving the indigenous language, while most other government agencies (including the courts of law) have continued to operate in English. The Irish Department of Education is a partial exception to this generalization — much of its business is still conducted in Irish. Similarly, senior officials of the New Zealand Education Department have been encouraged to learn Maori in recent years, and since 1983 all New Zealand teachers' college students have been required to spend some time studying the language. The setting up by the Irish government in 1978 of an official body (the Bord na Gaeilge) to establish goals for the wider use of Irish, and to monitor progress toward achieving them, has been paralleled in New Zealand by proposals to establish a Trustee for the Maori language, who would have similar duties. The incoming Labour Party government in 1984 promised to prepare legislation to grant full official recognition to the Maori language; in June 1985, the Wellington Maori Language Board, supported by the New Zealand Maori Council and other Maori organizations, began proceedings before the Waitangi Tribunal, claiming that denial of such recognition was in violation of the provisions of the Treaty of Waitangi (which in 1840 transferred national sovereignty from the Maori chiefs to the British Crown).

The role of the school

In Ireland, the school has been the chief agency for generating ability in the Irish language on a national scale since the 1920s. All primary schools have had to devote at least one-fifth of the school day to the Irish language, with the immediate goal (despite differences in approach) of enabling their students to speak Irish fluently. At the secondary level, written proficiency and academic study of the language have increased in importance, but this in the main has affected academically oriented students. The emphasis on developing conversational ability seems to have received strong support from teachers; 91% of primary teachers participating in a 1975 survey, for example, agreed that this should be the key feature of school programmes in Irish (Lindsey, 1975: 106).

Although the ultimate goals of this conversational fluency have become somewhat obscure with the passage of time, it is clear that this approach owes much to the belief by some of the influential leaders of the Irish language revival movement, like Professor Timothy Corcoran, that, just as the National schools had destroyed the language, they could also restore it "even without positive aid from the home" (quoted in Titley, 1983: 140). For people like Eamonn De Valera the teaching of and through Irish in the schools was certainly part of a strategy to make Ireland once again an Irish-speaking nation. Sixty years later, some kind of national bilingualism with Irish in active use but not completely replacing English seems to be an officially acceptable (but as yet unattained) longer-term goal (see Bord na Gaeilge, no date: 1–3 and *passim*).

In New Zealand, a similar stress has been laid on the early development of oral proficiency in Maori. Among the "aims for Maori language learning" in the official draft syllabus for primary schools (N.Z Department of Education, 1983) are "to help your pupils learn and apply the Maori language to everyday situations", and "to maintain and extend, through your pupils, the Maori language and culture". The introduction to the syllabus expresses the hope that through it "we can gather and share with all New Zealanders some of the language and some attitudes and values from New Zealand's Maori inheritance".

This falls a little short of creating a Maori-speaking New Zealand, but it is clear that this knowledge of the Maori language, while of special importance to children who are ethnically Maori, is intended for everyone. Like its much more sophisticated Irish counterpart, the New Zealand syllabus starts at the new-entrant level, and covers all primary school classes. For significant numbers of Maori parents, however, this low-key approach is far from satisfactory. A number of well-attended national gatherings on educational issues have endorsed proposals which would greatly strengthen the position of the Maori language in the schools.[7] One such meeting in January 1984 called for bilingual classes and compulsory use of Maori in *all* New Zealand primary schools; another in April called for Maori language to become part of the compulsory core curriculum in secondary schools. The role envisaged for the school by the advocates of these moves was clearly analogous to the earlier Irish view: the school was to bring the language back to life. One teacher at a meeting called by the New Zealand Maori Council in March complained bitterly of the current academic approach to teaching Maori in secondary schools, saying that it "did not aim to save the language but preserve it like Latin and Greek", and that "the education system has invited you to be a mourner at the tangihanga (funeral) of your culture, your language — and yourself." (Reported in *Tu Tangata*, 18 July 1984 p. 12).

One of the serious conflicts in New Zealand (which also has its Irish equivalent) is that between the pragamtic concerns of the "average person", and the enthusiasm and idealism of a committed minority. Many New Zealanders, irrespective of ethnicity, are highly supportive of some special place for Maori language in education and the ceremonial aspects of national life, but are far from convinced that the language could actually displace English to any significant extent. They are happy for the language to be "preserved", by encouraging people in a few remote places to continue speaking it, and making it available in some form or another in the schools, provided it doesn't get in the way of more important things — like proficiency in English and mathematics.

An increasingly assertive Maori minority, however, requires much more from the schools than simply language teaching or language revival. Instead, it wishes the schools to assume a crucial role in the socialization of children, teaching them to *be* Maori as well as to speak Maori. This extends even to the tertiary level: Maori students at Victoria University in Wellington, for example, have been objecting to lecturers who are not of Maori ancestry teaching certain courses on Maori language or culture. This objection is not primarily a racial one — it expresses rather a wish on the part of the students to regain something they feel they have been deprived of, from someone who has a more direct and intuitive relationship to this cultural heritage.

School practice

In 1922 the Irish government decreed that the Irish language was to be "taught or used" in all National (state) schools, for not less than an hour a day, where there was a teacher competent to teach it; in 1934 sufficient teachers with some knowledge of Irish were available for the proviso to be dropped (Macnamara, 1971:70). For about 20 years, Irish was the sole language used in the infant classes; in 1948, English was allowed for about half an hour a day; by the 1960s, the use of Irish as the main teaching language in infant classes (outside the Gaeltacht) was being officially discouraged. In the rest of the primary school, however, Irish has most commonly been taught for an hour a day as a subject, and used along with

English in teaching some other parts of the curriculum, with English pre-dominating. The use of Irish as the sole language of the primary school reached its peak in 1939, when 704 of the 5,000 National Schools were Irish-medium. Since then, use of Irish across the curriculum has waned, and in most schools it has retreated to its hour a day, following a standard structured syllabus.

Irish remains a core subject at the secondary level, and it seems that it has never been regarded as much more than that in vocational schools or in courses for students with limited academic aspirations. A large number of academically oriented secondary schools, especially those run by religious orders such as the Irish Christian Brothers, however, taught mostly or entirely in Irish, and the number of these declined less rapidly than the all-Irish National schools. The interest at the secondary level was supported by a system of bonus marks and other incentives for students writing examinations in Irish, by a pass in Irish being compulsory for the granting of many qualifications, and proficiency in Irish being a prerequisite for entry into or advancement in the civil service and other state agencies. Many of these sanctions and incentives were removed during the 1960s and early 1970s however, and the proportion of secondary school pupils taught even one other subject through Irish had declined to about 2% by 1973 (Tovey, 1978: 19).

Maori has been progressing in the opposite direction. Before 1960, no New Zealand primary school had an officially recognized Maori language programme, and even the one or two schools which did include Maori in their curriculum would have devoted the equivalent of only a few minutes a day to it, apart from music lessons and other incidental activities. In secondary schools, however, Maori had long been taught as a subject, but mainly in the church-related Maori boarding schools and in secondary schools located in predominantly Maori districts. The influx of Maori people into the cities and larger towns after the Second World War eventually led to a demand that Maori language be made available more widely, and also to an increasing need for Maori to be treated as a second language, as the proportion of native-speakers of Maori among those studying the language declined.

Most New Zealand secondary schools now offer tuition in Maori language, either directly or with the assistance of the Department of Education's Correspondence school. Since 1980, two or three urban secondary schools have responded to parental pressure by experimenting with the use of Maori as a teaching medium in subjects such as mathematics and social studies, and one Maori boarding school has committed itself to teaching entirely through Maori within the next few years. In most cases, the students involved are native-speakers of English. Interest in Maori at the secondary level is not confined to pupils of Maori ancestry; of the 1,992 candidates who sat the School Certificate examination in Maori in 1982, 28% were classified as non-Maori.

At the primary level, interest in the "elements of the Maori language" progressed rapidly to demands for full-scale bilingual education, and in 1976 the Minister of Education authorized the implementation of a bilingual primary school in one of the remaining Maori-speaking areas. Three more bilingual schools were authorized in 1980, and another three in 1984. All but one of these schools are in predominantly Maori communities. However, a number of other primary schools in ethnically mixed districts are also developing unofficial bilingual programmes, in which all their pupils participate. A few urban schools are also setting up special bilingual units for Maori-speaking pupils arriving in rapidly increasing numbers from the "language nests".

The demand for tuition in Maori has fast outstripped the supply of teachers and the ability of the Department of Education to provide resources. As a result, most schools have been left to devise their own programmes. Help has been provided by advisors on Maori language and education attended to the regional education boards, and by a corps of itinerant teachers of Maori, formed by the Education Department in the 1970s, who work with teachers in groups of schools. Work on a structured syllabus is also nearing completion. Although no precise figures are available, it is likely that more non-Maori children are involved in these school programmes than are Maori children; certainly, one aim of "conventional" Maori language teaching has become to spread knowledge and appreciation of the language throughout the nation.

The time available for Maori language, except in the bilingual schools, is currently much less than that for Irish in Ireland, however. Recent proposals by the Minister of Education for revision of the core curriculum in primary schools and the first two years of secondary schooling may have the effect of reducing the amount of time which can legitimately be spent on teaching Maori, as it is proposed to allocate the "language" section of the syllabus specifically to "English language". Discretionary hours would be increased from 7% to 12% of classroom time at the primary level, however, although few schools would want to use all this allocation for Maori language teaching. Since the teaching language for subjects other than English is not specified, unofficial bilingual education projects would not be greatly affected by the proposed changes.

Since 1960, the teaching or use of Maori in New Zealand classrooms has thus expanded steadily, if unevenly, as a result of increasing pressure from parents and community groups. During the same period the place of Irish in Irish primary schools has declined, and stabilized at a level far above that currently occupied by Maori in most New Zealand schools at present, but far below the level which many Maori parents and students are now seeking for their ancestral tongue. In both countries the school has assumed (or been given) a major role in transmitting the language to its potential speakers, and thus what happens (or does not happen) in the schools is of critical importance to the future viability of both Irish and Maori.

School effectiveness

Attempts to revive Irish through the schools pre-date independence. The first all-Irish schools were voluntary institutions set up outside the national system, and there is good evidence that they were responsible for a significant rise in the number of younger Irish speakers in several parts of the country in the period 1906–1922. Since independence there has been a strong association in survey and census results between high levels of education and high levels of proficiency in Irish. (O Riagain, 1982: 39). In 1978, it was estimated that about 10% of the English-speaking population of Ireland had been made truly bilingual (that is, had acquired native-like proficiency in Irish) through the schools (Another 20 or 30% had become partially fluent (Tovey, 1978: 17; O Riagain, 1982: 40).

Recent more detailed research into achievement levels in the primary schools has shown that the objectives of the primary school syllabus in Irish are being met fully by only a minority of students, and that levels of achievement were dropping perceptibly throughout the 1970s (Greaney, 1978; Harris, 1982b) A similar decline has been evident at the secondary school level, and in both cases, an important contributing factor has been the smaller number of children whose exposure to Irish has extended beyond the letter of the core syllabus. Examination successes, for example, are three times higher among pupils of all-Irish schools than those from other schools (O Riagain, 1982: 41; cf. Lindsey, 1975: 97). Nonetheless, most children leave with at least minimal competence (in terms of the syllabus requirements) in spoken Irish.

The schools have not, however, been able to reverse or even arrest the decline in the number of native-speakers of Irish. Even in parts of the Gaeltacht, Irish has become something of a school language. This has been a major problem in the rest of Ireland since the schools were made responsible for propagating Irish. The consequences of confining Irish to the classroom are well illustrated by this reminiscence by John Macnamara (1971: 73):

"When I was about eight years old, I went into a shop to buy sweets with my sister who was three years older than I. The lady behind the counter, to my great surprise, asked us why we were not talking Irish. We just hung our heads, as children do. But outside I asked my sister what the lady meant. She explained to me that we were learning Irish at school so that we would talk it all the time. And I asked her quite honestly: 'Is Irish for talking?'"

No extensive analysis has yet been possible of the degree to which the teaching of Maori in schools has produced fluent speakers, nor of the success or failure of the bilingual schools in encouraging Maori-speaking communities to remain so. But what evidence there is points to a situation very like the Irish one: some English-speaking children certainly have become bilingual as a result of the school's efforts, but not very many. A very large number of children have learned a great deal more Maori than they would have otherwise, but few have opportunities to use the language outside the classroom. The drift towards English in the Maori-speaking communities continues; some families have undoubtedly been encouraged by the new approach to the language in the school to remain Maori speaking — others may in fact have started to use more English at home, in the belief that the school can now take care of Maori (cf. Benton, 1980, 1984b). Since 1982, however, the *kohanga reo* movement has appeared on the scene, adding a new community dimension to the language revival movement in New Zealand to which the schools themselves are being forced to respond.

Home, school, and community

Public opinion surveys have consistently revealed wide levels of support among the Irish public for the idea that Irish should be widely spoken in the country, although not for its replacing English (Macnamara, 1971: 82; Lindsey, 1975: 97). No similar surveys have been carried out in New Zealand, although in 1973 a poll commissioned by a weekly magazine found that Maori would have been by far the most popular choice if only one language other than English were to be taught in New Zealand schools. It is also the only language actually offered in secondary schools which attracted a steady increase in enrolments in the 1970s, when second language study was rapidly declining in favour.

Nonetheless, neither Irish nor Maori is widely spoken as a home language. For most of this century proficient speakers of Irish and Maori have had to contend with an important statistical fact: however numerous they may be, their chances of finding someone to talk to in their mother (or adopted) tongue, outside a few linguistic strongholds or special occasions, have been quite remote. For example, it is probable that there are about 100,000 fluent speakers of Irish in the greater Dublin area — which means that any one of them has about a 1% (one-tenth of one-tenth) chance of encountering another Irish speaker serendipitously. (O Riagain & O Gliasain, 1979: 5). Even people who live in areas where there are higher numbers of Irish speakers will spend much of their day conversing with people who are comfortable only in English. The plight of the Maori-speaker is even more acute. At a generous estimate, about 30,000 of the 90,000 people of Maori ancestry, and a few hundred others, now living in the greater Auckland area, may have an excellent command of Maori. The rest, and, 700,000 other people, have to resort to English — which makes the Maori speaker's chances of finding a conversation partner without trying quite remote: about one in 750.

Of course, many adults can cope with such pressures through clubs, friendship networks, and choices of residence and workplace. But children are likely to be very heavily influenced by the majority language of the neighbourhood and the mass media. In Ireland and New Zealand this is generally English, and the language used between children and parents is likely to be English even if the parents themselves continue to use Irish or Maori. Many parents of course, would like to speak the other language but feel their Irish (or Maori, as the case may be) is inadequate. The schools and the home are thus locked into a vicious circle of mutual dependence: each needs the other to create a favourable environment for development of real proficiency in the second language, and both need the support of other social institutions to provide adequate opportunity and motivation for making use of this proficiency.

It is this latter support which has been conspicuously lacking in Ireland and New Zealand for over a century. Despite the rhetoric of political and cultural leaders about the importance of the indigenous language, the language of political and economic power has always been English. English has also been the language through which one can escape from rural poverty — to the cities, to England, the United States, Australia. English is the language of the courts, of administration (with some symbolic exceptions), of commerce, of the church, and of the mass media. Even when proficiency in Irish (or Maori) has enabled an individual to obtain power or influence, that power or influence has almost always been exercised principally through English. The social structures of both Ireland and New Zealand have thus been overwhelmingly powerful anglicizing forces, which the school systems have been ill-equipped to counteract, and which individuals and families have had even less chance of resisting.

Community innovations: The all-Irish schools and Nga Kohanga Reo

In both Ireland and New Zealand the language revival movements achieved their initial influence through the work of individuals and voluntary organizations like the Gaelic League, Te Reo Maori Society, and various local and special interest groups. State support (much more extensive in Ireland than New Zealand) came later, and in some ways undermined the work of the voluntary groups by shifting the responsibility for action away from individuals and the local community to particular state institutions. The weakening of state support in Ireland, and the lethargic response of the state to demands made on it in New Zealand, has acted as a stimulus for the enthusiasts themselves to take the initiative for language revival at the grass-roots community level.

One such community initiative is the all-Irish school movement. These primary schools, where the teaching language is entirely Irish, were first set up in the time of British rule, and were an educational manifestation of Irish nationalism. After independence, the promotion of an all-Irish primary education was taken over by the state, with, as we have seen, mixed success. As state enthusiasm waned from the 1950s, however, new all-Irish schools have started to emerge as alternatives to the conventional approach to Irish in the National Schools. Of the 14 all-Irish schools in the Dublin area in 1978, for example, eight had been established since 1969, as a result of parental demands, and, in some cases, despite resistance from the Department of Education (Tovey, 1978: 23).

Allied with the all-Irish school movement are all-Irish pre-school groups (Naionraí). Some of these are attached to the all-Irish schools (although they operate autonomously), and others are located in private homes or other facilities. Some of the children entering these schools and pre-school groups already have some knowledge of the Irish language, but most are native-speakers of English. The ideas underlying this approach to the propagation of Irish seem to have been articulated most forcefully by Timothy Corcoran, who had a major influence in shaping the early educational policy of the Irish Republic, but they certainly did not originate with him, and they are not uniquely Irish:

"The ideal age, in his opinion, for children to acquire fluency in a second language was between three and seven years. For this age group he envisaged a system of infant schools manned entirely by native Irish speakers teaching the spoken language. There would be very little reading, no writing, and much emphasis on songs. English would be forbidden . . . . With such a system Corcoran confidently predicted that Irish would become a 'permanent pos-

session' within a year and within three years, 'a second nature'."
(Titley, 1983: 140)

Exactly the same assumptions underly the *kohanga reo* ("language nest") movement in New Zealand. This emerged from a meeting of Maori leaders in 1981, sponsored by the Department of Maori Affairs, to discuss Maori concerns and suggest courses of action. The loss of the language was a major topic, and the idea of an all-Maori-language pre-school group, which could compensate for the inability of younger parents to speak Maori, attracted enthusiastic support. The way for such a move had been prepared by the establishment of a few bilingual schools as a result of community pressures — two in Maori-speaking areas and two in areas where most children spoke only English — and by the promotion of new methods of teaching Maori to adults at home and in community groups with some financial and technical help from the Department.

The first "nests" were established early in 1982, and the Department of Maori Affairs issued leaflets and guidelines explaining the aim of the enterprise and how it should be undertaken. Small cash grants have been made by the Department to help set the groups up, and further assistance has been made available through Department of Labour work schemes for unemployed school-leavers and adults. However, the organizational burden and ultimate financial responsibility rests with the local group. This has been important, as not only has it ensured that local control and initiative have been maintained, but it has also barred the Department of Social Welfare from arbitrarily imposing child care regulations on some individual centres — they have been able to classify themselves as groups of relatives rather than child-care or pre-school institutions, and thus escape many bureaucratic nets. The Department of Maori Affairs has also theoretically distanced itself from the movement by setting up an autonomous trust to be the national co-ordinating body.

The "nests" are described in Maori Affairs documents as "a whanau or family method for proper child development"; parents are assured that through these centres "the highest possible level of child growth is assured. In addition, the centres will produce children who can command both the Maori and the English languages by the age of five years" (Department of Maori Affairs, 1982a). It is assumed that no one in New Zealand can avoid learning English; Maori is therefore the only language which is permitted in the centres — as the official guidelines put it "there must be rules applied to visitors and certainly to the supervisors that at all times only the Maori language is spoken and heard by the growing child" (Department of Maori Affairs, 1982b: 9). Parents are urged to bring their children to the centres as soon as possible after birth, and let them continue to visit the *kohanga reo* after they start school at five.

From four or five experimental centres early in 1982, the number of functioning *kohanga reo* had increased to 287 by June 1984 (Department of Maori Affairs, 1984b). Even in this short period of time, the "nests" had enabled parents to put considerable pressure on the school system. Newspaper headlines like "Bilingual influx worries teachers" (*Dominion*, 27 July, 1983) soon became comparatively commonplace. There is a rather bitter irony here — 30 years ago, a high proportion of Maori children arrived at school unable to speak English, but little thought was given then to using Maori as a teaching language. Now, the presence of children who have become bilingual before entering school is the cause for some alarm. One reason is that these children now live in urban areas; another that parents have become conscious of the fact that their pre-school efforts can quickly be destroyed by an English-only school system, and they themselves are now sufficiently confident and well-organized to try to do something about this.

Towards the end of 1984, the Department of Education organized intensive in-service courses to help junior-school teachers cater for *kohanga reo* children. In the 1985 Budget special provision was made for extra staff for official bilingual schools (eight such schools had been approved by that time), and for bilingual "language assistants", a new category of para-professionals to assist teachers in areas where there were significant numbers of *kohanga reo* children among the new entrants.

Irish research has found that the presence of children at voluntarily chosen all-Irish schools has increased the amount of Irish used in the home, and stimulated the development of networks of Irish speakers, thus extending the work of the school into the home and community (O Riagain, 1982: 42; O Riagain & O Gliasain, 1979: 124–26, 140). In both Ireland and New Zealand the voluntary association of parents in educational endeavours has therefore proved successful in creating some of the conditions necessary for acquisition *and* maintenance of a *de facto* minority language in adverse circumstances in a modern industrial society. The next step — one crucial for the success on a national scale to which each movement aspires — is to force changes in the linguistic power structure. The establishment of the Bord na Gaeilge has given the Irish revival movement a chance — perhaps the last one — to influence policy and behaviour in a wide variety of public institutions. This same model has already come to the attention of Maori language organizations.[8]

Counter-forces

Mention has already been made of some of the social and economic pressures on individuals and families — relative isolation of Irish and Maori speakers within the total population, lack of opportunities to use Irish or Maori freely in a wide variety of occupations, and so on — all of which have undermined the long-term effectiveness of the work of the schools. It must again be emphasized that these pressures affect Irish-speakers and Maori-speakers wherever they may be. The economic dependence of bilingual Irishmen and New Zealanders on the English-speaking "mainstream" affects the Gaeltacht communities and their New Zealand equivalents in much the same ways. Emigration from Irish- and Maori-speaking areas leads to a twofold language loss — most of the emigrants will switch to English as their main language in their new environment, and will themselves become forces for increased use of English, especially among their children, when visiting and being visited by their relatives from the bilingual areas. Increased tourism has also greatly increased the need for Gaeltacht people to speak English regularly (and further eroded the position of Irish); television is mainly an English-language medium in both countries, and again reinforces the dominance of English on a local as well as a national basis. Thus it is not surprising that a 1973 survey found that of those people in the Gaeltacht who came from homes where Irish was used "always" or "often", less than three-quarters had maintained that level of usage in their current homes (Tovey, 1978: 10–11). Exactly the same trends have been observed in Maori-speaking districts in New Zealand (Benton, 1984b).

John Macnamara (along with other commentators) has claimed that the Irish language revival movement is essentially a "middle-class" phenomenon, and that the workers and Gaeltacht people "continue to demonstrate that the Irish society is essentially English-speaking and that the material advantage in the long run lies with English" (1971: 85). Certainly, the material advantage in the short run would appear to lie with English, for many of these people. However, there is still a significant amount of "working class" support for some aspects of the revival movement. In the 1970s, support for Irish was highest among professionals and also government employees of *any* status, from labourers to departmental heads. Those most antagonistic to Irish were the commercial, industrial, and rural elite (Tovey, 1978: 21–22) — that is, the groups that had least to gain from disturbing the *de facto* dominance of the colonial language. At the same time, while the Dublin all-Irish schools taken together were attended by a higher than average proportion of children from comfortably-off families, some of these schools had relatively high proportions of children from working-class families (O Riagain & O Gliasain, 1979: 26–32). The *kohanga reo* movement owes its growth to widespread support from the least advantaged segment of New Zealand society, and most of the Maori/English bilingual schools at present serve economically depressed communities (cf. Douglas & Douglas, 1983).

Quite a number of obstacles have been placed in the way of encouraging a revival of Irish or Maori by the schools themselves, and by the education system. If the authoritarian methods "shaped by the harsh, draconian proposals" of Professor Corcoran made some Irish classrooms in previous generations "brutal and terrifying" places (Titley, 1983: 140–41), this would not have done much to inspire a love for the Irish language. Now, however, the all-Irish schools have been gaining popularity because they are seen as pleasant alternatives to the largely English-language national schools. In New Zealand, the all-English school system is now clearly perceived by many Maori parents as a major factor in negating their efforts to maintain the language at home or through the *kohanga reo*; the response has been an increasing insistence on the provision of bilingual education in urban as well as in rural areas, coupled with threats to establish an independent Maori school system. (The first of these schools was set up at the Hoani Waititi Marae, near Auckland, in 1985.)

Concern about overall standards of educational achievement, most extensively summarized in John Macnamara's work (e.g. Macnamara, 1966) was in part responsible for the massive retreat from Irish in the primary schools in the 1960s. However, even without such a stimulus, the position of Irish in the system as a whole would have become less tenable as secondary education expanded in scope and numbers of pupils, while development of text books and other curriculum materials in Irish for secondary schools lagged far behind. Because English remained the language of commerce and industry, many parents supportive of primary education in Irish were undoubtedly hesitant to allow their children to be subjected to excessive amounts of Irish at the secondary level. This not only inhibited the development of an adequate and well-supported Irish-medium secondary curriculum, but also arrested the linguistic development in Irish of many children who had made good progress in mastering the language at the primary school. The same troubles are currently causing concern with English/Maori bilingual education in New Zealand.

In New Zealand, a major obstacle to the wider acceptance of Maori as a subject (let alone a teaching medium) in the secondary schools has been the scaling system employed in the external School Certificate examination, taken at the end of the third year of secondary schooling. Under the present system, the proportion of students given a passing mark in any given subject is dependent on the relative performance of the students concerned in the other subjects which they have also taken.[9] If the students as a group have not done well in their other subjects, fewer will pass the subject under review. English is a key factor in this equation, and the comparatively low proportion of Maori students above the fiftieth percentile in this subject helps to lower the pass rate in Maori (which is taken by many Maori students).[10] This of course gives the subject, and the language, a "bad name" academically, and increases apprehension about giving it a more prominent role in the secondary curriculum.

Neither country appears to have given adequate attention to teacher preparation or in-service training for teachers in teaching in and through a second language. The Irish system coped much better with this until the 1960s: the teachers' colleges were mainly Irish medium, and native-speakers of Irish from special preparatory high schools were guaranteed places in them. When this arrangement was abandoned, recruitment from the Irish-speaking areas declined sharply, and the switch from Irish to English as the main language in the teachers' colleges meant that most students for whom it was a second language had little chance to improve their command of Irish (Macnamara, 1971: 70; Tovey, 1978: 18). In New Zealand a special scheme to train native-speakers of Maori as specialist Maori-language teachers for secondary schools was phased out when the immediate objective had been reached, rather than expanded to become a full-scale course leading to a teachers' certificate which could have helped increase the number of fluent Maori-speakers in primary schools as well. "Credential inflation" has also been a problem in New Zealand: over the years, the minimum and *de facto* standards of entry for teachers' colleges have been raised just as the proportion of Maori-speakers with the previous minimum qualification has begun to increase — thus re-imposing rather than removing obstacles to recruitment.

In both Ireland and New Zealand there has been a strong belief that the real work of language revival ought to be done by volunteers. The then New Zealand Minister of Maori Affairs summed this up when he remarked early in 1984 that the spectacular growth of the *kohanga reo* was just what he expected: "In 1980 . . . I said I was confident that there are too many people willing to work for the Maori Language to allow it to die" (Department of Maori Affairs, 1984a: 2). The New Zealand Department of Education, in an official statement about the *kohanga reo* (1984a), expressed a similar faith in the efficacy of voluntary labour: "The department hopes that the further interest in the Maori language that the development of *kohanga reo* has aroused . . . will be sustained through those community members who have been taking an active role because of their fluency and ability in Maori, and that they will, find ways to help in the local schools". At the same time, the primary teachers' organization, the N.Z. Educational Institute, was becoming increasingly anxious about the lack of resources available to both the *kohanga reo* and the schools which their "graduates" would be entering (NZEI, 1984).

This belief that the people can (or ought to be able to) "do it" with a minimum of outside intervention (not to mention finance) has often been coupled with a form of benign neglect even when state support has been made available. John Macnamara comments that even when rules protecting or requiring the use of Irish have been made, "in applying most regulations the prevailing attitude has been *pas trop de zele*" (1971: 65). Colman O Huallachain (1977: 149–54) has pointed to another reason for the lack of dedication on the part of officialdom for developing viable and acceptable policies for the propagation of the Irish languages — the Irish civil service is in many ways a clone of its British counterpart and ancestor, and hardly equipped to prosecute such a course of action. Fundamentally, those charged at the highest levels with developing and implementing policies for the restoration of Irish do not believe that this is either possible or desirable. Much the same, I fear, could be said of their New Zealand colleagues. As an Irish poet put it several centuries ago:

> mar do rith eader bodaigh i mbrogaibh
> na daimhe isteach
> *(it's as if oafs in boots have come running in*
> *instead of dancers.)*

Lessons and prospects

Unfortunately, once they have arrived, the oafs in boots are very difficult to get rid of, and the damage they do is far from easy to repair. The Irish experience has shown very clearly that compulsory acquisition of a language does not necessarily lead to its continued use. The revival or maintenance of a language is a social enterprise which cannot be delegated to one social institution, the school, with any reasonable hope of long-term success.

In both Ireland and New Zealand committed language enthusiasts are in a minority, which in part explains the confusion in aims and vacillation in practice on the part of government officials and politicians ostensibly supporting the Irish and Maori languages. In New Zealand the position is complicated by the dual role of Maori — at one level it is a national symbol, at another the language of a particular ethnic group. But the Irish situation is not radically different from this: both the Maori population and the residents of the Gaeltacht have had to come to terms with the twin ascriptions of backwardness and privilege, and with being "preserved" for the benefit of their compatriots and the tourist industry. Native-speakers of Maori and Irish alike also have to contend with the possibility that their languages will be "taken over" by second language learners who in many ways are far removed from the roots of Gaeldom and Maoritanga.

A key lesson of the Irish experience which is also being learned in New Zealand is that although the language cannot survive without the help and co-operation of the schools, a bilingual society will come into being (or remain in being) only if the efforts of the schools are supported in the home and by many other social institutions. The establishment of the Bord na Gaeilge in Ireland, and similar proposals being made in New Zealand, indicate that these facts are now recognized by some policy-makers and advocates of language revival. The extent to which this recognition will be reflected in administrative practice and social action remains to be seen.

Meanwhile, many people in both countries, while warmly accepting the symbolic and ceremonial functions of Irish and Maori, continue to regard proposals for reviving the everyday use of these dying languages as a romantic dream, and nothing more. Public policy in both countries, more often than not, seems to have been based on such a view. It may well be that linguistic forces, like economic forces, are not susceptible to conscious control by individuals or by nations, except when such attempts at control follow in fact the general direction of the force. The propaganda of modernization would certainly support such a view, and classify the Maori and Irish languages as relics of an irretrievable past.

If this be so, those working for language revival through the schools and in the wider community are perhaps exemplifying the spirit of the Maori proverb "Kia mate ururoa, kei mate wheke *(it is better to die fighting like a shark than to be clubbed to death like an octopus)*. After all, some sharks do get away.

Notes to Chapter 6

1. The use of schools to revive the Welsh language in the anglicized areas of Wales offers the closest analogy to the Irish situation, but has two significant differences: Welsh is used as a medium of instruction in subjects other than Welsh, and attendance at these schools is voluntary. Furthermore, for much of this century, there has been a far greater proportion of the Welsh population using Welsh as a home language than has been the case with Irish in Ireland.

2. A full account of the development of current policies regarding the use of the Maori language in New Zealand schools is given in Benton 1981.
3. For example, in August 1983 a Bill containing the following clause was narrowly defeated (43 votes to 41) in the New Zealand House of Representatives: "Every school in receipt of state funds shall make available tuition in the Maori language where this is requested by any pupil". In January 1984 a large gathering of Maori people involved in the *kohanga reo* movement (discussed later in this paper) passed resolutions calling for the provision of "adequate" Maori language programmes, and the compulsory use of the Maori language, in all primary schools (Department of Maori Affairs, 1984a).
4. According to Macnamara, 1971: 78. My personal observations in 1983 did not give me reason to believe that the proportion of Irish-language programming had increased markedly in the meantime.
5. These have been the Maori Language Bill, 1980, the Maori Affairs Amendment Bill, 1981, and the Maori Language Bill, 1983. The latter also proposed a "Trustee for the Maori langauge . . . to report to the Minister on desirable programmes and facilities and also to monitor the overall progress towards the achievement of the aims of this Act". All were supported by opposition parties and independent members of the House of Representatives, but opposed and defeated by the government majority.
6. See Benton (1984c) for an extended discussion of official policy towards the Maori language in New Zealand; the legal status of Maori is outlined in detail in Benton (1979b).
7. Department of Maori Affairs, 1984a; *Tu Tangata* 16 (February 1984); *Tu Tangata* 18 (July 1984).
8. For example, the text of the Bord na Gaeilge Act was included in submissions to the Parliamentary Select Committees studying a new draft of the Maori Affairs Bill in 1984 by Nga Kaiwhakapumau o te Reo (Wellington Maori Language Board).
9. Those fifth-form students sitting the examination for the first time, and taking English and three or more other subjects are included in the calculations; others are fitted in to the scaled marks according to their rank ordering among those sitting each subject.
10. The scaling system is arranged in such a way that overall about half the students will pass. In 1982, the overall pass rate for the English was 51%. However only about 27% of Maori students taking English passed; this helped to depress the proportion of Maori candidates passing Maori to 41%, and of all candidates to 44%. In 1985, the system was adjusted to ensure that no more than 50% of candidates failed any major subject (including Maori).

References

BENTON, R. A. 1979a, *Who Speaks Maori in New Zealand?* Wellington: NZCER.
— 1979b, *The Legal Status of the Maori Language.* Wellington: Maori Unit, NZCER.
— 1980, Changes in Language Use in a Rural Maori Community. *Journal of the Polynesian Society,* 89.4: 455–78.
— 1981, *The Flight of the Amokura: Oceanic Languages and Formal Education in the South Pacific.* Wellington: NZCER.

— 1984a, Te Rito o te Korari: Maori Language and New Zealand's Cultural Identity. In: G. MCDONALD & A. CAMPBELL (eds), *Looking Forward: Essays on the Future of Education in New Zealand*, pp. 69–87. Wellington: Te Aro Press.

— 1984b, Bilingual Education and the Survival of the Maori Language. *Journal of the Polynesian Society*, 93.3.

— 1984c, Smoothing the Pillow of a Dying Language: Official Policy Towards the Maori Language in New Zealand since World War II. In: A. B. GONZALEZ (ed.), *Panagani: Language Planning, Implementation and Evaluation*. Essays in honour of Bonifacio P. Sibayan on his 67th birthday. Manila: Linguistic Society of the Philippines. Pp. 24–39.

BORD NA GAEILGE no date, Action Plan for Irish 1983–1986. Dublin: Bord na Gaeilge.

DEPARTMENT OF MAORI AFFAIRS 1982a, *Te Kohanga Reo: the Language Nest* (Pamphlet). Wellington.

— 1982b, *Te Kohanga Reo* (Handbook). Wellington.

— 1983, Te Kohanga Reo: Interim Report to 31 October 1983. Wellington. Unpublished document.

— 1984a, *Nga Kaupapa me nga Whakaaro: te Kohanga Reo Wananga a Iwi i Tu ki Turangawaewae Ngaruawahia 20–23 Hanuere 1984*. Wellington.

— 1984b, Te Kohanga Reo Whanau Centres Operating 22 June 1984. Wellington. Unpublished document.

DOUGLAS, E. M. K. & DOUGLAS, R. B. 1983, Nga Kohanga Reo — A Salvage Programme for the Maori Language. Paper presented to Early Childhood Conference, Hamilton.

GREANEY, VINCENT 1978, Trends in Attainment in Irish from 1973–1977. *Irish Journal of Education*, 12.1: 22–35.

HARRIS, JOHN 1982a, National Assessment of Speaking Proficiency in Irish. *Contemporary Perspectives on the Teaching of Irish*, 14–26. Dublin: Bord na Gaeilge.

— 1982b, Achievement in Spoken Irish at the End of the Primary School. *Irish Journal of Education*, 16.2: 84–116.

LINDSEY, JAMES, F. 1975, Irish Language Teaching: A Survey of Teacher Perceptions. *Irish Journal of Education*, 9.2: 97–107.

MACKEY, W. F. 1982, *Language Policy in Ireland and Canada — A Comparative Survey*. Dublin: Bord na Gaeilge.

MACNAMARA, J. 1966, *Bilingualism in Primary Education: A Study of Irish Experience*. Edinburgh: Edinburgh University Press.

— 1971, Successes and Failures in the Movement for the Restoration of Irish. In: J. RUBIN & B. H. JERNUDD (eds), *Can Language be Planned?* Pp. 65–94. Honolulu: University Press of Hawaii.

N.Z. DEPARTMENT OF EDUCATION 1983, *Tihe Mauri-Ora: Draft Syllabus Primary Maori Language*. Wellington.

— 1984a, Te Kohanga Reo. *N.Z. Education Gazette*, 63.2: 1.

— 1984b, A Review of the Core Curriculum for Schools. Wellington.

N.Z. EDUCATIONAL INSTITUTE, 1984, Urgent Discussions on Resources for Kohanga Reo. *Nat Ed Newsletter* 22 February: 3.

O HUALLACHAIN, C. L. 1977, An Aspect of the Time Factor in Language Policy and its Implementation: the Irish Experience. In: B. P. SIBAYAN & A. GONZALEZ (eds), *Language Planning and the building of a National Language*, 138–54. Manila: Linguistic Society of the Philippines.

O RIAGAIN, P. 1982, The Influence of Social Factors on the Teaching and Learning of

Irish. In: *Contemporary Perspectives on the Teaching of Irish*, 36–53. Dublin: Bord na Gaeilge.

O RIAGAIN, P. & O GLIASAIN, M. 1979, *All-Irish Primary Schools in the Dublin Area*. Dublin: Institiuid Teangeolaiochta Eireann.

TITLEY, E. B. 1983, Rejecting the Modern World: the Educational Ideas of Timothy Corcoran. *Oxford Review of Education*, 9.2: 137–45.

TOVEY, H. 1978, *Language Policy and Socioeconomic Development in Ireland*. Dublin: Institiuid Teangeolaiochta Eireann.

7 Namibian educational language planning: English for liberation or neo-colonialism?

ROBERT PHILLIPSON, TOVE SKUTNABB-KANGAS &
HUGH AFRICA

The purpose of this chapter is to contribute to the ongoing work of educational language planning for Namibia. We shall draw on experience from a wide range of countries and groups so as to highlight those factors which can be decisive for success or failure in education in multilingual contexts. One key factor is choice of languages for educational purposes. As SWAPO (South West Africa People's Organization) has opted for English as an official language for independent Namibia, it is important to decide what role English should play in education and what the role of the mother tongues should be. Will English secure liberation or will it serve as a bridgehead for neo-colonialism?

English and French are often called *languages of wider communication* (LWC) (Fishman *et al.*, 1977). The languages are closely related to the countries and cultures from which they originated, which we shall refer to as *cultures of wider communication* (CWC). The spread of these languages in recent centuries and their indigenization in different parts of the world are central aspects of colonialism, imperialism and present-day internationalism. While large CWC countries like the United States, Britain and France are or pretend to be monolingual countries in which the education system aims at monolingualism in the LWC, most African countries are multilingual. Even so, most African educational language planning aims at monolingualism in an LWC (Bokamba & Tlou, 1980).

It is our contention that it serves the interests of LWC speakers and the CWCs to promote the use of LWCs in Africa. Most LWC researchers and educational experts are consciously or unconsciously biased in favour of the LWC and monolingualism, and even when well-intentioned, their advice reflects this. We also contend that educational language planning in Africa must aim at bi- or multilingualism, as advocated by African researchers like Afolayan (1984), Africa (1980), Bokamba & Tlou (1980), Mateene (1980a, 1980b) and Tadadjeu (1980). We therefore regard it as axiomatic that *over-use of the former colonial language and under-use of mother tongues* as media of education reproduce inequality, favour the creation or perpetuation of elites, promote dependency on the CWC, and prevent the attainment of high levels of bi- or multilingualism (Chishimba, 1984; Mateene, 1980b).

Language policy decisions are often taken in very unfavourable circumstances, when nations are "developing" away from a phase of underdevelopment, economically and politically (Rodney, 1972). *Namibia*, the "last colony" (Green *et al.*, 1982) is still illegally occupied by South Africa, and exploited by multinational capital, despite numerous attempts by the United Nations to end this state of affairs (SWAPO, 1981). Language planning for Namibia is therefore under way outside the country, concurrently with a liberation war (Chamberlain *et al.*, 1981). As the armed struggle has been in progress for nearly 20 years, there has been time for elaborate formulation of the political, social, economic and educational goals of SWAPO, which is recognized as the only legal representative of the Namibian people by the United Nations. SWAPO plans to establish a "non-exploitative, non-oppressive, classless society" (SWAPO, 1983). Policy and plans for a liberated Namibia are articulated in a number of publications from the United Nations Institute for Namibia in Lusaka, an independent research and teaching centre.

SWAPO has decided that *English* is to be *an official* language in independent Namibia, and that the *mother tongues* will be media of education at the lower primary level and not neglected thereafter (SWAPO, 1982: 40; Commonwealth Secretariat and SWAPO, 1984). The intention is to replace Afrikaans, currently the lingua franca in Namibia and the medium of education from upper primary level and sometimes earlier, which is seen as the language of oppression, by English, which is seen paradoxically as a language of liberation. At present less than 1% of the population of 1½ million have English as their mother tongue, while 15% have Afrikaans, and only a small proportion are fluent in English as a second or foreign language. There are seven main local language groups. The largest, Oshiwambo, accounts for roughly 45% of Namibians (Chamberlain *et al.*, 1981). Several of the languages were alphabetized a century ago (e.g. Kurvinen, 1877).

South African Bantu education policy has been to deliberately promote ethnolinguistic fragmentation as one instrument for enforcing apartheid. Language is one means of effectuating segregated and racist policies. The vast majority of Namibians drop out of the education system and 60% of the population is illiterate (for details see Ellis, 1984 and Mbamba, 1982). There are 70,000 or more Namibians in exile in refugee settlements in Angola and Zambia, adults and children. Their education forms part of SWAPO's attempts to try out strategies for educational change, to be implemented in independent Namibia. These attempts are informed by careful consideration of the experience of other countries.

International comparisons

Turning to this experience, we have chosen examples so as to be able to analyse some of the factors which seem to be decisive for the success or failure of an educational policy which could result in high levels of bilingualism. Many of our examples do *not* come from contexts which resemble the Namibian situation, for two reasons, one empirical, one methodological. The empirical reason is that although there are many parallels in other African countries and elsewhere, there has been too little longitudinal research into and evaluations of different educational models. The methodological reason is that it is easier to distinguish some of the principles which are generally valid by comparing dissimilar situations.

We will analyse different types of education under four headings: *segregation, mother tongue maintenance, submersion* and *immersion*. In three instances it is necessary to treat separately the programmes meant for majorities and minorities. The English-speaking group in Canada are in the majority, numerically and in terms of power (see Table 1). We also classify the Blacks in South Africa and occupied Namibia as a majority, even though they are at present still a powerless majority. In Soviet Uzbekistan the numerically dominant group in the republic, the Uzbeks (more than two-thirds of the population in Uzbekistan; Krag, 1983), and the six principal minority groups all have equivalent linguistic rights in education. They are together treated as a majority in our classification. These groups have the right to education through the medium of their mother tongues. They are not obliged to undergo schooling in the LWC, Russian. The Uzbekistan comparison is particularly relevant for the Third World because here literacy has over the past 60 years been successfully extended from a tiny elite minority to cover the entire population. All children complete 10 years of schooling, and this is soon to be extended to 11 years (Guidelines, 1984).

TABLE 1

	Programmes						
	Segregation LDS		Maintenance HDS		Submersion LDS		Immersion HDS
	L1		L1		L2		
						L2	
Dominant medium of education	Africa Namibia Bantu education	Europe Bavaria FGR Turkish migrants	Asia Uzbekistan 7 main groups	Europe/USA Sweden, USA, Finns, Chicanas	Africa Zambia All main groups	Europe Most WE indig. and immig. min.	North America Canada anglophones
Linguistic goal	Dominance L1	Dominance L1	Bilingualism	Bilingualism	Elites: L2 dom., masses: L1 dom.	Dominance L2	Bilingualism
Societal goal	Apartheid	Repatriation	Equity and Integration	Equity and Integration	Perpetuation stratification	Assimilation, marginalization	Ling. and cult. enrichment, job prospects
Majority/Minority	Majority	Minority	Majority	Minority	Majority	Minority	Majority
Status of group (high/low)	Low	Low	High	Low	High	Low	High
Country industrialized/under-developed (Ind/Und)	Und.	Ind.	Ind.	Ind.	Und.	Ind.	Ind.
Group has been (C) or is (C+) colonized by L2 country	C+	–	C	C	C	C/–	–
Language of group — official	+	–	+	–	+	–	+
— standardized and has teaching materials	+	+	+	+	–	+	+
L2 official	+	+	+	+	+	+	+
L2 standardized and teaching materials	+	+	+	+	+	+	+

Note: LDS = Low Degree of Success. HDS = High Degree of Success.

Namibia is, like the majority of Third World countries and like Soviet Uzbekistan, multilingual. At present elementary schooling is provided in 12 languages (Zimmermann, 1984). Whether education can be provided in the future in a larger number of mother tongues, those with few speakers, or whether this is impracticable, is a complex issue which cannot be adequately pursued here.

For each programme we assess the *degree of success*, in attaining high levels of bilingualism and school achievement, and crudely label the programmes as leading to *high* or *low* levels of success. Next we identify whether the *medium of education* is the mother tongue (L1) of the pupils or a foreign or second language (L2). Finally linguistic and societal goals of the programmes are broadly characterized (for details see Skutnabb-Kangas, 1984, Chapter 6). Our classification builds more on results than on declarations of intention and may not therefore tally with the officially declared goals.

Our example of a *segregation* model for a *majority* population is the Bantu education now given at the elementary level to Namibians through the medium of L1s, producing poor results, meaning scholastic failure for the majority, and low levels of cognitive/academic proficience in both languages (Mbamba, 1982). This fits with the linguistic goal, dominance in L1, and the societal goal, perpetuation of apartheid.

Our example of *segregation* for a *minority* is the education of migrant Turks in Bavaria, West Germany, through the medium of Turkish, again with low levels of success. The linguistic goal is dominance in Turkish. The societal goal is to prepare the migrant pupils for forced repatriation when their parents' labour is no longer needed or when they themselves become "too expensive" for West Germany (Skutnabb-Kangas, 1984).

In contrast to segregation programmes, *mother tongue maintenance* programmes show high levels of success. The medium of education is L1, as in segregation programmes, but the goals are different. The linguistic goal is bilingualism, the societal goal is equity and integration. An example of *maintenance for a majority* is the mother tongue medium education given in the Soviet republic of Uzbekistan to the seven main language groups. Examples of *maintenance for minorities* are the Finnish medium classes for the Finnish migrant population in Sweden and such Spanish medium programmes in the U.S. as the San Diego and Carpinteria programmes (Cummins, 1984). All these result in high levels of bilingualism and school achievement. All three groups in the examples used have a history of colonization by the L2-power, i.e. the Uzbeks, the Tadjiks etc. by Russia, the Finns by Sweden, and the Chicanas by the U.S.A. This common history of colonization makes these cases more directly comparable to contemporary Africa.

The segregation and maintenance programmes referred to have had the mother tongue as medium of education. In the remaining two types of programme, submersion and immersion, the medium of education is a second or foreign language (L2).

An example of a *submersion* programme for a *majority* is education through the medium of a former colonial language in many African countries, e.g. Zambia. For the vast majority of the population, results are poor, linguistically (Africa, 1980) and academically (Chishimba, 1984). The official goal is to provide educational "opportunities to each person within the limits of his (*sic!*) capacity" (Ministry of Education, 1977: 5). The linguistic goal achieved is dominance in the LWC, English, for the elites, and dominance for the masses in their mother tongues (or the regional lingua franca), which the school does nothing to develop, and limited proficiency in English. The society is highly stratified, and education since independence has not altered this (Chileshe, 1982). This state of affairs is by no means unique to Zambia — in fact it generally holds throughout sub-Saharan Africa (Mateene, 1980b).

Submersion programmes for *minorities* are still by far the most common way of education for both indigenous and immigrant (linguistic) minorities. For instance in western Europe this means education through the medium of L2, the majority language, resulting in dominance in the majority language at the expense of the mother tongue, and poor school achievement. Societally this means assimilation for some and marginalization for the many (Skutnabb-Kangas, 1984).

By contrast, Canadian *immersion* programmes, in which *majority* children are educated through the medium of an L2, lead to high levels of bilingualism and success at school. The societal goals include linguistic and cultural enrichment and increased employment prospects for an elite (California State Department of Education, 1984; Swain & Lapkin, 1982).

We move now from the defining characteristics of these four types of programme to a set of descriptors which may have a decisive influence on the outcome of education.

Of the groups in our seven examples those in Uzbekistan, Zambia and Canada have in principle *high status* whereas the others are *low status* groups. The countries in five of the examples are *industrialized*, while Namibia and Zambia have been *underdeveloped*. In only two of the examples is there absence of a past or present *colonial relationship* between the L1 and L2 groups.

The last four descriptors relate to the *official status* of the languages and the degree to which they have been *standardized* and have *teaching and reference materials*.

All the languages of the groups concerned have some official status, with the exception of the immigrant languages (and most indigenous minority languages) in Europe and North America. With the one exception of Zambia the full range of the languages is standardized and at least some teaching materials exist. In the case of immigrant languages, some of the materials may come from the countries of origin. The potential for extending the written use of Zambian languages is as yet untapped (for academic arguments in favour of this see Kashoki, 1982 and Chishimba, 1984, for political arguments against it see The Prime Minister of Zambia in Commonwealth Secretariat and SWAPO, 1984). In all our examples the L2 both has official status and exists in standardized forms with teaching materials.

Provisionally generalizing on the basis of the evidence from the descriptors so far, we conclude that high levels of success in relation to bilingualism and school achievement can be achieved *either with L1 or L2 as the dominant medium of education, either by a majority or a minority group*, by groups with *either high or low status*, in contexts where the language *either has official status or does not*.

In all successful contexts the *linguistic goal* has been *bilingualism* and the *societal goal* has been a *positive* one *for the group* concerned. The mother tongues of the groups have been *standardized* and *teaching materials* have been *available*, which has also been the case for L2.

We also conclude that in all contexts with low levels of success the linguistic goal has been dominance in one of the languages, either the mother tongue or the L2, not bilingualism. The other language has been neglected or taught badly, even though in many cases it has official status, and is standardized, with teaching materials. The societal goal in all the contexts with poor results has been to keep the group or at least a bulk of them in a powerless subordinate position.

Prerequisites for efficient L2-learning and bilingualism

Now it is arguable that since the only constants so far distinguishing programmes leading to a high or low degree of success have been the linguistic and societal goals, and nothing more tangible, and since our classification of goals, especially if it does *not* tally with the officially declared goals, might be considered arbitrary, then there might be the suspicion that we first looked at the outcomes and then attributed negative goals to the programmes with poor results and positive goals to the programmes with good results, so as to make the classification neat. In order to examine this interpretation we turn now to how the programmes are organized. We will go through a set of 16 prerequisites for efficient L2-learning (Skutnabb-Kangas, 1984: 244), in order to see to what extent the different programmes are organized so as to create optimal conditions. Since the *de facto* linguistic and societal goals of a programme are reflected more in the way the programme is organized than in declarations of intention, our analysis can also serve to validate our characterization of the goals of the different programmes. Table 2 lists these factors and contains a positive or negative rating for each of the seven types of programme. The programmes are distinguished, as before, according to whether they lead to a high degree of success (HDS) or a low degree of success (LDS).

The factors have been grouped into four categories, organizational learner-related affective factors, and linguistic, cognitive, pedagogical and social factors related to respectively the L1 and the L2. To start with the *organizational factors: alternative programmes* (1) are only available in the maintenance and immersion contexts, i.e. the HDS programmes are optional. An Uzbek, a Finn in Sweden, or a Chicana in the U.S. who wants education through the medium of Russian, Swedish or English rather than the L1 can opt for this. An English-speaking Canadian child can choose between English-medium education or a French-medium immersion programme. Children in segregation or submersion programmes have no choice.

Factor 2 covers whether there are *in the same class* both *native speakers* of the medium of education and pupils for whom the medium of education is an *L2*. This is the normal situation in submersion programmes, disadvantaging the L2 learners. We consider that in Zambia the situation is comparable in that pupils' home background (i.e. class) may have a decisive influence on their proficiency in English. In all the other programmes pupils are, in relation to prior familiarity with the language, on an equal footing in that initially either they *all* know the language of instruction (segregation and maintenance) or none of them do (immersion).

The third factor shows that the HDS programmes have *teachers* who are both *bilingual* and well *trained*. Whereas the LDS programmes have either well trained monolingual teachers, who do not understand pupils' mother tongues, or else the training of teachers is inadequate, even if they are to some extent bilingual, for instance in Zambia (Chishimba, 1981).

Factor 4 shows that most of the LDS programmes lack *bilingual materials*. The materials actually used (factor 5) in them are imported or racist, thus imposing alien cultural values. It is now recognized (for instance in Zambia, Commonwealth Secretariat and SWAPO, 1984) that even teaching materials written in independent African countries perpetuate colonial or Western values (Chileshe, 1982; Higgs, 1979).

The *learner-related affective factors* suggest that a supportive learning environment and non-authoritarian teaching reduce *anxiety* (6). *Internal motivation* (7) is increased when the pupil is not forced to use the L2 (for instance because the teacher does not understand the L1) and can start producing L2 utterances only when ready for it. High motivation is also related to an understanding of and sympathy with the educational objectives and to sharing in responsibility for one's own learning. These are principles endorsed in SWAPO's educational policy (Angula, 1984; Commonwealth Secretariat & SWAPO, 1984: 20). High *self-confidence* (8) is related to whether learners have a real chance of succeeding in school, and to favourable teacher expectations. One of the conditions for this is that the teacher accepts and values the child's mother tongue. There is a high correlation across the board between a positive rating on these three viariables (low anxiety, high motivation and high self-confidence) and successful programmes.

The final sets cover *linguistic, cognitive, pedagogical and social language-related* factors. *Linguistic development in L1* (9) is inadequate when the mother tongue is taught badly as in segregation programmes or not at all as in most submersion programmes. Official Zambian policy permits the oral use of mother tongues to facilitate comprehension, but no attempt is made to teach or develop proficiency in the mother tongue.

Enough *relevant cognitively demanding subject matter* (10) to promote the common underlying proficiency for all languages (CALP, see Cummins, 1980) is provided in the HDS programmes. This is done in L1 in maintenance programmes and in L2 in immersion programmes. The input may satisfy this criterion in segregation programmes because the pupils at least understand the instruction. In submersion programmes this is less likely when both language and subject matter are unfamiliar.

In addition to L1 development in school, pupils also need the *opportunity to develop their mother tongues outside school in linguistically demanding formal contexts* (11). This opportunity exists for all indigenous groups, but not for immigrants. Some groups may therefore be able to compensate for inadequate school provision. A more general factor which influences whether the language learning situation is additive or subtractive (Lambert, 1975) is the degree to which *L2 teaching supports or harms L1* development (12). Only submersion programmes threaten the mother tongues in this way.

TABLE 2

	Segregation	Maintenance			Submersion	Immersion	
	LDS	L1	HDS		LDS	L2	HDS
Dominant medium of education	Bantu	Turks	Uzbekistan	Finns Chicanas	Zambia	W. Europe minorities	Canada
Organizational factors							
1. Alternative programmes available	–	–	+	+	–	–	+
2. Pupils equally placed vis-à-vis knowledge of ME	+	+	+	+	–	–	+
3. Bilingual (B), Trained (T) teachers	B	B or T	BT	BT	B	T	BT
4. Bilingual materials (e.g. dictionaries) available	–	+	+	+	–	–	+
5. Cultural content of materials appropriate for pupils	–	–	+	+	–	–	+
Learner-related affective factors							
6. Low level of anxiety (supportive, non-authoritarian)	–	–	+	+	–	–	+
7. High internal motivation (not forced to use L2, understands and sympathetic with objectives, responsible for own learning)	–	–	+	+	–	–	+

8. High self-confidence (fair chance to succeed, high teacher expectations)	−	−	−	+	+	−	+
L1-related linguistic, cognitive, pedagogical and social factors							
9. Adequate linguistic development in L1 (L1 taught well, badly or not at all in school)	B	B	−	W	W	−	W
10. Enough relevant, cognitively demanding subject matter provided	−?	+?	−?	+	+	−?	+
11. Opportunity to develop L1 outside school in linguistically demanding formal contexts	+?	−	+	+	−	−	+
12. L2-teaching supports (+) or harms (−) L1 development	+	+	−?	+	−	−	+
L2-related linguistic, cognitive, pedagogical and social factors							
13. Adequate linguistic development in L2 (L2 taught well, badly or not at all in school)	B	B	B	W	W	B	W
14. L2 input adapted to pupils' L2 level	+	+	−?	+	+	−	+
15. Opportunity to practise L2 in peer group contexts	−	−	−	+?	+	−	−
16. Exposure to native speaker L2 use in linguistically demanding formal contexts	−	+	−	+	+	+	+

Note: LDS = Low Degree of Success. HDS = High Degree of Success.

Linguistic development in L2 (13) is inadequate when the L2 is badly taught, as it is in all the LDS programmes. Also relevant is the degree to which *L2 input is adapted to pupils' L2 level* (14). It is difficult to adapt the input in this way in immigrant submersion contexts. The task is relatively more feasible when no pupils are native speakers of the medium of education, as in Zambia. Absence of *the opportunity to practise the L2 in peer group contexts outside school* (15) may be due to practicalities (immersion children not meeting many L2 children), to sheer racism (Turkish children being avoided by German children), or to a shortage of L2 native speakers, as in Zambia, or in Bantu education, where institutionalized racism aggravates the situation. *Exposure to native speaker L2 use in linguistically demanding formal contexts* (16) depends on the existence of L2 institutions staffed by native L2 speakers. Turks in West Germany cannot escape exposure to native German, whereas Zambians are exposed to a range of non-native Englishes, some of them appropriate regional models, some of them interlanguages.

The Namibian situation

As we can see from the chart, there is a clear difference between the programmes in that the HDS programmes with bilingualism as a linguistic goal and with positive societal goals have organized the teaching so that many of the conditions for efficient L2 learning are met. The LDS programmes do so to a much lesser extent. We shall now relate the different programme characteristics to *the Namibian situation* after independence in order to see where parallels exist, what could be done and what would be best avoided. We will consider which types of programme may be appropriate and lead to success.

We start with immersion programmes, since Namibians are a majority in their own country and since they are to be taught, at least later on, through the medium of an L2. From the descriptors it appears that the only significant difference between Bantu education and immersion is the status of the group. Just as we have marked "high" for Zambia, the Namibian groups should have high status after independence. There is thus in principle nothing in the descriptors to prevent success if Namibians were to be taught predominantly through the medium of an L2, English, from the very beginning.

Equally there is in principle nothing in the descriptors to prevent success if Namibians were to be taught predominantly through their mother tongues in a maintenance programme for a majority, like in our Uzbekistan example. On the basis of a consideration of the descriptors, two alternatives are open for Namibia, immersion and maintenance.

But matters look altogether different when we turn to the educational prerequisites as they will be in independent Namibia. In many parts of Namibia one language is prevalent, while urban areas are more multilingual. It may therefore be possible, at least in towns, to offer alternative programmes (factor 1). Any decision to use English only as the medium of education from the start of schooling would exclude any alternatives.

Most Namibian pupils would be *equally placed* either in programmes where nobody knows the medium of education, for instance English, or where everybody knows it, i.e. the mother tongues (2). Pupils whose mother tongue has relatively few speakers will need special support if mother tongue medium programmes cannot be organized for them. SWAPO needs to *train teachers* who are *bilingual* (3). Some teachers are currently being trained outside Namibia, but not in Namibian languages. Even teachers who are trained can have poor results, as in segregation and submersion programmes, when they lack in-depth knowledge of the pupils' L1. *Bilingual materials* need to be developed (4) — and again it is the Namibian languages that most require attention. Racism and alienating *cultural values* need to be eradicated from teaching materials (5). This applies in its most acute form in apartheid textbooks (for examples see Ellis, 1984), but also to those emanating from transnational, mainly British publishers, which dominate the African market. All these organizational factors represent problems which can be solved, as has been done in both the Canadian immersion and the Uzbekistan maintenance programmes for majority populations.

All the *learner-related affective factors* which are negative in Bantu education can become positive in independent Namibia (just as they are in Canada and Uzbekistan) if SWAPO educational policy is implemented and the teachers are trained accordingly. All these changes are extremely demanding to implement, and African experience shows how difficult it is to achieve them. In principle, however, they are possible. But it is *not possible* to change all the *language-related factors* so as to create optimal conditions. Mother tongues and English can be taught well at school (factors 9 and 13), enough relevant L1 material and adequately adapted L2 input can be provided (factors 10 and 14), and if institutional structures are developed in Namibian society in the major Namibian languages, opportunity for formal L1 development outside school can be organized (factor 11).

However, as long as English is the language of world capitalism, it is going to threaten the mother tongues (factor 12), lead to their displacement, stigmatization and underdevelopment (Skutnabb-Kangas & Phillipson,

1985). English is the key link between world capitalism and the local elites via the economic, military and cultural interests that unite them. English tends to replace the mother tongues of the elites, the Afrosaxons (Mazrui, 1973). The only way to counteract this threat to the mother tongues is to organize education so as to strengthen them maximally. This means among other things using them as dominant media throughout the school. As regards the remaining factors (15 and 16), there is little opportunity to practise English with native speakers informally or formally, because there are almost no native English speakers in Namibia.

Our analysis shows that several of the preconditions for an immersion programme for L2-medium teaching from early on do not exist in Namibia. If English is made the medium from the start, or from early on, the situation becomes one of submersion, just as in Zambia. Here the results in English, even for those few who reach the cut-off points of the 7th and 12th grades, are not better than for children who have had English as a subject only in other countries (Africa, 1980) — except that these children have developed their mother tongues and understood the subject matter instruction while many Zambian children have not. By contrast, most of the preconditions *are met* in a maintenance programme of the Uzbekistan type.

The politics of educational language policy

This discussion of educational research and experience in a range of contexts has attempted to adduce principles of such generality and predictive power that they can be of assistance to educational language planning for Namibia. There is substantial evidence that leading SWAPO educationalists are *forming policy* in an informed, sophisticated way (Angula in Commonwealth Secretariat & SWAPO, 1984; Geingob in Chamberlain *et al.*, 1981; Tjitendero, 1984). Clearly the *implementation of policy* presents huge problems, which a liberation war, exile and refugee life traumatically exacerbate. There is evidence from many African countries of good policy not being implemented and of an increased use of LWCs after independence (Bokamba & Tlou, 1980; Kalema, 1980; Mateene, 1980a, b). Equally there is massive evidence that educational "aid", of the kind that Namibia, like many Third World countries, is likely to be obliged to accept, has not achieved its intended goals. This is of course also true of "aid" to industry, health and many other fields. Quite apart from the multitude of practical implementation problems, there are warning lights indicating that the initial policy was misconceived in many comparable contexts. Neo-colonial links and research imperialism mediated by CWC experts are in part responsible for this.

If research is to contribute to the solution of social problems, then both the research issues and the social reality have to be correctly diagnosed and integrated. Thus when planners for Namibia correctly identify the need for a massive functional literacy campaign and extensive learning of English (Green, no date; Ellis, 1984) they appear to over-rate English and to under-rate the mother tongues. Even committed planners who are trying to serve the needs of the whole nation, not just the elite, may fall into this trap, because of the widespread and superficially appealing maximum exposure fallacy, which incorrectly holds that the more of an L2 people are exposed to, the more of it they learn (Cummins, 1983).

Bi- or trilingualism has been advocated as a national goal for multilingual African countries (Afolayan, 1978; Tadadjeu, 1980). If bi- or trilingualism for every individual is to be a national goal in independent Namibia, then use must be made of all Namibian languages in institutional structures in all domains of life. Educational means must be chosen so as to lead to these goals. Thus if education is the birthright of all, is to save people from poverty by being closely linked to production, is to promote social change, and to train Namibians to staff a sophisticated economy (all declared SWAPO goals), then a strategy is needed which takes the research evidence and the local cultural, linguistic and ecological situations as their starting-points, also when choosing languages.

The OAU, founded 1963, has one article in its charter stipulating that the official use of foreign languages will be only provisionally tolerated. The OAU Inter-African Bureau of Languages exists to "assist and encourage the use of indigenous African languages for educational, commercial and communication purposes on a national, regional and continental level" (document SC/CULT/6/2.70, quoted in Kalema, 1980: 1). In practice there has been a gradual shift "in the direction of europeanisation of the media of instruction with a concomitant neglect of the teaching of African languages" (Bokamba & Tlou, 1980: 49). "The foreign colonial languages are more favoured now then they were before independence" (Mateene, 1980a: vii). "The use of vernaculars in education has been gradually phased out" (Bokamba & Tlou, 1980: 49). Tanzania is an exception to this rule in sub-Saharan Africa, as is Somalia (for details see Scotton, 1981).

Opting for English as a national language inevitably leads to an over-rating of English and an under-rating of the mother tongues, in a way which parallels how racism operates in other contexts. The argumentation used to legitimate the continued use of LWCs in Africa is the ideological underpinning of neo-colonialism, taking the place of military occupation (Galtung, 1980). References to the supposed superiority of a European language, or its use in international relations, or its neutrality vis-à-vis competing local languages are one-sided and misleading. The arguments, and the underlying attitudes, are comparable to those used in imperialist anthropology, history and literature, and follow the same logic as racism. Racism is typically affirmed

— by means of *self-exaltation* on the part of the dominant group which creates an idealistic image of itself
— the *degradation* of the dominated group, and the suppression and stagnation of its culture, institutions, life-styles and ideas
— by systematic *rationalization* of the relationships between both groups, always favourable to the dominant group (Preiswerk, 1980).

There is a serious risk of the same processes applying when a former colonial language, which inevitably serves CWC interests, is retained as the main medium of education. Judging African languages according to European norms (e.g. in relation to "development" or modern vocabulary) invariably involves exaltation of the LWC and degradation of local languages. Claiming that a LWC can cement national unity and transcend local ethnolinguistic differences ignores the relationship of local LWC speakers to the CWC. Equally, ethnolinguistic homogeneity is not a prerequisite for national unity, nor can it result from decrees which try to simplify a complex linguistic reality (Kashoki, 1982; Afolayan, 1984: 13). This kind of rationalization is in the interests only of the local elite and the CWC. For refutation of the arguments conventionally adopted by apologists for LWCs, see Bokamba & Tlou, 1980 and Mateene, 1980b.

The main thrust of our argument is to indicate the dangers of premature adoption of English as medium of education in Namibian education and to stress the need to strengthen and support the Namibian languages. Our analysis is also confirmed by evidence from Asia, for instance India (Pattanayak, 1981) and the Philippines (Smolicz, 1983). However our chapter should not be interpreted as in any way contesting SWAPO's decision to adopt English as an official language. If as many Namibians as possible are to learn English, educational policy decisions on the best means to reach this goal will benefit from an explicit clarification of the ideological purposes that various programmes serve. The same method, for instance using the mother tongue as medium of education, can function quite differently in politically different situations. When the South African divisively motivated mother tongue policy is terminated, conditions may be appropriate for the kind of mother tongue programme that has succeeded in Nigeria (the Ife project, see Afolayan, 1984) with, for those who continue beyond elementary education, ease of transfer to using English as a medium. Or the mother tongues can be used as mediums of education right through the education system.

including higher education, as the OAU Inter-African Bureau for Languages recommends (Mateene, 1980b: 23). English should be taught as a (foreign language) school subject throughout the education system, and high levels of achievement can be predicted if the overall language policy is well conceived and implemented.

We summarize our analysis in four claims:

1. English as an official language in Namibia will be assisted if Namibian languages are maximally used inside and outside the education system.
2. Resistance to the use of mother tongues is an expression of a colonized consciousness, which serves the interests of global capitalism and South Africa, and the bourgeoisie and petty bourgeoisie who are most dependent on capitalist interests.
3. Namibia should follow the example of those multilingual states which have alternative language programes leading to bilingualism.
4. Educational aid from "donors" should be long-term and explicitly accept Namibian multilingual goals.

References

AFOLAYAN, A. 1978, Towards an Adequate Theory of Bilingual Education for Africa. In: J. E. ALATIS (ed.), *International Dimensions of Bilingual Education.* Washington, D.C.: Georgetown University Press.

— 1984, The English Language In Nigerian Education as an Agent of Proper Multilingual and Multicultural Development. *Journal of Multilingual and Multicultural Development,* 5: 1, 1–22.

AFRICA, H. 1980, *Language in education in a multilingual state: a case study of the role of English in the educational system of Zambia.* Ph.D. dissertation. Toronto: University of Toronto.

ANGULA, N. 1984, English as a Medium of Communication for Namibia: Trends and Possibilities. In: COMMONWEALTH SECRETARIAT & SWAPO (eds), *English Language Programme for Namibians,* 9–12.

BOKAMBA, E. G. & TLOU, J. S. 1980, The Consequences of the Language Policies of African States vis-à-vis Education. In: K. MATEENE & J. KALEMA (eds), *Reconsideration of African Linguistic Policies.* Kampala: OAU Bureau of Languages, 45–66.

CALIFORNIA STATE DEPARTMENT OF EDUCATION 1984, *Studies on Immersion Education: A Collection for United States Educators.* Sacramento: California State Department of Education.

CHAMBERLAIN, R., DIALLO, A. & JOHN, E. J. 1981, *Toward a Language Policy for Namibia. English as the Official Language: Perspectives and Strategies.* Lusaka: United Nations Institute for Namibia.

CHILESHE, J. 1982, Literacy, Dependence, and Ideological Formation: The Zambian Experience. Unpublished paper, University of Sussex.

CHISHIMBA, M. M. 1981, Language Teaching and Literacy: East Africa, *Annual Review of Applied Linguistics*, II, 67–89.
— 1984, Language Policy and Education in Zambia. *International Education Journal*, 1:2, 151–80.
COMMONWEALTH SECRETARIAT & SWAPO 1984, *English Language Programme for Namibians*, Seminar Report. Lusaka, 19–27 October 1983.
CUMMINS, J. 1980, The entry and exit fallacy in bilingual education. *NABE Journal*, 4, 25–60.
— 1983, *Heritage Language Education: A Literature Review*. Toronto: Ministry of Education, Ontario.
— 1984. *Bilingualism and Special Education: Issues in Assessment and Pedagogy*. Clevedon: Multilingual Matters.
ELLIS, J. 1984, *Education, Repression and Liberation: Namibia*. London: World University Service and The Catholic Institute for International Relations.
FISHMAN, J. A., COOPER, R. L. & CONRAD, A. W. 1977, *The Spread of English. The Sociology of English as an Additional Language*. Rowley, Mass.: Newbury House.
GALTUNG, J. 1980, *The True Worlds. A Transnational Perspective*. New York: The Free Press.
GEINGOB, H. 1981, Foreword, In: R. A. CHAMBERLAIN *et al.*, *Toward a Language Policy for Namibia. English as the Official Language: Perspectives and Strategies*, v.
GREEN, R. H. no date, Toward Independence and Self-Reliance: Some Person-power Development Considerations, duplicate.
GREEN, R. H., KILJUNEN, K. & KILJUNEN, M. (eds) 1981, *Namibia. The Last Colony*. Harlow: Longman.
Guidelines for Reform of General and Vocational Schools, Approved by the Plenary Meeting of the CPSU Central Committee on April 10 and by the USSR Supreme Soviet on April 12, *Moscow News*, Supplement to Issue No. 21 (3113) 1984, Moscow.
HIGGS, P. L. 1979, *Culture and Value Changes in Zambian School Literature*. Ph.D. Dissertation, Los Angeles: University of California.
KALEMA J. 1980, Report on Functions and Activities of the OAU Inter-African Bureau of Languages. In: K. MATEENE & J. KALEMA (eds), *Reconsideration of African Linguistic Policies*, 1–8.
KASHOKI, M. E. 1982, Achieving Nationhood Through Language: The Challenge of Namibia. *Third World Quarterly*, 4:2, 282–90.
KRAG, H. L. 1983, Die Sowjetunion — Staat, Nationaltätenfrage und Sprachen-politik. *Sprache und Herrschaft*, 13:II, Wien.
KURVINEN, P. 1877, *ABD Moshindonga, Omukanda Uatango koshindonga ua piangoa. — Ondonga kielen ABD. Ensimmäinen kirja Ondonga kielellä*. Helsinki: Suomen Lähetysseura.
LAMBERT, W. 1975, Culture and Language as Factors in Learning and Education. In: A. WOLFGANG (ed.), *Education of Immigrant Students*. Toronto: Ontario Insti-tute for Studies in Education.
MATEENE, K. 1980a, Introduction. In: K. MATEENE & J. KALEMA (eds), *Recon-sideration of African Linguistic Policies*. Kampala: OAU Bureau of Languages, vi–vii.
— 1980b, Failure in the Obligatory Use of European Languages in Africa and the Advantages of a Policy of Linguistic Independence. In K. MATEENE & J. KALEMA

(eds), *Reconstruction of African Linguistic Policies*. Kampala: OAU Bureau of Languages, 9—41.

MATEENE, K. & KALEMA, J. (eds) 1980, *Reconsideration of African Linguistic Policies*. Kampala: OAU Bureau of Languages, OAU/BIL Publication 3.

MAZRUI, A. A. 1973, *The political sociology of the English Language*. The Hague: Mouton.

MBAMBA, M. A. 1982, *Primary Education for an Independent Namibia. Planning in a Situation of Uncertainty and Instability*. Stockholm: Almqvist & Wiksell.

MINISTRY OF EDUCATION 1977, *Educational Reform: Proposals and Recommendations*. Lusaka: Republic of Zambia Ministry of Education.

PATTANAYAK, D. P. 1981, *Multilingualism and Mother-Tongue Education*. Delhi: Oxford University Press.

PREISWERK, R. (ed.) 1980, *The Slant of the Pen: Racism in Children's Books*. Geneva: World Council of Churches.

RODNEY, W. 1972, *How Europe underdeveloped Africa*. London: Bogle l'ouverture.

SCOTTON, C. M. 1981, The Linguistic Situation and Language Policy in Eastern Africa. *Annual Review of Applied Linguistics*, II, 8–20.

SKUTNABB-KANGAS, T. 1984, *Bilingualism or Not: The Education of Minorities*. Clevedon: Multilingual Matters.

SKUTNABB-KANGAS, T. & PHILLIPSON, R. 1985, Cultilinguistic Imperialism — What can Scandinavia Learn from the Second and Third Worlds? In T. SKUTNABB-KANGAS & R. PHILLIPSON (eds), *Educational Strategies in Multilingual Contexts*, ROLIG-papir 35, Roskilde: Roskilde Universitetscenter.

SMOLICZ, J. J. 1983, National Language Policies in Australia and the Philippines — a Comparative Perspective, Paper at the 7th Conference of the Asian Association on National Languages, Kuala Lumpur, Malaysia, August 1983.

SWAIN, M. & LAPKIN, S. 1982, *Evaluating Bilingual Education: A Canadian Case Study*. Clevedon: Multilingual Matters.

SWAPO 1981, *To Be Born a Nation: The Liberation Struggle for Namibia*. London: Zed Press and Luanda: Department of Information and Publicity, SWAPO of Namibia.

— 1982, Preliminary Perspectives into Emergent Educational System for Namibia. Luanda: Department of Education and Culture, SWAPO of Namibia, May 1982.

— 1983, *Education for the Future: Programmes, prospects and needs*. Luanda: Department of Education and Culture, SWAPO of Namibia.

— 1984, *Education: For All! National Integrated Educational System for Emergent Namibia*. Luanda: SWAPO of Namibia.

TADADJEU, M. 1980, *A Model for Functional Trilingual Education Planning in Africa*. Paris: Unesco.

TJITENDERO, M. P. 1984, Education for Liberation: Process of Development. Paper at Bremen University, April 24, 1984, Bremen.

ZIMMERMANN, W. 1984, Language Planning, Language Policy and Education in Namibia. *International Education Journal*, 1:2, 181–96.

8 National language policy in the Philippines

A comparative study of the educational status of "colonial" and indigenous languages with special reference to minority tongues

J. J. SMOLICZ

The overview

The attempt to build monolingual states was often based upon identification which many peoples had developed between the consciousness of being a separate national group and the native tongue. The language thus often became a symbol of its national identity and the core value of its culture. This link between cultural identity and language persists to this day, and is likely to continue in the future. What is at question is not whether language may be regarded as the most important element of a given culture — indeed, its carrier and core value (Smolicz, 1979,1980) — but whether this identification between language amd a cultural group requires in each instance the creation of a separate political entity for its protection and development. It should be possible for a number of linguistic groups to co-exist within the same political organism without fear that their cultural heritage is thereby threatened, and that the only recourse to ensure survival is to separate into yet another little state, however precarious its economic base or geographic position.

It is the contention of this chapter that there is no intrinsic need for such a nexus between a language and a state. It, therefore, follows that attempts to artificially suppress minority languages through policies of assimilation, devaluation, reduction to a state of illiteracy, expulsion or genocide are not only degrading of human dignity and morally unacceptable, but they are also an invitation to separatism and an incitement to fragmentation into mini-states. The danger is that if this is not realized in time, needless suffering, discrimination, tension and strife may be inflicted upon the whole population. This applies to the dominant group which attempts to achieve a monolingual state by imposing its own mother tongue upon all others, as well as to those minority groups which try to preserve their languages by adopting either a separatist or secessionist stance. In this kind of struggle, the culture-creative powers of a group are needlessly re-directed to culturally destructive pursuits that consume energies which could have been used to advance the languages and cultures of all concerned.

It is the principle underlying this chapter that each state, in this case the Philippines, usually needs some kind of a national language that would act as a "lingua franca" for communication between all its citizens. This should not imply, however, the disappearance of all alternative modes of verbal expression. On the contrary, people whose mother tongue is different from the national language should be given the opportunity to develop their first or native tongue. In such a multilingual setting community languages other than the national one would not be "secret" tongues, but "open" and available to interested individuals from other groups, including those from the group whose home language had been declared as national.

Linguistic pluralism for individuals, diglossia or societal bilingualism for the state, have long been accepted in many parts of the world, and nowhere more perhaps than in Asia. But in other countries bilingualism (and especially biliteracy) is still looked upon with suspicion and may be discouraged through prohibitive or discriminatory regulations in the educational system and other organs of administration. This suspicion of bilingualism and the deeply engrained belief in a monolingual state can be observed in countries such as the U.S., Australia, or Great Britain, which for long periods of their history have lived under the assumption that citizens spoke but one native tongue, and that all other languages were "foreign", in that their use could only be justified by reference to interaction with outsiders or aliens. The idea of "community languages" other than English still finds little acceptance in such Anglo-Saxon-dominated societies, while in Germany, for example, 4.6 million "guest-workers" speak languages (such as Turkish, Italian or Greek) which are inaccessible to "ordinary" German schoolchildren who are required to study "foreign" languages that have been officially defined as English or French. Some of the countries mentioned above have now acquired substantial linguistic minorities, caused by arrivals from the "New Commonwealth" in the U.K., or the flood of Latin Americans that have supplemented the "older" ethnics in the U.S. Lack of sufficient recognition of the rights and aspirations of linguistic minorities may create for both of these countries serious "centrifugal" problems in the future. Australia, also finds itself in this group, with a quarter of its population now drawn from a non-English speaking background.

In Asia there has been a traditional recognition of multilingualism which many European states lack. This does not mean that Asia has been free of strife which at times has been "internally generated", while at others it could be attributed to an unfortunate importation of the outdated nationalistic European model of a monolingual nation-state. It may be argued that some aspects of this belief in the need for one national language as a symbol of national independence may now be found in the Philippines, as that country makes strides to free itself from the former "colonial" tongues — Spanish (now almost phasing itself out of existence) and English (still used in many domains, such as higher education and scientific training in the school). In their efforts to establish Pilipino as the national tongue, the authorities appear to have placed the emphasis almost entirely on the Pilipino–English balance; the other languages of the Philippines (spoken daily by almost two-thirds of the population) are being completely lost from sight.

Language policies in the Philippines[1]

In the Philippines the process of educational transmission is particularly hampered by the linguistic confusion involving the entire Filipino educational system. In this respect we can witness the full impact of different social and cultural values, and the way they affect the acquisition of knowledge through the changing directions of the educational policy in the country.

In theory, there are three types of linguistic media that can be considered as possible means of transmission of knowledge, since the country continues to have three "official" languages English, Spanish, and Pilipino. The last of these, which has been declared as "national", is very largely based upon Tagalog. It must be recognized, however, that Tagalog is but one of several indigenous or Filipino languages of the country. The other major Filipino languages are: Cebuano, Ilokano, Hiligaynon, Bicol, Waray, Kapampangan, Pangasinan. These eight languages (including Tagalog) account for over 85% of the population, with the rest of the people speaking some 75 other "tongues" and 300 "dialects".

In the Philippines, for historical as well as linguistic reasons, there is some confusion about the spelling of the name of the "national" language. Even the spelling of the country itself is variable and while "Philippines" is the English version, "Filipinas" is the Spanish one, and Pilipinas the official indigenous name. Although the indigenous languages of the country are generally referred to as the Filipino languages, the "national" variety of the dominant native tongue Tagalog is called "Pilipino" (with a "P"). The situation was further complicated when in 1973 the new Philippine Constitution declared that, in the future, the "common national language (is) to be known as Filipino" (with an "F"). Since this provision of the constitution has not yet been proclaimed by the National Assembly, the implication has been drawn that in the meantime Pilipino will continue as the "interim" national language (Llamzon, 1983; Perez, 1983). There appears to be no consensus as to what language "Filipino" really is, except that it is generally assumed to be based upon "Pilipino", but with the addition of some words and/or constructions from the other indigenous languages. Thus it would seem that Tagalog is now acting as the nucleus of "Pilipino", and that in future "Pilipino" will act as the nucleus for "Filipino". What is fairly clear, however, is that the national language, irrespective whether it is spelled with a "P" or "F", is very close to Tagalog and that the name "Tagalog" and "Pilipino" are often used interchangeably.

When in 1898, after over three centuries of their colonial rule, the Spaniards were expelled from the Philippines by the Americans, a major effort was made to introduce the teaching of English to the country. This move was directed not only against Spanish, but against all the Filipino languages, which were outlawed from the school. This educational drive for English reached its peak during the 1920s and early 1930s when the teaching of English claimed a major part of the curriculum.

Manhit (1980: 47–48) reminds her readers of the not so distant past when not only did English instruction in the junior school increase by "leaps and bounds" but even,

> "students and teachers, once within the school grounds, were required to use no other language but English. Woe unto anyone caught speaking his/her language. Punishment was suspension from classes or deduction of grades."

After the bills of 1916 and 1924 that promised "independence" (but without specifying its future date), it was officially required that the government "shall provide for the maintenance of a system of public schools conducted in English". As a result of such legislation, the percentage of total instruction time allotted to English subjects in junior grades rose from approximately 40% to close to 60% of the school time. As Manhit (1980: 47) comments, in consequence of arrangements that precluded the use of any native language that would be "detrimental to the spread of English", and the refusal of the American teachers to "use any other language but English as a medium of instruction", Filipino school children were subjected to massive language indoctrination campaigns:

"Thus six hours a day, five days a week learners were in realistic situations in which of necessity they had to listen to and speak and think in English."

Such "pressure cooker" or "immersion" techniques undoubtedly helped to establish literacy in English among wide circles of Filipino population and, while they failed to eradicate the native languages from domestic and other extra-curricular usage, they effectively delayed the literary growth of the Filipino languages (including Tagalog), as well as their modern development in the field of science and technology. The results of these efforts are partly reflected in the 1960 census when 39.5% of the population claimed to be able to speak English, and only 2.1% to speak Spanish, while those reporting the ability to speak Tagalog amounted to less than half of the population (44.4%).[2]

Attempts to develop a national language

As far back as 1908, the Philippine Commission made a recommendation to establish a language institute for training of teachers (both Filipino and American) in the several native tongues of the Philippines. This move was thwarted as a threat to English, and the initiatives to formulate a policy that related to languages which the people actively spoke in their homes had no legislative consequences until shortly before the Second World War.

The pressures for the recognition of the Filipino languages gradually increased, but much hesitation surrounded the initiatives to establish a national language of the Philippines; indeed, the move to have Tagalog formally accepted in that position failed at the 1934 Constitutional Convention. Instead, the Convention merely agreed that steps should be taken "toward the development and adoption of a common language based on one of the existing native languages" (Constitution of the Philippines, Act. XIII, Sec. 3). The Constitutional Convention held in 1971 also showed deep divisions of opinion and E. A. Constantino (as reported by Bautista, 1981: 6) has recalled,

"the hostility towards Tagalog-based Pilipino (. . .) a hostility so fierce that there was even the danger that a foreign language like English might be adopted as the Philippine national language."

Bautista admits that in order to,

"forestall such a possibility, the University of the Philippines linguists (. . .) broached the proposal of forming a national language through the 'universal approach', that is from a fusion of elements of existing Philippine languages and dialects. And that was how Article XV, Section III (of the Constitution) came to be: 'The National Assembly shall take steps towards the development and formal adoption of a common national language called Filipino'."

Constantino (1981: 28–31) remains firm in his belief that such a "universal approach" can be successfully adopted in the Philippines since, in his view, it has been applied before and can be applied again. However, Bautista (p. 7) recognizes that many linguists remain "skeptical" about the feasibility of applying such a "fusion" approach. One can only conclude that Tagalog has been once again steered successfully through the Convention under the guise of "Filipino", with only a vague promise that this term will somehow do justice to the other indigenous languages of the Philippines.

The protagonists of Pilipino/Tagalog now assume that the "Filipino" of the Constitutional Convention is to be based on Pilipino in the same way that Pilipino has been based upon Tagalog (Perez, 1983). They do this by invoking the extreme facility of Pilipino/Tagalog to borrow words from other languages, although such words appear to come more often from Spanish or English than from the other indigenous languages of the Philippines (which seem only to supply some occasional words connected with food or other specialized domestic pursuits). New developments in Tagalog, as it is spoken in the Manila area, are also claimed as evidence of the flexibility of Pilipino and its divergence from Tagalog in its ethnic heartland. The fact remains, however, that Tagalog Philipino is another name for Tagalog as a modern literary language, and that its advocates (motivated perhaps by their desire to use it as a tool of national unity against English) would like to continue this development, but this time under the new title of Filipino. (Some of the people concerned even seem unaware of the implications for the change of nomenclature from Pilipino to Filipino and continue to use the "Pilipino" label.)

Whether one refers to it as "Pilipino" or "Filipino", the national language continues to bear an unmistakable resemblance to its progenitor and this has sometimes been unconsciously acknowledged even in official publications. For example, in the recent proceedings of a symposium devoted to the development of Pilipino (Gonzalez & Bautista, 1981: ii) it was noted that since some chapters were presented in Pilipino, English translations were provided in the appendix "for the benefit of those non-Tagalog readers who feel more comfortable reading in English".

In this connection it should be noted that Tagalog is not the mother tongue of the largest linguistic group in the country, although it does have more speakers in the country as a whole than its nearest rival Cebuano (which has a greater number of native speakers). Nevertheless, despite efforts to popularize it, according to estimates of 1967, less than two-thirds of the population were actually able to speak Tagalog, while only approximately a quarter regarded it as their mother tongue. The figures released in 1972 (for 1970, by Regions and Provinces) show that while in the country as a whole 52% of the population could speak Pilipino/Tagalog, this varied from 98% in Manila to 70% in Palawan, 55% in Batanes and Pangasinan, 38% in Ilocos Sur, 34% in Iloilo, 29% in Cebu, 24% in Bohol and 18% in Sulu.[3]

Bilingual policy and "linguistic gap"

Over recent years, determined efforts have been made to spread Tagalog/Pilipino throughout the school system, and these efforts have been intensified since the adoption of a "bilingual policy" that has left no room for any other native tongue as the "educational partner" for English. Initially, some education in the "vernacular" took place at elementary school level. With the proclamation of the "bilingual educational policy", however, all the other major Filipino languages were phased out from the curriculum and effectively banned from any kind of educational role in the school. Instruction was to be in English and Pilipino only, while a strict demarcation of domains was effected by the decision to have all science and mathematics taught in English, while social sciences and related disciplines were to be taught in Pilipino, which was also to be taken as a school subject in its own right. Other Filipino languages were not only prohibited as languages of instruction, but they were not even to be taught as subjects in any form, whether at elementary, secondary or tertiary levels. Application of the policy has been made easier by the centralized organization of the Filipino system of public instruction and the rigid application of centrally controlled school curricula.

In practice this means that in schools of a province, such as Negros Occidental, where almost all the pupils, as well as the great majority of teachers, are Ilongos and speak a variant of Hiligaynon in their homes, schooling begins in what are virtually two foreign languages: English and Pilipino. (On the island of Negros only slightly more than a quarter of the population were able to speak Pilipino/Tagalog in 1970: 29% in Negros Occidental and 24% in Negros Oriental, while ability to speak English in 1960 was limited to 40% in both parts of the island.) Middle class pupils usually bring with them some knowledge of English, but the children from the "barrios" in the countryside can usually speak only a very limited form of English, and their knowledge of Tagalog is restricted to what they have learned from the television screen, or comics that are written in a linguistic hybrid known as "Taglish".

Even after completing their elementary education, and leaving school, the barrio children, especially those from isolated and impoverished rural areas, speak most halting English, or are too shy to speak English at all. To such young people the Pilipino language also remains "basic" and intellectually "non-internalized"; at the same time, they do not become fully literate in their mother tongue, although they may attempt to write in Ilongo by applying, through their own efforts, the rules of spelling and grammar that they have learned for Pilipino. Such efforts may at best result in semi-literacy and represent a precarious method of acquiring the ability to read and write in one's home language. Even teachers themselves are often uncertain of how to write in their native tongue, and resort to English in family correspondence. The latter option is, of course, hardly open to most village children, who would find it too difficult to try to compose long texts in English. Unfortunately they cannot compensate for this deficiency in other ways, since they lack the command of literate forms of both Pilipino and their native tongue. Hence there are children who finish school without being fully literate in any language.

Under such conditions of linguistic confusion in their formal education, it is not surprising that the learning of scientific concepts in particular appears so laborious and unrewarding. The learning process must indeed be opaque when the route for the percolation of science is obscured by ignorance of the linguistic medium that should normally facilitate such transmission. This gap in communication is camouflaged by the assumption that children speak sufficient English for the teaching of elementary science. In making this assertion, educational authorities ignore the fact that while science curricula have become steadily more demanding and sophisticated, the time allotted to English education has decreased due to the increased time assigned to Pilipino. In this regard, research demonstrates a steady deterioration in the knowledge of English among university entrants (Manhit, 1980, 1981). At the same time, science curricula assume a steadily increasing ability to comprehend English texts.

It is indeed, surprising that there has been no greater public questioning of the "bilingual policy". Public comments on this issue have been more muted than would normally be expected in an ethnically and linguistically plural society. One possible reason for this may be that those who could have been expected to be most vocal (i.e. the professional and middle class groups in society) are the least disadvantaged. Pupils from the upper echelons of society use English in their homes, attend private schools, and often come from Manila and other Tagalog-speaking areas of the country. Private schools, which in the past did not always match the academic achievements of the public educational system, are now getting ahead by their greater reliance upon English and the delayed introduction of Pilipino, which is frequently treated more as a subject to be taught, than as a medium of communication and instruction. When social sciences are taught in Pilipino, this subject is frequently least liked and shows a low level of achievement among middle class students of all linguistic backgrounds.

In Tagalog areas, such as Bulakan, English is normally introduced during the second term of the first year of elementary education. Even in such a Tagalog/English bilingual setting, teachers find English texts too advanced, in that they assume a background in English which many country students conspicuously lack. Testing of pupils from higher elementary grades in science by the Science Education Centre of the University of the Philippines is still in an experimental stage but low test scores, as well as personal interaction with pupils, reveal a significant "linguistic gap" in English, which curriculum planners frequently ignore.

If such difficulties are experienced in the application of the bilingual policy in relation to students who begin their formal education with Tagalog as their home language, the problems are magnified for those Filipinos who speak other Filipino languages in their homes. These difficulties are, however, less apparent in Metro Manila, since in this area one finds a steady generational shift to Tagalog among all non-Tagalog groups. This shift is most clearly seen in children of "mixed marriages", where one of the parents has Tagalog as his home language, but the effect is also observed among children from families where parents are of different, but non-Tagalog background. In Metro Manila assimilation to Tagalog is encountered even among children from homogeneous non-Tagalog backgrounds. For example, in families where both parents are Bikol, Ilokano, or Kapampangan, a typical linguistic pattern is established whereby parents continue to speak to each other in their original language, but to their children in a mixture of their native vernacular and Tagalog, while the children almost invariably answer in Tagalog. The proportion of English used in conversation is often a function of the socio-economic position and status of the family, and attendance at a "more elite" private school.

Metro Manila can, therefore, be regarded as a giant linguistic melting pot with Tagalog acting as a unifying agency that displaces, rather than supplements, the usage of other Filipino languages which can be viewed as "passing transients" in the capital. This state of linguistic assimilation, away from the ethnic language or vernacular and towards the dominant (if not the "majority") tongue, is reminiscent of assimilation into English and the gradual erosion of minority languages in Australia, and other Anglo-Saxon based countries. It should be stressed that this situation prevails in the

Philippines solely in Metro Manila and in some other urban centres located in linguistically mixed areas and those of more recent migration (such as parts of Mindanao and Palawan).

One of the tacit assumptions of the government's bilingual policy is that such linguistic "unification" will eventually occur in the country as a whole. This is implicit in the slogan "one people, one country, one language". The evidence, however, suggests that this is an erroneous assumption in relation to most of the non-Tagalog provinces of the Philippines. The proportion of the population with ability merely to speak Pilipino, generally as a second language, showed only a fairly small increase from 1960 to 1970. This increase was from 23% to 34% in Iloilo, 42% to 55% in Pangasinan, 28% to 52% in Ilocos Norte, 18% to 29% in Cebu, but from 28% to over 40% in Davao where population movements were noted. In Sulu the jump was from 11% to 18% and in Leyte from 18% to 28%.

The population of these non-Tagalog areas (and especially the young) are acquiring a smattering of Pilipino through the educational system and the mass media, but this is mostly at a rather superficial level. Even when a deeper understanding of Pilipino is occasionally acquired, this is not at the expense of the ability to speak and identify with the mother tongue. Nor is it at the expense of English, which continues to be used for more intellectual matters, in the case of educated elite of all linguistic backgrounds. In the meantime, the mistaken assumptions of the "bilingual policy" are creating in schools (especialy among the rural poor) a problem of functional semi-illiteracy and, through the stress on Pilipino, an attenuation in the know-ledge of English, which is supposed to act as the medium for the study of science. The price of this policy is being paid by those most in the need of educational support, namely the poorer sections of the community in the provinces, whose failure in school is partly induced through the misunder-standing of their linguistic needs.

The viability of the non-Tagalog Filipino languages

The first point which the new educational policy must take into account is that non-Tagalog (or non-Pilipino) Filipino languages (as spoken by over two-thirds of the Filipino people) are not going to disappear overnight, or in the forthcoming generations. *The attempt to introduce all the Filipino population to Pilipino as a national language can and should therefore continue, but not at the expense of the eradication of the other Filipino tongues, or their reduction to domestic vernaculars with no literature, no status, and no domains save the home or the marketplace.* An "Alice in Wonderland" policy of pretending that there are only two "educational" languages in the country, namely English and Pilipino, undermines the linguistic stability of Filipino children, most especially children of rural and working class background from non-Tagalog speaking homes. The resulting instability is related to the insufficient stress on the mastery of English on the one hand, and the attempt to force non-Tagalog Filipino languages into extinction through a process of "transitional degradation" on the other. This involves an attempt to force back the "vernaculars" from their early beginnings at literary development into a state of domestication or "kitchen status", and even right up to their eventual disappearance. The policy in question has failed to eradicate the languages concerned, but is causing linguistic destabilization among those Filipino pupils who already suffer economic and educational deprivation. The failure to effectively transmit "educational knowledge" is only one facet of this state of deprivation and underprivilege.

Earlier in the chapter it was argued that one reason for the apparent acceptance of the bilingual policy in education by the non-Tagalog speaking provinces was that those in a position to oppose it were least affected by its negative consequences. A further reason for this relative quiescence of public opinion can be deduced from an examination of current Filipino school practices. This involves a systematic by-passing of the official directives by many schools, especially in the private sector. For example, in Leyte in a number of Catholic schools a linguistic approach has evolved which corresponds more closely to the capabilities and needs of the people whose home language is Waray-Waray; whose knowledge and interest in Pilipino are rather tenuous; and whose acquaintance with English is initially very peripheral. Waray-Waray is used as the language of instruction in the first four grades of elementary school, while English is intensively taught as a subject. In grades 5 and 6, English becomes the principal medium of instruction and Waray-Waray is only used as an auxiliary in situations demanding further linguistic elaboration. In secondary education English takes over as the sole means of instruction, while Pilipino is taught as a subject. At the college level and at universities, all education is in English, although there exists a department of Pilipino studies.

There is no teaching of Waray-Waray *per se* at any stage of education, although books of poems and occasional periodicals testify to the continued vitality of the mother tongue of the people (Quetchenbach, 1974). Language used in church may often be a good guide to the desires and needs of a given population. This is specially true of the Catholic church in its post-Vatican II stage of development, which has involved substitution of the spoken languages for the formerly ubiquitous Latin. In the southern Philippines religious services are almost invariably said either in English or in the local language, be it a form of Hiligaynon or Waray-Waray. Tagalog/Pilipino is hardly ever used, indicating that the faithful do not regard it as either their mother tongue, or as a "superior" liturgical language, since the latter role is filled by English. Hence church usage, which is closely attuned to the aspirations of the people, confirms the resiliance and continued dynamism of the non-Tagalog languages on their "home ground".

In this type of situation an outside observer, accustomed by the example of Belgium or Quebec to the assertiveness of linguistic groups who perceive their position as inferior or under threat, may wonder at the placid acquiescence by the various Filipino groups to the elimination of their tongues from education, and seek an answer from the local population. When pressed to explain the omission of any kind of formal instruction in their mother tongue, people such as teachers, adopt what can be taken as a characteristic Filipino way of dealing with awkward questions: they deflect it without giving a direct answer. This is done, for example, by saying, "We treasure our own language so much that we wish to keep it for ourselves at home." Another interpretation was provided to the author by the large audience of teachers at one of the private schools in Cebu, where speakers explained the non-teaching of Cebuano as due to their insufficient confidence in the maturity of their home tongue as a literary language and their sense of its inadequacy in the learning situation.

Linguistic emancipation and the quest for recognition and autonomy

It should be noted that similar feelings of inferiority afflicted many European linguistic groups in the past, so that Polish did not become a literary tongue and did not shake off its subservient status to Latin until the sixteenth century. Baltic languages, such as Latvian and Lithuanian, did not begin to develop as literary tongues until well into the nineteenth century. The diffidence among speakers of the various Filipino "vernaculars" is therefore quite understandable, especially in view of the long period of subordination to the Spanish language in administration and education (1565–1898) and subsequent imposition of English as the literary language of the country. The present policy of achieving "Filipinization" through Pilipino (Tagalog) as the only national language and the exclusion of the other Filipino languages from the school has the effect of further strengthening this diffidence.

The example of Europe shows, however, that such a lack of confidence in the maturity of one's native tongue is not likely to last forever. If the Philippines' authorities feel impelled to follow the European nineteenth century fashion that stipulated that each state should possess a single distinct national language, it will be only a matter of time before similar notions are adopted by the non-Tagalog provinces of the Philippines. The acceptance of this axiom would invoke its corollary, namely, that each major linguistic group should be able to organize itself into an autonomous province or even into an independent state. It is, therefore, most likely that in time the Philippines will follow the pattern of Spain, where even the centuries-old imposition of Castilian as the national language of Spain has now to give way to the demands of regional populations that have "rediscovered" their ethnic languages as the most effective rallying call for regional autonomy or even national independence. This trend has occurred not only in the traditional separatist provinces such as the land of the Basques (where the situation resembles the Filipino dilemmas in relation to the "Islamic South"), but also in Catalonia, Galicia and even in Andalusia. In consequence of such "ethnic revival", the term "Spanish" language has virtually "disappeared" from the official nomenclature and been replaced in public parlance by Castilian, Catalonian, Galego, etc. Similarly, it can be expected that in due course non-Tagalog provinces will likewise deny the name of "Pilipino" to the present national tongue and will demand the recognition and teaching of their own languages (which will no longer appear as some inferior "vernaculars" or "dialects").

It would therefore seem prudent to forestall this kind of "ethnic offensive" before it acquires elements of bitterness, by reversing the current "Tagalog only" policies and reintroducing other Filipino languages into schools. The non-Tagalog provinces already witness the preferential treatment of Islamic regions, including teaching of a foreign language, such as modern Arabic, by the Filipino educational system in the southern parts of the country in response to the more determined stand of the local population: it would be a pity if the authorities acted only when subjected to such pressures, instead of initiating necessary reforms out of their own accord. Such reforms would not only satisfy the legitimate regional and ethnic aspirations of the provinces, but also take into account the strictly educational needs of the non-Tagalog speakers.

Double linguistic barrier

The present situation where scientific and other kinds of knowledge are shielded or screened from the pupils by the imposition of a double linguistic barrier of two tongues that the child does not learn in his own home, should be eliminated to allow more than a semblance of equality of educational opportunity for children who use Filipino languages other than Tagalog in their homes, and who do not come from the privileged homes where English usage enables the children to enter the world of science with some degree of confidence.

The question is not only a matter of equality for the barrio children and the rural poor from the Ilocos, Bicol, Negros, Panay or Pampanga. It is also the question of the wastage of human resources in the country and the disquieting spectacle of the steady deterioration not only of the knowledge of the English language *per se*, but of science taught through the medium of English. The perpetual calls for "evaluation programs" to gauge the current state of "scientific progress" and "technological innovation" among the "rural poor" will remain but empty slogans so long as the basic need to overcome the double linguistic barrier is not eradicated. At present the needs of the country in educational and economic progress, as well as the equality of opportunities for rural children in the provinces, are being sacrificed on the altar of out-dated values whose aim is to reassert national identity by inflating the use of Pilipino at the expense of English. The fact that the majority of Filipinos do not use Tagalog as their tongue is ignored.

The main need at present is to alter the bilingual policy so as to arrest the decline in educational standards. This cannot occur until Philippine authorities realize that the linguistic trends towards Filipino homogeniza-tion that are currently taking place in the capital city are not a true reflection of the country as a whole, and that there are no signs that "provincial" languages are likely to disappear from either popular use or sentiment. In such a situation any future plans for replacing English with "Pilipino only" in school science or in university education would only serve to further lower the educational standards of the country and further increase the educa-tional gap of opportunity between Manila and the non-Tagalog provinces, which already begin to sense that the only way to relieve their lot and excite an interest on the part of the central government is to threaten secession and foment unrest.

Educational support for literacy development in the home language

In order to forestall such developments, educational policies must take into account the fact that non-Tagalog Filipino languages cannot be kept in the back room for ever, and that since they give every sign of persistence, they require educational support for literacy development. Such recognition of regional cultural variation is perfectly compatible with the overall system of over-arching Filipino values. Such Filipino shared or over-arching values as love of native land, consciousness of common origin and history, and the particularly strong family networks, also include the use of Pilipino as a national language for all Filipinos. But the people should also be permitted to develop their mother tongues, side by side with the national one. (For a discussion of over-arching values and core values, see Smolicz, 1980, 1981a,

1984). If the present concessions to the Islamic population in the South are deemed to eliminate friction and strengthen cohesion through toleration of legitimate diversity, the same holds true for the Christian provinces of Luzon or the Visayas which share many more values with the Tagalog regions.

The way to national cohesion lies in the satisfaction of regional identities, a conclusion already being adopted in Europe by Spain, Germany, Italy and, rather tentatively and hesitantly by Great Britain. The educational policy must therefore ensure the continued and improved teaching of English to allow the Philippines to keep an "open window" onto the wider world, while at the same time encouraging the development of the national language Pilipino, but not at the expense of legitimate linguistic usages and aspirations of almost two-thirds of the population. This would entail the teaching of the major Filipino languages at school according to the home usage of the pupils. In this way languages such as Ilokano or Hiligaynon would be used as languages of instruction in elementary education in their respective regions, as well as being taught as "subjects proper", so that the pupils would learn them in a grammatical form and appreciate their nascent literature, as well as being encouraged to contribute towards it. At elementary school stage English and Pilipino would be taught as school subjects.

At secondary school stage science could be taught in English, at least for the foreseeable future, while both the regional language and Pilipino would continue to be taught as legitimate subjects in their own right. It is not appropriate to phase out the regional language at secondary level since one cannot lock out a language for ever at the "junior stage" without evoking among its speakers a feeling of inferiority and undermining their cultural identity. Social sciences at secondary level could be taught either in the regional language or in Pilipino, depending on the linguistic ability and wishes of the pupils and their parents.

At the university stage the balance between English and Pilipino would depend upon the subject, capabilities of staff, as well as student needs, although in science it is most likely that the instruction would be in English. However, all major colleges and universities should establish departments in regional languages so as to allow cultural creativity to flourish in the home language of the students.

National language policy in a multilingual setting

In the Philippines, linguistic assimilation is hardly tacit, because the bilingual educational policy outlaws from the school all languages other than English and Pilipino. Its consequences are hardly ever openly discussed, however, and a discreet veil is drawn over the continued existence of other Filipino languages; in a similar manner, the non-use of such languages at the school and university level is also passed over in silence. This silence is hardly ever broken even by the occasional publication of literary works in those "unrecognized" languages (e.g. Quetchenbach, 1974), since these are generally regarded as purely local productions that may be of sentimental value, but which are of hardly any importance in the life of the nation as a whole. Here, too, the assumptions are monolingual in relation to "native" languages, so that even if the policy makers do not openly contemplate the actual disappearance of the non-Tagalog Filipino languages, they seem intent on incarcerating them in the narrow confines of the home, and arresting their literary development.

Such linguistic policies are based upon the erroneous vision of a monolingual nation-state, in spite of the fact that this vision is outdated in the modern world, and quite inapplicable to a multilingual and multicultural society such as the Philippines. Short-sighted policies of this type are inflicting educational harm upon minorities, preventing both minority and majority children from participating in more than one language and culture and thus impoverishing the children's intellectual development and narrowing their cultural horizons. It is also sowing seeds for future discontent through the perpetuation of the notion of superior and inferior languages and cultures.

Hence the policy of monolingualism in relation to the indigenous or community languages of a society that is multilingual represents a policy of educational discrimination and political instability. This conclusion does not minimize the importance of a national language, but the acceptance of such a language should not be at the expense of the legitimate aspirations of less powerful or less assertive sections of the population to retain and develop their native tongues. This aspiration should be regarded as a right (and not a privilege), a right which the dominant group already enjoys to the full, but needs to learn how to accord to others. An enlightened national language policy must encourage all groups to be open to other languages and cultures, in order to dispel any assumption of superiority or exploitation, whether in the economic, cultural or linguistic fields of national policy.

As far as the Philippines are concerned, the acceptance of multilingualism (both internally directed in respect to non-Tagalog Filipino languages, and externally in relation to English) should be regarded as a goal that does not conflict with the evolution of Pilipino as the national language of the country. The political and social stability of the country, as well as an equitable distribution of educational opportunities, requires acceptance of the principle that one can be *literate* in one's mother tongue and still be fluent in Pilipino and uphold it as the national language of the country.

In terms of language phases, the situation in the Philippines has shown a significant variation. The pluralistic pre-colonial phase preceeded the Spanish-dominated epoch which, at least linguistically, did not penetrate very deeply into the population as a whole. During the "English-only" period, in the first half of this century, the Americans attempted to make as many people as possible monolingual, or at least mono-literate in English. The current phase can be regarded as the enforced propagation (almost by green-house type methods of cultivation) of Pilipino into a national language, often by presenting it as essentially different even from literary Tagalog, and as the only medium of expression for all intellectual development in the country. In the future one must hope for the emergence of an *internal multilingual phase* which accepts the presence of other Filipino languages, including their right to literary development, alongside Pilipino/ Tagalog as the national language of the country, and English as the international language which has special significance for science and technology.

In this way, the Philippine needs to proceed to the goal of *acceptance of the co-existence of the national language as the medium of communication between all the citizens, together with a variety of other community languages that have a right to intellectual and educational development.* This right is enshrined in the United Nations Charter of Human Rights for all linguistic groups — majority and minority — as well as in the UNESCO Convention against Discrimination in Education adopted in 1962.

The situation in the Philippines is further complicated by the existence of indigenous mountain or "hill-tribe" people of the Philippines, whose languages are now also attracting the attention of educationists and linguists (Elkins, 1981; Fransisco, 1981). "The Philippine Cultural Minorities", as they are frequently called, were also described in two special issues of the *Philippine Quarterly of Culture and Society* (1974, 1977). In this connection it should be noted that the term "cultural minorities" in Filipino parlance does not usually refer to the major non-Tagalog speaking groups in the country, but to "the predominantly non-Christian groups of varying degrees of cultural development, that is, the pagans and Mohammedanized Filipinos (Muslims), who form 8% of the present population of the Philippines" (Tenazas & Ramas, 1974).

On linguistic data from census questions

The need for changes in the current linguistic policies of the Philippines can be illustrated, at a practical level, in the way census data on languages are being collected, or on the way they are withheld or made inaccessible to an ordinary reader. The *1981 Pocketbook of Philippine Statistics* (1981) which contains 17 chapters of tables, provides information, for example on "selected characteristics of Air Visitor Arrivals" and their numbers by nationality (Tables 8.1 and 8.2), as well as data on the Annual Production of Fertilizers (Table 6.4), but in its General Statistics, Social Statistics and Education sections does not find space to give any information on the current state of the various Filipino linguistic groups. In fact, it was found simplest to locate linguistic information gathered in previous Filipino censuses from the records of the International Center for the Study of Bilingualism at Laval University in Quebec.

An over-arching framework of values

Those who are opposed to linguistic pluralism, whether in the Philippines or not might argue that the proliferation of other pluralistic societies languages could lead to political instability and undermine national identity. The cohesion of the state does not, however, depend on having a basically monolingual population; the examples of Ireland and Lebanon show that a common language (whether English or Arabic) has not prevented slaughter in both those countries. On the other hand, states such as India or Switzerland show less ethnic antagonism despite the complex linguistic mosaic of their population. In Yugoslavia linguistic differences between Serbian and Croatian are relatively minor (some linguists claim them to be the same language), and yet the two ethnic groups are in a state of tension that is mainly caused by other, non-linguistic, cultural factors.

Multicultural and multilingual states have little choice in the matter: to ensure stability they must achieve a degree of consensus, since in its absence, the dominant group would have to rely on some form of manipulation or coercion to maintain the state. To achieve consensus, an ethnically plural society must have evolved a set of *shared* values that *over-arch* the various ethnic groups (Smolicz, 1983). If the ethnic groups concerned are to remain culturally viable, and if the state is to remain a stable one, we must have a dynamic equilibrium established between the over-arching values of the country, on the one hand and ethnic values, on the other. The dominant group may contribute the major component of the over-arching values, but, once these have been accepted by the other groups, they are no longer the property of that group alone, but the common possession of all citizens. For example, in a country such as Australia all groups (and not just the British) accept English as an over-arching value, but not at the expense of their native tongues, but as a supplement to them. In this way ethnic groups can fit into an over-arching framework, while conserving their core values which are usually characterized by such features as a distinct language, family or clan tradition, or religion.

In such a dynamic setting, the over-arching framework is forever changing and adapting, not only due to the creativity of the members of all groups and diffusion from outside, but also because of the input from a variety of majority and minority ethnic sources, although it is likely that the dominant group will prove the most important contributor. That is possible provided there is a consensus about fundamentals, so that the dominant group does not attempt to rupture the core values of the minorities, while the minority values fall within the range that is compatible with the over-arching framework and do not involve exclusivist notions that would prevent any possibility of an overlap. Tiny minorities with values that are essentially opposed to the over-arching framework may be tolerated, but the "tolerance ratio" would be disturbed if groups with diametrically opposed value-systems entered the country in larger numbers since this would upset the equilibrium and violate consensus.

Fortunately for the country discussed in this chapter, most (if not all) of the constituent ethnic groups fall within the over-arching framework. This is of vital importance for pluralist societies which are still evolving and whose independence is still of relatively recent vintage (Smolicz, 1982). In the Philippines, family loyalties and love of the scattered and beautiful archipelago of islands seem to evoke a positive response from all groups. In both societies the over-arching values are still in a state of crystalization, and a discussion of the extent to which, for example, Christianity and its secular residues underlie their cultural fabric are a matter of debate. (During its colonial period Catholicism was certainly the over-arching value that the Philippines shared with Spain, since for the Spanish empire the Catholic religion took precedence in the core value hierarchy over language, which Spain did not manage to transplant as successfully as it did in the case of religion.)

What seems clear, however, is that Pilipino in the Philippines is already accepted as a national language. What has not yet perhaps been grasped by the dominant group is that this must be understood in relation to co-existence of such a national language with the native tongues of ethnic minorities. Such co-existence is essential since these languages are frequently the core values of distinct cultures, and if they were to atrophy, the cultures concerned would also crumble, leaving behind a residue which would not lead to cohesion but to resentment at the implied state of inferiority of minority group members.

Bilingualism of individuals and diglossia in the state are perfectly compatible with the development of a stable Filipino society. It is only the denial of diversity that breeds separatism and undermines cohesion, which is guaranteed by the free acceptance of the over-arching framework of values by all the ethnic groups in society.

Notes to Chapter 8

1. This chapter was written in its original draft while the author was a Visiting Fellow at the Science Education Center of the University of the Philippines (February–April 1982). The author wishes to express his sincere gratitude to the Director of the Center, Professor Dolores F. Hernandez for her encouragement of this study and for her incisive comments that directed it towards investigating the languages of the Philippines. The first draft of this section formed part of a larger monograph entitled *Science, Education and Values: Cultural and Linguistic Barriers to Education in the Philippines* that was published by Science Education Center of the University of the Philippines, Quezon City, May, 1983.
2. All data for 1960 are taken from 'Census of Population and Housing 1960 — Summary Report' (Philippines). These figures were obtained from the records of the International Centre for the Study of Bilingualism, Laval University, Quebec.
3. All linguistic data from the 1970 census were released by the Statistical Office of the Philippines (NCSO) in 1972 and were originally published in "Pilipino in the year 2000", *Essays in Honour of Santiago A. Fonacier* (pp. 265–66). All such records were obtained by courtesy of the International Centre for the study of Bilingualism, Laval University, Quebec, Canada.

References

BAUTISTA, M. L. S. 1981, An Explanatory Note: Round-Table Conference on Philippine National Language Development. In: A. GONZALES & M. L. S. BAUTISTA (eds), *Aspects of Language Planning and Development in the Philippines*. Manila: Linguistic Society of the Philippines.

CONSTANTINO, E. A. 1981, The Work of Linguists in the Development of the National Language of the Philippines. In: A. GONZALES & M. L. S. BAUTISTA (eds), *Aspects of Language Planning and Development in the Philippines*, Manila: Linguistic Society of the Philippines.

ELKINS, R. E. 1981, Personal communication on the language of the Manopo.

FRANSISCO, J. R. 1981, Indigenous Learning Systems: The Philippines. In: L. BRILLANTES SORIANO (ed.), *Indigenous Learning Systems for Deprived Areas*, Proceedings of a SEAMEO Regional Seminar at the Center for Educational Innovation and Technology (INNOTECH) Manila, Philippines, pp. 124–43. See also "Opening Statement", pp. 1–19.

GONZALES, A. & BAUTISTA, M. L. S. 1981, *Aspects of Language Planning and Development in the Philippines*. Manila: Linguistic society of the Philippines.

LLAMZON, T. 1983, The Status of Pilipino in Metro Manila: 1968–82. Paper presented at the Seventh Conference of the Asian Association on National Languages (ASANAL) University of Malaya, Kuala Lumpur, August 1983.

MANHIT, B. J. 1980, The Case for Reading: A Socio-political Perspective, *Educational Quarterly*, Vol. 26, No. 4, pp. 32–41.

— 1981, Alternatives for functional literacy: a socio-psychophilosophical perspective, *Education Quarterly*, Vol. 27, No. 4, pp. 1–25.

PEREZ, A. Q. 1983, Vocabulary Development of Pilipino. Paper presented at the Seventh Conference of ASANAL, Kuala Lumpur. August 1983.

QUETCHENBACH, R. T. 1974, *Lineyte-Samarnon Poems: A Collection*, Tacloban City, Philippines. (This book represents a collection of works from Waray poets gathered from magazines and books that have been published in Leyte since 1934. Each poem is published in Waray-Waray and English. There are no Tagalog translations.)

SMOLICZ, J. J. 1979, *Culture and Education in a Plural Society*. Canberra: Curriculum Development Centre.

— 1980, Language as a Core Value for Culture, *R.E.L.C. Journal of Applied Linguistics* (Singapore), Vol. 11, No. 1, pp. 1–13.

— 1981a, Core Values and Cultural Identity, *Ethnic and Racial Studies*, Vol. 4, No. 1, pp. 75–90.

— 1981b, Culture, Ethnicity and Education: Multiculturalism in a Plural Society. In: J. MEGARRY, S. NISBET & E. HOYLE (eds), *World Year Book of Education 1981: Education of Minorities*. New York: Nichols Publishing Co. See also "Cultural Pluralism and Educational Policy: In Search of Stable Multiculturalism", *Australian Journal of Education*, Vol. 25, No. 2, 1981, pp. 121–45.

— 1982, Cultural Values and Internally-Generated Innovation in the South East Asian Context, *Innotech Journal*. SEAMEO, Regional Center for Educational Innovation and Technology, Vol. 6, No. 1, pp. 43–55.

— 1984, Multiculturalism and an Overarching Framework of Values, *European Journal of Education*, Vol. 19, No. 1, pp. 11–24.

SMOLICZ, J. J. & HARRIS, R. MCL. 1977, Ethnic Languages in Australia, *International Journal of the Sociology of Language*, No. 14, pp. 89–108.

SMOLICZ, J. J. & LEAN, R. 1979, Parental Attitudes to Cultural and Linguistic Pluralism in Australia: A Humanistic Sociological Interpretation, *The Australian Journal of Education*, Vol. 23, No. 3, pp. 227–49.

SMOLICZ, J. J. & SECOMBE, M. J. 1984, Multicultural Television for All Australians, *International Journal of the Sociology of Language*.

TENAZAS, R. C. P. & RAMAS, L. L. 1974, A Map of the Better-Known Cultural Minorities of the Philippines, *Philippine Quarterly of Culture and Society*, San Carlos Publications, Vol. 2, Nos. 1–2, p. 3.

9 Linguistic consequences of ethnicity and nationalism in multilingual settings

CHRISTINA BRATT PAULSTON

Introduction

This chapter presents an analytical framework for explaining and predicting the language behaviour of social groups as such behaviour relates to educational policies for minority groups. The paper argues a number of points: (1) if language planning is to be successful, it must consider the social context of language problems and especially the forces which contribute to language maintenance or shift. (2) The linguistic consequences for social groups in contact will vary depending on the focus of social mobilization, i.e. ethnicity or nationalism. (3) A major problem in the accurate prediction of such linguistic consequences lies in identifying the salient factors which contribute to language maintenance or shift, i.e. answering the question "under what conditions". Rational policy-making requires that all these factors be considered in the establishment and understanding of educational policies for minority groups.

The theoretical model is grounded on a wide variety of data: my own fieldwork data and school visits on five continents; impressions and observations from my own work with training teachers from ethnic groups and directing doctoral dissertations on language shift and spread; and examination of some 30 case studies of social and political groups in multilingual situations.

The organization of the chapter seeks to present basic linguistic facts before presenting the arguments for the analysis, which are based on those

117

facts. After some initial comments about language planning and language problems, a major section of the chapter discusses the possible linguistic consequences of ethnic groups in contact, namely language maintenance, bilingualism or shift. A shorter section on language (and religion) as social resources in competition for social advantage follows. The chapter concludes with a discussion of ethnicity, ethnic movements, ethnic nationalism and geographical nationalism and how they result in differential outcomes of language maintenance and shift. A concluding section makes a few general comments for policy-makers on the setting of educational policies for minority groups.

Language planning and language problems

Most scholars limit the term language planning to "the organized pursuit of solutions to language problems, typically at the national level" (Fishman, 1973: 23–24). The degree of "organized" varies; a language planning process which shares Jernudd's specification of the orderly and systematic (a) establishment of goals, (b) selection of means, and (c) prediction of outcomes (Jernudd, 1973: 11–23) is an exception rather than the rule. Heath makes clear in her study of language policy in Mexico (1972) that language decisions are primarily made on political and economic grounds and reflect the value of those in political power. Linguistic issues *per se* are of minor concern. Since the matters discussed are overtly those of language, there is frequently confusion about the salient issues discussed in language planning, whether they are, in fact, matters of political, economic, religious, sociocultural or linguistic concerns, or even moral concerns. OECD's (Organization for Economic Co-operation and Development) interest in the educational policies for minority social groups serves to emphasize the legitimate and important economic implications such language policies have; one can even argue that the most important factor influencing language choice of ethnic groups is economic, specifically one of access to jobs (Brudner, 1972).

Language choice is one of the major language problems, whether it be choice of national language (as in Finland and Israel), choice of national alphabet (as in Somalia) or choice of medium of instruction (as in Norway). In Israel, social conditions and religious attitudes towards Hebrew and the Promised Land made possible the rebirth of Hebrew and its implementation as a national language. "As to the success of the Hebrew revival, it was probably due largely to the prevalence of the required conditions" (Nahir, 1984: 302); that is Israel serves as an example of social forces facilitating national language planning. In contrast, Peru during the Velasco government officialized Quechua as a national language (Mannheim, 1984) with resounding failure of implementation. In Peru, as in much of Latin America, race is defined primarily by cultural attributes: wear a long braid, and many faldas, wide Indian type skirts, and speak Quechua and you are Indian; cut your hair, wear European style clothing and speak Spanish, and you become if not white, at least mestizo (Patch, 1967). To embrace Quechua would be to declare oneself Indian with all the accompanying socioeconomic stigmatization, and such planning held no hope of successful implementation. Peru serves as an example of language planning which goes counter to existing socio-cultural forces.

The problem is of course to be able to identify relevant social forces and predict the outcomes they will have. For example, contrary to expectation, choice of medium of instruction in the schools, especially for minority groups,[1] has very little predictive power in the final language choice of the ethnic group. The difficulty is that we have a very poor grasp of what the relevant social forces are and what the corresponding educational, social and cultural outcomes will be. Three points need to be made here. The major point to understand about language as group behaviour[2] is that language is almost never the causal factor, never the factor that gives rise to, brings about, causes things to happen, but rather language mirrors social conditions, mirrors man's relationship to man. It is quite true that denying Blacks access to schooling as was common in the U.S. South in the last century made them unfit for anything but menial jobs, but Black illiteracy was not the cause of Black/White relations and exploitation, it was the result of it.

The corollary to this simple, yet hard to grasp point is that bilingual education (mother tongue education, home language education, i.e. education in the national language plus the ethnic group's own language) is in itself not a causal factor. One reason there is no conclusive answer in the research on BE of the seemingly simple question whether a child learns to read more rapidly in a second language if first taught to read in his primary (Engle, 1975: 1) is that medium of instruction in school programmes is an intervening variable rather than the independent variable it is always treated as. One cannot hope to achieve any consensus in research findings by examining intervening variables without identifying the independent variables (Paulston, 1975). Schools and schooling can facilitate existing social trends, but they cannot be successful counter to social and economic forces. English medium schools were the major language learning facility for the children of the European immigrants to the United States, but the same schools have not been successful in teaching English to Navajo children on the reservations and they have had their fair share of failure in Chicano education. "Under what social conditions does medium of instruction make a difference for school children in achieving success" remains one key question.

The third point relates to the possible linguistic outcomes of the prolonged contact of ethnic groups within one nation, the typical background situation which necessitates special educational policies for minority groups. There are not many possibilities: the three main ones are language maintenance, bilingualism, or language shift. Another possibility is the creation of pidgins and creoles but they entail bilingualism or shift and will not be further considered in this chapter. For an overview of the range of language problems and their intended treatments, see Nahir's "Language Planning Goals: A Classification" (1984).

Language maintenance and language shift

To the study of language maintenance and shift, we need to add two other related topics, language spread (Cooper, 1982) and language death (Dorian, 1981; Dressler & Wodak-Leodolter, 1977). Cooper defines language spread as "an increase, over time, in the proportion of a communication network that adopts a given language or language variety for a given communicative function" (1982: 6). Most language spread probably takes place as lingua francas, as LWC's (language of wider communication), and English is a good example (Fishman, Cooper & Conrad, 1977). On the whole, such spread is neutral in attitudes.

But languages also spread for purposes of within-nation communication, and when they do so, not as an additional language like English in Nigeria, but as a new mother tongue, then language spread becomes a case of language shift. When such language spread through shift takes place within groups who do not possess another territorial base, we have a case of language death. Languages do become extinct, and the many dead Amerindian languages are now a mute witness to the spread of English (Bauman, 1980). Language shift, especially if it involves language death, tends to be an emotional topic; and economists and other social scientists who are not basically interested in language and culture *per se* will simply have to accept that it is often fairly futile to insist on a reasoned view in matters of language shift where it concerns the opinions and attitudes of the speakers of the shifting groups. Linguists and anthropologists frequently belong in this category as well.

In addition, the data base is very small. For example, in Gal's fine dissertation (1979) the ten page bibliography only contains *six* entries which mention shift or maintenance in the title. I know of no major study on language maintenance, presumably because it is not considered problematic.

Still there are some generalizations we can make about language shift and maintenance which seem to hold in all cases. One of the primary factors in accounting for subsequent course of mother tongue diversity, to use Lieberson's phrase, lies in the origin of the contact situation (Lieberson, Dalto & Johnston, 1975; Schermerhorn, 1970). Voluntary migration, especially of individuals and families, results in the most rapid shift while annexation and colonialization where entire groups are brought into a nation with their social institutions of marriage and kinship, religious and other belief and value systems still *in situ*, still more or less intact, tend to result in much slower language shift if at all.

The mechanism of language shift is bilingualism, often but not necessarily with exogamy, where parent(s) speak(s) the original language with the grandparents and the new language with the children. The case of bilingualism holds in all cases of group shifts, although the rate of shift may vary with several bilingual generations rather than just one.

A thoroughly documented fact is that language shift frequently begins with women, as manifest in choice of code (Schlieben-Lange, 1977); in choice of marriage partner (Gal, 1979; Brudner, 1972); and eventually in the language in which they choose to bring up their children (Eckert, 1983). The most common explanation is that women who are in a subordinate position in society, are sensitive to issues of power, including the language of power, but there really exists no generally accepted explanation.

Maintained group bilingualism[3] is unusual. The norm for groups in prolonged contact within one nation is for the subordinate group to shift to the language of the dominant group, either over several hundred years as with Gaelic in Great Britain or over the span of three generations as has been the case of the European immigrants to Australia and the United States in an extraordinary rapid shift. It was exactly the language shift and attempts to stop it which have caused much of the trouble in Quebec (from French to English [Gendron, 1972]) and Belgium (from Flemish to French, [Verdoodt, 1978]).

Language shift is often treated by laymen and social scientists alike as an unarguable indicator of cultural assimilation, and it is often the painful thought of foresaking the culture and values of the forefathers that is at the root of the strife over language shift. Assimilation is a much more complex issue than language shift, but a few points need to be considered. First, we need carefully to make the distinction, in Schermerhorn's terms (1970), between social and cultural institutions. Economic incorporation of an ethnic group with access to the goods and services of a nation, the common goal of minority groups and the most common reason for migration in Europe (some also claim religious freedom or refugee status), is different from cultural assimilation and the giving up of values and beliefs. It is primarily to the perception of forced assimilation that the issue of the medium of instruction in the national language becomes tied, and so many Chicanos bemoan the loss of Chicano culture with the loss of Spanish. But there is not necessarily an isomorphic relationship between language and culture; Spanish is the carrier of many other cultures besides Chicano, and less commonly accepted, language maintenance is not necessary for culture and ethnicity maintenance, as indeed Lopez (1976) documents for the Chicanos in Los Angeles. In other words, it is possible for groups to maintain their own ethnic culture even after language shift, as we see in groups like the English gypsies and many AmerIndian tribes.

Although most ethnic minority groups within a nation do shift language, they will vary in their degree of ethnic maintenance and in their *rate* of shift. Some causal factors can be identified. For example, in Pittsburgh the Greeks shift over a four generation span compared with the three generation shift of the Italians. Some factors which contribute to the slower Greek shift are (a) knowledge and access to a standardized, written language with cultural prestige and tradition, which is taught by the Greek churches in Pittsburgh, and (b) arranged marriage partners directly from Greece (who then are monolingual in Greek). The Italians in contrast speak/spoke a non-standard, non-written dialect with no prestige, and they shared their Roman Catholic churches with the English-speaking Irish, typically with Irish priests and sisters, so they found no language maintenance support in the churches. Nor was there any pressure for endogamy as long as the marriage was within the Roman Catholic Church.

Ethnic groups also vary in, quite vaguely, ethnic pride or ethnic stubbornness in culture maintenance — even after they have shifted language and become socially incorporated into a nation. Alba says in the preface to his book about Catalunya: "Catalonia is not especially notable for anything except its persistence — its stubbornness in existing despite the most adverse conditions" (1975: ii). The survival of Catalan may best be explained as a result of nationalism but it does exemplify the notion of stubbornness, as Alba calls it, in group maintenance.

Groups also vary in group adhesion and there is wide intra-group variation in members' attitude toward language maintenance and cultural assimilation. A case in point is Robert Rodriguez' beautiful, autobiographical but controversial *Hunger of Memory* (1982) in which he argues for assimilation — and against bilingual education. Carillo's comments on this work are worth citing:

> "Mexican–American children were a minority in the schools. There was a strong pressure to assimilate; the overwhelming presence of the dominant anglo society was enough to cause this pressure. Add to this the impression of a sensitive child that the rewards of the society were limited to those who were members of the dominant culture, and you can begin to understand Rodriguez' conflicting feelings about learning English, maintaining his Spanish, assimilating to anglo society, and maintaining his ties to Mexican–American culture.
>
> Today, growing up Mexican–American in California is very different. As the minority group has grown, it has influenced the dominant culture significantly. . . . Today, a Mexican–American child in California has many options on the scale from complete assimilation to strong pride in Mexican–American culture." (1984: 9, 30)

Carillo does not write as a social scientist but as a participant Chicano and ESL (English as a Second Language) professional, and he documents his perception of social change, in the host culture as well as the minority group, in his defence of the much criticized Rodriguez.[4] Carillo's point about many options available stresses the need for flexible educational policies.

Where shift does not take place, it is for three major reasons:

(a) Self-imposed boundary maintenance (Barth, 1969), always for reasons other than language, most frequently religion, e.g. the Amish and the orthodox Jewish Hassidim. The Hassidim are perfectly aware of the role of English but their choice is for group cohesion for religious purposes:

> "Many [Lubovitch] families elect to send their children to the Yiddish speaking school [no English curriculum]. In so doing, they increase the possibility of upward mobility within the ethnic group and decrease the probability that these children will gain the secular and technical skills necessary for employment in the economy of the larger society. All Lubovitchers are aware of the potential usefulness of secular skills and an English curriculum, but few . . . families elect the bilingual school for their children." (Levy, 1975: 40)

Such extreme measures of language maintenance are very unusual and never undertaken over time only for the sake of language itself.

(b) Externally imposed boundaries, usually in the form of denied access to goods and services, especially jobs. The Black community of the past in the U.S. is an example. Geographic isolation (which is theoretically uninteresting but nevertheless effective) is also a form of external boundary which contributes to language maintenance, as Gaelic in the Hebrides or Quechua in the Andes.

(c) A diglossic-like situation where the two languages exist in a situation of functional distribution where each language has its specified purpose and domain and the one language is inappropriate in the other situation, as with Guarani and Spanish in Paraguay (Rubin, 1968) or with Modern Standard Arabic and the mother tongues in the Maghreb (Grandguillaume, 1983).

We see then that the major linguistic consequence of ethnic groups in prolonged contact within one nation is language shift of the subordinate groups to the language of the dominant group. The major dependent variable is the rate of shift. But this shift only takes place if there are opportunity and incentive for the group to learn the national language. There are probably many kinds of incentives (the data base here is very inadequate) but the two major ones are (1) economic advantage, primarily in the form of source of income, and (2) social prestige. In Brudner's terms (1972), jobs select language learning strategies, which is to say wherever there are jobs available that demand knowledge of a certain language, people will learn it. Without rewards, language learning is not salient. Sometimes language shift is held to be problematic (Quebec), sometimes it is encouraged as national policy (France), sometimes it is resisted by the ethnic groups (Catalan) and sometimes encouraged (European immigrants to Australia and the United States), but it is invariably to the social conditions one must look to understand the attitudes and values which accompany language shift.

Another less common result of languages in contact is language maintenance, frequently with bilingualism, and it is always for reasons other than appreciation of the language *per se*. The third consequence is prolonged group bilingualism. This chapter is not the place for a thorough discussion on the nature of bilingualism (Albert & Obler, 1978; Grosjean, 1982; Hornby, 1977; Lambert, 1972; Mackey, 1976; Miracle, Jr., 1983), but it should be mentioned that full-fledged, balanced bilingualism is the exception rather than the rule. Bilingualism spans a range from passive, imperfect knowledge of dead sacred languages (Sanskrit, classical Arabic, classical Hebrew, Suryoyo, etc.) to the linguistic competence necessary for simultaneous interpretation (but even so U.N. interpreters only translate into one language, not back and forth). Degree of proficiency has little to do with language attitudes, and the sacred languages particularly assert a vast influence on attempts to orderly language planning (e.g. choice of alphabet in Somalia). When we talk about bilingualism and bilingual education as an educational policy, we should therefore be careful to consider the degree and functional possibilities of the linguistic competence of the group discussed. I have observed "mother tongue" education for Assyrian children in Sweden who could not even count to ten in their mother tongue but were fluent in the national language.[5] In the same country, I have seen classes for Turkish primary students who knew very little Swedish. The highly varied nature of bilingualism forces us to face the problem whether equity in education will allow the same educational policies for all ethnic groups. Indeed, the United States Supreme Court has suggested that equal treatment does not constitute equal opportunity in the matter of education of ethnic minority children compared to mainstream children. One can easily take that argument a step further and consider that the various ethnic groups may merit differential treatment.

Language and religion as social resources

Language can be seen as a resource which is available to ethnic groups in their competition for access to the goods and services of a nation. All groups do not avail themselves of language as a symbol in their fight for independence or economic shares or for whatever goal they see as in their best interest. When they do, language can be a very effective power base as the nationalistic movements in Europe in the last century bear witness to. Language loyalty was so often romanticized during these movements, that one does well to remember that there is nothing inherently "natural" about group language loyalty, but rather that it is a deliberately chosen strategy for survival.

Mohammed Kabir documents these points in an important dissertation on "Changing Faces of Nationalism in Bangladesh" (1985, ms). His claim is that the economy is the crucial factor in bringing about changes in a nation, and as change occurs, so do members' loyalties and their bases therefore. Members choose political identity and mobilize particular strategies depending on their particular demands. So language, ethnicity, and religion are available resources and are chosen as identity bases variously over time as strategies to achieve specific demands.

Bengal, Kabir's case study, was populated by the same ethno-linguistic group, roughly half of whom were Muslim and the other half Hindu. Eventually the Hindu group came to dominate education and agriculture. In 1905 Bengal was split into East and West Bengal against the opposition of the Hindus, and in 1912 Bengal was reunited this time against the will of the Muslims. The 1940 Lahore resolution granted Pakistan sovereign state so Muslims could have a separate homeland, and consequently the East Bengali claimed Muslim status to join Pakistan and become free of Hindu competition. But power became concentrated in West Pakistan, and the Bengali had little or no share in education and other social-economic spheres. In spite of the Bengali constituting 54% of the population, Urdu was the only national language of Pakistan, and this time the language controversy was the beginning of the separatist movement. Muslims in East Bengal joined with Hindus in separatist demands based on Bengali linguistic identity, and Bangladesh achieved independence in 1971 as a linguistic unity. To date, no one has raised the point of a united Bengal, because, Kabir points out, neither group (Hindu and Muslim) perceives reunification to be in their best interest.[6]

We see then an example of a group, East Bengal Muslims, who when they perceived such action best suited to their purposes and demands, claimed religious status and identity and Pakistani nationalism, later linguistic-ethnic nationalism and separatism and, at present, status for Bangladesh founded on religio-linguistic identity. Throughout the course of the last 100 years, language and religion have been available resources, variously utilized in the battle for survival in a harsh world.

Immigrant groups are not very different from the Bengalis. When they see learning the national language well and fluently in the best interest of their children (and there are social institutions available like the schools and the church, which can help them do so), there are very few problems associated with the educational policies for minority groups. Within the single city-state of Singapore with her four official languages and three major religions, there is no sign of ethnic strife or educational problems (Crewe, 1977). In fact, the ex-colonial English is favoured as medium of instruction by many (MacDougall & Foon, 1976). I must admit that I looked very carefully for competition along ethnic lines but saw none. The simple explanation is to be found in Singapore's very strong and expanding economy. There is enough of the good of this life to go around for everybody, and competition takes place on the basis of individual qualities, not along ethnic lines.

But when these same immigrant groups instead of socioeconomic opportunity see stigmatization, economic exploitation and systematic unemployment, they are perfectly likely to use the original mother tongue as a strategy for mobilization. Language boundary maintenance reinforced with religion is an even stronger tool. The Turks in Europe have frequently followed this latter process (Sachs, 1983). It is not that mainstream members and those from assimilated former ethnic groups like the Poles and the Slovaks in Pittsburgh don't face difficulties in a declining economy; it is rather that they don't feel a we–they injustice and antagonism and also that they have (through language shift) lost language as a resource for mobilization strategy. As I write this, City Council has decided to merge the Police Force and the Fire Fighter units in Pittsburgh. Both groups perceive this as being against their best interests and are violently opposing the new policy. As both groups share the same ethnic mix, language and ethnicity were not available resources and instead both groups mobilized along the lines of their labour unions. Had ethnicity been an available resource, they very likely would have mobilized along ethnic lines to judge from Elazar & Friedman's (1976) case study of teachers in Philadelphia who did just that and who were able to successfully defend their jobs in that fashion.

Almost 20 years ago, Glazer asked: "Just why America produced *without* laws that which other countries, desiring a culturally unified population, were not able to produce *with* laws — is not an easy question" (1966: 360). There is a fable by Aesop which holds the answer to that question and which best illustrates the points I have been trying to make. The sun and the wind see a man with a cloak (read language) walking along the road. They decide to enter a contest to see who can first cause him to shed his coat. The wind tears at him for hours but the man only wraps himself more tightly in his cloak. The sun takes over and spreads her benevolence over the man who after a short time divests himself of his cloak. Moral: In hard times, man will cling to his language and ethnic group; in times of plenty, man pays little attention to resources like ethnic languages.

Ethnicity and nationalism

Introduction

The past discussion has dealt exclusively with the course of language and the linguistic consequences of ethnic minority groups in prolonged contact within one nation. But groups can find another focus of social mobilization than ethnicity, and in the rest of this chapter I shall argue that there are four distinct types of social mobilization, which under certain specified social conditions result in different linguistic consequences: ethnicity, ethnic movements, ethnic nationalism and geographic nationalism. I am attempting a theoretical framework which will allow us to explain and to predict the language behaviour of groups who have access to or are exposed to more than one language. I have argued earlier that such an understanding is vital to helpful educational policies and successful language planning in general.

This chapter represents the first attempt to organize these thoughts in writing, and as always some revision will be in order. I have long thought about the social mobilization of religious groups within this framework and eventually opted for considering religion as a social resource similar to language. Linguistic groups may choose a religious identity as the main base in strategies of competition, but they do so as pre-existing ethnic or national groups. *For purposes of explaining language behaviour of groups*, I doubt that religion needs to be considered a primary force of group cohesion. More data will help support, modify or disprove this point. Religious groups are also theoretically problematic because of the preponderence of "irrational" behaviour where it is difficult to predict behaviour on the notion of acting in their own best interest.

A definite weakness of the framework is the present inability to incorporate the social organization of tribes and clans when those tribes exist within a single ethno-linguistic group spread over several nations, such as Kurdistan. Somalia has a tribal social organization but with one language within one nation, and so adherents for the various alphabets simply take on aspects of special interest groups which is not theoretically problematic. Nigeria's tribes are isomorphic with ethnic groups and can be so understood. It may be that Kurdish behaviour is more explainable with a better understanding of facilitating or constraining social conditions. More data and more reflection are needed on the linguistic consequences of this fairly unusual social organization.

Another weakness is the lack of consideration given to the role of pan-movements in language maintenance. The role of English and French in pan-Africanism, the role of classical and literary standard Arabic in pan-Arabism, and the role of the Chinese character writing system all share certain features one of which is maintenance beyond what might reasonably have been expected. Future development of the topic of this chapter will have to consider both tribes and pan-movements within the same framework.

Earlier explanations

The focus of social science research and its scholarly writing as it relates to the language behaviour of social groups has very much reflected actual events in the real world. The one-nation-one-language national movements of nineteenth century Europe provided the beginning of this field of literature, where *nationality* often was used synonymously with *ethnic group* (Deutsch, 1953).

Fishman has argued for a distinction between *nationalism* and *nationism* in his "Nationality–Nationalism and Nation–Nationism" (1968) where he attempts to sort out some of the terminological confusion accompanying *nationalism*. He suggests that "the transformation . . . of tradition-bound ethnicity to unifying and ideologized nationality . . . be called nationalism" (1968: 41) and that "wherever politico-geographic momentum and consolidation are in advance of sociocultural momentum and consolidation [be called] *nationism*" (1968: 42). He goes on to discuss the different kinds of language problems such recent nation-states face. Van den Berghe in the same volume (1968) also addresses the terminological confusion. He suggests:

> "that tribe[7] and its derivatives be scrapped altogether. To refer to a political movement based on ethnicity, I shall use the term 'nationalism' (e.g. Yoruba nationalism, . . .). To refer to political movements that use the multinational state as their defining unit, I shall speak of 'territorialism' (e.g. Nigerian territorialism, . . .)."
> (1968: 215)

Fishman's and van den Berghe's linking of ethnicity with nationalism is typical of the thinking reflected in this set of scholarship.

The concern for nationalism was followed by an interest in ethnicity. Glazer & Moynihan point out in the "Introduction" to their *Ethnicity: Theory and Experience* that the word *ethnicity* made its appearance in the *Oxford English Dictionary* first in the 1972 *Supplement* where the first recorded usage is of David Riesman in 1953. They suggest "that a new word reflects a new reality and a new usage reflects a change in that reality". They continue:

> "The new word is 'ethnicity' and the new usage is the steady expansion of the term 'ethnic group' from minority and marginal subgroups at the edges of society — groups expected to assimilate, disappear, to continue as survivals, exotic or troublesome — to major elements of a society." (1975: 5).

This concern and focus of research on ethnicity and ethnic minority groups is not only an English language world phenomenon although the term ethnicity may not be used. To mention just a few representative publications, *Recherches Sociologiques* of Louvain-la-Neuve published in 1977 a special issue on "Langue et Identité Nationale" which deals with language maintenance of ethnic minority groups in Europe. So did the Second International Conference on Minority Languages in Åbo/Turko, Finland in 1983 (Molde & Sharp, 1984). *Lenguas y Educacion en el Ambito del Estado Español* (Siguan, 1983) deals with the emergent concern for the educational problems of linguistic minority groups in post-Franco Spain. UNESCO just published a special issue of *Prospects* on "Mother Tongue and Educational Attainment" (14:1, 1984).

This resurgence of ethnic awareness brings into question the goal of complete assimilation for these groups. Elazar & Friedman discuss this new development of ethnic affirmation (in groups who have all shifted to English) in their *Moving Up: Ethnic Succession in America* (1976). They point out that ethnic identity has often been seen as a problem that must somehow be overcome. Social scientists have often considered religious and ethnic groups as "vestiges of a primitive past that are destined to disappear" (1976: 4), but recent "writers on the 'new pluralism' have argued that racial, religious, and ethnic groups *are* a basic component of our social structure" (p. 5) who affect our institutions and are at times more powerful than economic forces in their influence.

What Elazar & Friedman are discussing in their study of ethnic groups reflects not only a "change in reality", in Glazer & Moynihan's term, but also a paradigm shift (Kuhn, 1970) from equilibrium theory to a conflict perspective. This shift in focus on ethnicity is provocatively explored in John Bennett's *The New Ethnicity: Perspectives from Ethnology* (1975a) whose shift in basic theoretical outlook also reflects the change in the phenomenon of ethnicity. The old notion of ethnicity looked on ethnicity as a group-cultural phenomenon where ethnicity was taken to refer to shared norms, artifacts, values, and beliefs within a "culture-population-group frame of reference" (Bennett, 1975b: 4), groups mobilizing around cultural symbols (R. G. Paulston, 1977: 181), of which language when it was available formed one of the most obvious. The major function of the new ethnicity can be seen as "a set of strategies for acquiring the resources one needs to survive and to consume at the desired level" (Bennett, 1975b: 4); above all, it differs from the old ethnicity in that it is "a cognitive ethnicity, a self-chosen ethnicity" (Bennett, 1975b: 9).

And that is roughly where we stand today with the scholarship on the background situation to language problems and educational policies of linguistic subordinate minority groups.[8]

A new theoretical framework

I suggest now that there is merit in reconsidering the literature and that instead of entwining the concepts of ethnicity and nationalism, we would be better served in our endeavours to understand the nature of educational language policies, if we were to differentiate the two. I suggest four types of social mobilization, which come close to forming a continuum rather than four distinct types: (1) Ethnicity which very much corresponds to the notion of old ethnicity: (2) Ethnic movement which is based on the concept of the new ethnicity: (3) ethnic nationalism and (4) geographic nationalism which correspond to Kohn's closed and open nationalism (1968) as well as to Fishman's nationalism and nationism (1968) (see Table 1 on pp.132–33).

It is perfectly possible for social groups to embrace a different type of mobilization at different stages of their history and to move back and forth on the continuum of types; the Flemish have at various times occupied all four niches. No sense of evolution or development is implied in the notion of stage, only time in the historical sense, nor is any ameliorative value implied by any type; ethnicity and nationalism are simply descriptive labels for sets or syndromes of behaviour, attitudes and perceptions of groups of peoples. Given certain social conditions, they will behave in certain predictable fashions in regard to language, which behaviour it is my purpose to explore.

It is, however, an unavoidable fact that nationalism as a social pheno-menon is a stigmatized behaviour in present day Europe for reasons of historical events during the last century. It is understandable that a region that has experienced the excesses of National Socialism and found economic recovery in a united Euorpe hesitates to again encourage nationalism. To use nationalism as a concept analytically for organizing sets of behaviours is, however, very different from advocating nationalism as a political and economic system, but it should be recognized that the concept of nationa-lism may be difficult to use in the present day European climate. I do not intend these comments as a criticism of the analytical power of nationalism, only as a recognition of possible tactical drawbacks when explaining educa-tional policies.

Ethnicity

"An 'ethnic group' is a reference group invoked by people who share a common historical style (which may be only assumed), based on overt features and values, and who, through the process of interaction with others, identify themselves as sharing that style. 'Ethnic identity' is the sum total of feelings on the part of group members about those values, symbols, and common histories that identify them as a distinct group. 'Ethnicity' is simply ethnic-based action' (Royce, 1982: 18).

TABLE 1 *Linguistic consequences of social mobilization in multilingual settings*

	Ethnicity	Ethnic Movement	Ethnic Nationalism	Geographic Nationalism
			Territory	
(1) Defining characteristics	As identity	As strategy in competition for scarce resources	Closed nationalism (Kohn) exclusive	Open nationalism
	Unconscious learned behaviour	Goal: socioeconomic advantage		Intellectual leaders Middle class Loyalty (important)
	Shared ancestors; roots		Common enemy Taught behaviours	
	Taken for granted Not goal oriented No violence	Cognitive Self-chosen Militant Violent	Goal: independence, political self-determination	
	Common values and beliefs	Charismatic leader Language as rallying point Boundary maintenance	External distinction Internal cohesion (Haugen)	
	Survives language shift			
		Glorious Past		
			Cultural self-determination	
		etc.		etc. as identity

Less ◄——————— Legislation Involved ———————► More

	Ethnicity	Ethnic Movement	Ethnic Nationalism	Geographic Nationalism
(2) Facilitating or constraining factors	? Under what social conditions? E.g. Participation in social institutions, schooling, exogamy, military service, religious institutions; mass-media; roads and transportation; travel, trade, commerce, war, evangelism; occupations; in-migration, back-migration, urbanization, etc.			
(3) Linguistic consequences	Language shift	Language shift but slower rate	Maintenance national language as powerful symbol	Maintenance national language
Also: Language spread Language death Language reformation			Language planning-academies	
			Strong language attitudes	
				Standardization Modernization Literacy-teacher training Language problems: Choice of national language

Ethnicity tends to stress roots and a shared biological past and the common ancestors (factual or fictional). The basis of personal identity is cultural (including religion), and ethnicity is a matter of self-ascription. The cultural values and beliefs, which are held in common, are unconsciously learned behaviour, and ethnicity is just taken for granted. The members tend to feel comfortable with past and future, and there is no opposition and no violence involved.

There is in fact little power struggle and not much purpose with ethnicity, and so the common cause is assimilation and concomitant language shift, like the Walloons, who were brought to Sweden in the 1600s to develop the iron industry, have completely assimilated into Swedish culture (Douhan, 1982). Ethnicity will not maintain a language in a multilingual setting if the dominant group allows assimilation, and incentive and opportunity of access to the second language (L_2) are present. Some general factors of social conditions which influence access to the L_2 are:

(a) Participation in social institutions, primarily universal schooling, exogamy, and required military service, and often religious institutions.
(b) Access to mass-media, especially TV.
(c) Access to roads and transportation versus physical isolation, like islands and mountains.
(d) Travel, including trade, commerce, war, and evangelism.
(e) Some occupations.
(f) Demographic factors, like size of groups, vast in-migration, continued migration, back-migration, urbanization.

The major social institution facilitating L_2 learning in a situation which favours language shift is without a doubt public schooling. With children from socially marginal groups like the Navajo Indians (Rosier & Holm, 1980; Spolsky, 1977) bilingual education tends to be the more efficient form of public education, but with children from socially favoured groups, education in the national language is a viable alternative, as the vast literature on the Canadian immersion programmes for middle class children attests to (Cohen & Swain, 1976; Lambert & Tucker, 1972; Swain & Lapkin, 1982). There is a vast literature on the pros and cons of bilingual education, and the issues are too complicated to discuss in this paper (see, e.g. Center for Applied Linguistics, 1977; Cummins, 1976; Hartford *et al.*, 1982; N. Epstein, 1977; Paulston, 1980; Spolsky, 1972).

A social institution for adults which can contribute markedly to L_2 learning is the Armed Forces. In Peru, military service paired with the necessary travel to the coast district has been the major means of learning

Spanish for many Quechua young men, former school drop-outs. In Zaire, during the colonial times of the Belgian Congo, Flemish officers did not insist on French, and the Armed Forces became a major force in the spread of Lingala, a local pidgin which became the language of the army.

Exogamy, marrying outside the ethnic group or other social unit, obviously necessitates language shift for one partner, at least within the family. This shift typically is in the direction of the language of the socio-economically favoured group. This is exactly what happened in French Canada, but the French-speaking Canadians held political power and through legislation have been able to protect the position of French. Language maintenance and shift in regions where political and socio-economic power is divided between the ethnic groups is difficult and prob-ably impossible to predict. Exogamy, showing definite trends of direction, is the most positive indicator of incipient shift. Once it is clear whom the children of migrant workers in Europe will marry, the setting of educational policy will be much facilitated. If they commonly marry nationals of the host culture, there will be no need of special or different educational policies for their children. If, however, they marry exclusively within their own ethnic group, learn the national language poorly and show other trends of strong culture maintenance (arranged marriages with partners from the home country, vacations in the home country, etc.), then a strong case can be argued for the case of bilingual education.[9]

Demographic data are troublesome. Apart from concerns about relia-bility and validity of the database (de Vries, 1977; Thompson, 1974) and methods of analysis (see Section II, "Demography" in Mackey & Ornstein, 1979), we don't really know what constitutes a critical mass in language maintenance of an ethnic group. We recognize that maintenance is easier for a large group, but we don't know how large is large. Clearly other factors like elitist status and prestige are at work here as well.

Most of the other factors are self-explanatory although I should point out that there exists no hard quantificational data base, and this list has been collected from a reading of case studies where these conditions are often treated observationally and anecdotally. No doubt there are additions to be made.

Ethnic movement

The major difference between Ethnicity and Ethnic Movement is when ethnicity as an unconscious source of identity turns into a conscious strategy, usually in competition for scarce resources. An ethnic movement is ethnicity turned militant, consisting of ethnic discontents who perceive the world as against them, an adversity drawn along ethnic boundaries. While ethnicity stresses the content of the culture, ethnic movements will be concerned with boundary maintenance, in Barth's terms, with "us" against "them". It is very much a conscious, cognitive ethnicity in a power-struggle with the dominant group for social and economic advantage, a struggle which frequently leads to violence and social upheaval. Many ethnic movements have charismatic leaders (probably always born a member of the ethnic group) like Stephen Biko in South Africa and Martin Luther King, but they need not have an intellectual elite or a significant middle class.

Movements need rallying points, and language is a good obvious symbol if it is available. (It may not be. The IRA, the Irish Republican Army, uses English.) So is religion. Original mother tongues and sacred languages are powerful symbols and may serve to support men in their struggle for what they perceive as a better life.[10] But note that language as a symbol need not be the ethnic group's original mother tongue. Both Stephen Biko and Martin Luther King used English and partially for the same reason — the diversity of African languages. The symbol in Biko's case was the choice of language, English rather than Afrikaans; in King's case the symbol lay with the characteristic style of Black English rhetoric, many of which features originated with the West African languages.

When an ethnic movement draws on religion as a resource for identity base as strategy in social competition, when cognitive ethnicity is joined with religious fervour, the likely consequence is one of language maintenance, probably of a sacred language (only). Sacred languages tend with great diligence to be kept unchanged.[11] The result is that sacred languages often are not spoken and only exist in written form. Groups maintaining a sacred language like the Assyrians will typically shift their everyday language to that of the surrounding community so that we find Assyrians all maintaining Suryoyo (a form of Aramaic) but speaking Arabic, Turkish, Swedish or American English. Maintaining two extra languages seems too cumbersome a task.

There are exceptions. Pre-Israeli Jews maintained both Hebrew and Yiddish (or Hebrew and Ladino) but as a result of externally imposed boundary maintenance, of the environing community's refusal to let them assimilate. (Ladino was after all the result of an earlier assimilation into Spanish culture.) When allowed to assimilate, Yiddish disappeared and that explains why Yiddish was maintained in Slavic East Europe but not in Germany, i.e. as a factor of degree of social enclosure (Schermerhorn, 1970). The drop out rate is likely to be high for such religious groups if the host community allows assimilation, as it is for the Amish and as Bennett cites for the New York Hassidim.

Ethnic movements by themselves probably cannot maintain a language but will affect the rate of shift so that the shift is much slower and spans many more generations. Such a long state of bilingualism affects the structure of the languages involved (Thomason & Kaufman, forthcoming), as Spanish expressions in Peru like *no mas* and diminutives like *chicititito*, which are calqued on Quechua (Albo, 1970; see also Pfaff, 1981). What is less understood and really not studied at all is the degree to which such groups keep their communicative competence rules[12] and apply their own rules of appropriate language use to the new language. An Arab who speaks fluent Swedish but stands as close, touches as much, interrupts as often, etc. as it is appropriate to do in a conversation in Arabic will have a confusing and probably irritating effect on a Swede who has very different rules for using language. We know virtually nothing about this aspect of language shift, but it is easy to speculate that cognitive ethnicity is more likely to guard cultural ways of using language and we know that different standards for using language (like appropriate loudness of voice) easily becomes a source of friction between groups. This topic merits study because the different communicative competence rules show up clearly in the classroom (Philips, 1970), and the children suffer as a consequence, since the teacher's rules are always held to be the "right" ones. Certainly educational policies should be taken to include teacher training. We know with dismal certitude teachers' misinterpretation of the social meaning of the language used by children with different group norms for speech. All teachers of ethnic minority children, whether they are members of the ethnic group or not, need a working understanding of communicative competence and its implications for the classroom.

Nationalism

When ethnic discontents turn separatist, we get ethnic nationalism. For nationalism, there seems to be as many definitions as there are scholars of nationalism, basically because, in Shafer's words (1972), nationalism has many faces. The following definitions will give a sense of the range of phenomena scholars have attempted to identify:

> "[Nationalism is] a consciousness, on the part of individuals or groups, of membership in a nation, or of a desire to forward the strength, liberty, or prosperity of a nation." (Royal Institute of International Affairs, 1939)

Arab nationalism emphasized other facets:

> "The nation . . . is a wider conception than the state, greater than the people, and more meaningful than the fatherland. It is not necessary for a nation to have one state or one fatherland [this is peculiarly Muslim], or to be composed of one people, but it must have its own language [some do not], its own history, its own ideals, its own shared aspirations, its own shared memories, and its own natural links which bind its members in two respects, the moral and the economic." (Abd al-Latif Sharara, 1962: 228)

African nationalism yet again differs:

> "African nationalism is a feeling among the African people. It is not only a feeling against something, but also for something. It is a feeling against European rule . . . . This is the fundamental feeling of African nationalism — the African feeling against Eurocracy, in favor of Afrocracy. . . . African nationalism is therefore essentially a political feeling. . . . (Sithole, 1960)

Shafer, who has brought together these definitions (1976), concludes elsewhere that it is impossible to fit nationalism into a short definition (1972: 5). Kohn points out that while all instances of nationalism will vary according to past history and culture, present social structure and geographical location, all forms of nationalism still share certain traits (1968: 64). Cottam's insistence that nationalism not be dealt with as a thing reified but rather interpreted as a manifestation of nationalistic behaviour is very useful here as he identifies some of the shared traits in his definition of nationalist "as an individual who sees himself as a member of a political community, a nation, that is entitled to independent statehood, and is willing to grant that community a primary and terminal loyalty" (Cottam, 1964: 3; lecture notes, January 15, 1984). Group cohesion to the end, a goal-orientation of self-determination, a perceived threat of opposing forces, and above all access to or hope of territory are characteristics of all national movements. What is important to remember and what both Royce's and Cottam's definitions stress is that ethnicity and nationalism both are sets of syndromes of behaviour, perceptions, and attitudes of a group of people. Given certain social conditions, they will behave in certain predictable fashions, including language behaviour which is our present interest.

Ethnic and geographic nationalism share all these features. The goal is independence, their own political status and social institutions on their own territory. The most common ideal is the nation-state but there are others. Catalunya, Quebec, and Flemish Belgium are content to remain part of a larger state as long as they can safeguard their own social and cultural institutions of which language (and language maintenance) becomes a very prominent symbol. When use of their own language is denied, other cultural acts acquire a national symbolism way beyond their actual significance. To illustrate, during Franco anti-Catalan days, to cheer for Club Barcelona when the soccer team played Real Madrid became a political statement as was dancing the sardana after Sunday mass.

The improvement of one's own lot in life or at least of one's children's is probably a common goal of all national movements; the motivation, like in ethnic movements, is one of perceived self-interest, a self-chosen state. Very often nationalism takes place as a protest against oppression, against a common enemy, whether it be against a (dominant) group within the same state or against another state. Euskadi, the Basque nation within Spain, is an example of the first type and it introduces another problem of interpretation of degree of intensity of a national movement. The Basques range from terrorists and separatists to assimilists with language shift more common than admitted. There is typically a great emphasis on loyalty and group cohesion, which are consciously taught behaviours, taught through social institutions like school, church, and army, with typical symbols the flag,[13] the national anthem, and above all the language. To admit to language shift is to be disloyal, and this very deep-seated feeling of disloyalty is an additional problem in eliciting valid survey data in this type of research (Thompson, 1974).

Goals in national movements, besides general independence, tend to be quite definite and specific. These goals are often legitimatized by or based on historical past events or conditions. During the Finnish school strike in Stockholm during February of 1984, when Finnish parents kept their children out of school in support of their demand for Finnish medium schooling in kindergarten through university level courses, the reason given was that Finland is bilingual in Swedish–Finnish and that Sweden should reciprocate. It is a demand legitimized on the national law of the ethnic immigrant group and its past history and is much more characteristic of nationalism rather than of ethnic movements which tend to base their claims on a rationale of equity with others within the nation-state.

Whether a defining characteristic or a necessary social condition, a national movement must have a well developed middle class in which condition it differs from ethnic movements. Alba's (1975) anecdote of the Catalan workers who considered issues of language immaterial is representative. "We don't care if we are exploited in Castilian or Catalan", was their rejoinder, and they aligned themselves with the workers' unions and the socialist party rather than mobilize themselves along national lines. Without a stake in property, nationalism is not perceived to further one's self-interest.

Royce considers the similar situation of the Basques. The ETA, the Basque national organization is led by members of the middle class. The lower class perceived no advantage in a Basque movement and the concerns and economic interests of the elite are primarily state/national and international. The regional economic interests are in the control of the middle class who feel that they carry an unfair share of Spain's economic burden with no adequate compensation. "The important point in this case is that the impetus for ethnic nationalism came from the sector whose privileges and power depended on the economic well-being of the Basque provinces. Basque nationalism was the obvious way to maintain their position" (Royce, 1982: 104).

The crucial difference between ethnic movement and ethnic nationalism is access to territory; without land one cannot talk about Basque nationalism. It is also access to territory that gives viability to a separatist movement. We can talk about Chicano nationalism but without territory such a movement, were it genuine, is doomed to failure. Mostly such phraseology masks conceptual confusion and what is intended is a label for what in fact is an ethnic movement fighting for equal access to goods and services (Oriol, 1979).

Ethnic nationalism and geographic nationalism share a great many features as is obvious from the previous discussion. The difference between them is probably the same as Hans Kohn outlines for "open" and "closed" nationalism (1968: 66). In ethnic or closed nationalism the ethnic group is isomorphic with the nation-state. The emphasis is on the nation's autochthonous character, on the common origin and ancestral roots. In ethnic nationalism language can come to carry an importance way beyond any proportion of its communicative functions. The typical claim is that the deep thoughts and the soul of the nation can only be adequately expressed in the common mother tongue. Hitler's Germany was the most extreme form of ethnic nationalism with its emphasis on racial exclusivism and rootedness in the ancestral soil. (It is an interesting observation that the leaders of national movements need not be original members of that nation; Hitler, Stalin, and de Gaulle did not have their original roots in the state of which they became national leaders.)

Kohn calls "open" nationalism a more modern form; it is territorially based (hence geographic nationalism) and features a political society, constituting a nation of fellow citizens regardless of ethnic descent. The so-called great immigration countries of Canada, Australia and the United States are good examples. As Kohn comments, they rejected the notion of a nation based on a common past, a common religion or a common culture. Instead "[Americans] owe their nationhood to the affirmation of the modern trends of emancipation, assimilation, mobility, and individualism" (1968: 66).

In ethnic nationalism, language is a prime symbol of the nation but that is not necessarily so with geographic nationalism. Actually the United States does not even legally have a national language. Canada has two national languages but English and French are not thought of as national symbols of Canada. Rather, the maintenance of a common language was primarily undertaken for pragmatic LWC purposes. At the same time, although one cannot change one's genes, one can learn a new language, and in a nation which does not care about genes but uses language to define its membership, as does Catalunya, learning the new language obviously held both practical and symbolic significance: knowing the national language became the hallmark of membership and in-group status. The combination of voluntary migration, the social incentives of in-group membership, and easy access to the new language has tended to result in very rapid bilingualism, often with consequent shift.

Some considerations for policy makers

M. Pompidou is said to have commented that a politician can ruin himself in three ways, with women, by taking bribes, and by planning. Women, he said, is the most pleasant way, gambling the quickest, and planning the surest. What this anecdote illustrates is the uncertainty inherent in planning at the national level, a fact recognized by any experienced politician at the same time as he faces the necessity of such long range planning.

I have argued in this chapter that the uncertainty of language planning in education will be reduced if the planners consider the social context of language problems and especially the social, cultural and economic forces which contribute to language maintenance and shift. The most elegant educational policies for minority groups are doomed to failure if they go counter to prevailing social forces, especially the economic situation. This is as true for maintenance efforts in an economically incorporating group as it is for shift efforts to the national language for a socially marginal group. In OECD countries, the language planning efforts most likely to be successful are those which are supported by economic advantage (or similar social incentives) for the minority groups.

At the same time, planners need to acknowledge and respect the fact that there are other points of view on language maintenance and shift than the strictly pragmatic aspects argued in this chapter. Religious groups take language maintenance seriously without any immediately obvious incentives, and so do a few ethnic groups. Nations vary in their actual tolerance of religious disparity, but the principle of religious freedom is well recognized in the OECD countries. Simply, it is one of respect for the self-determination of a group to hold the values and beliefs as it chooses. Similarly we should hold the truth self-evident that an ethnic group has a right to its own language if it so chooses. The point made in this chapter that ethnic groups very rarely opt for continued language maintenance if the social conditions favour a shift to the national language is no counter-argument to the ethical principle of a right for minority groups to cultural self-determination. However, planners need to realize that the social costs of such continued language and culture maintenance tend to be high to the minority group members, and consequently parents and children may be at variance on this point, a situation which enormously complicates the setting of educational policy.

While moral decency dictates the language rights of minority groups, it does not necessarily follow that the state is under any obligation to economically support such rights nor does it follow that minority groups have a right to impose their language on the nation. The context of the situation and its historical development will hold the key to such problems, which are invariably political in nature rather than linguistic. Honest planning does not confuse the two.

While the social factors may at times seem of such overwhelming importance in influencing the outcomes of language planning that one is tempted to dismiss any efforts of setting educational language policies for minority group children as quite futile, this perception is far from accurate. National efforts or indifference in teacher training, textbook development and other implementational stages of national policies do make a difference. The implementation of educational policies for minority groups is the area where the difference between the various planning efforts actually shows up and where planning will have tangible effects on the lives of individual children. The implementation of educational language planning is a topic clearly outside the scope of this conference, but my point is that policy makers, political as well as educational should be cognizant of what is feasible inside as well as outside the classroom. We know surprisingly little about how the features of implementation fit into any typology of language planning and bilingual education, which can help us predict and understand educational success or failure. Clearly, it is a possible next step for CERI/

OECD to explore this aspect of "Educational Policies and the Minority Social Groups".

Acknowledgements

This paper was given at the Conference on The Educational Policies and the Minority Social Groups Experts' Meeting organized by CERI/OECD at OECD headquarters, Paris, January 16–18, 1985.

Notes to Chapter 9

1. I am following the terminology of the conference in using the term *minority* but want to point out that in dealing with language outcomes, subordinate status is frequently more important than mere numbers.
2. Most studies on bilingual education are done from a psychological perspective with the individual as the unit of research. In this chapter I am solely interested in the language behaviour of *groups*.
3. By group bilingualism I mean a group where all or most of the individual members are bilingual. This is not necessarily true of countries who legally recognize more than one national language. For example, German speaking Swiss do not typically speak French and Italian as well.
4. I should make clear that Rodriguez is criticized for ideological reasons by proponents for bilingual eduction, not for the quality of his writing.
5. Segregation in the name of bilingual education is a serious concern.
6. Indeed, almost all group language behaviour can be explained on the assumption that people act in their own best and vested interest. This assumption does not always apply to religious groups, at least not in any obvious way. The Hassidim and the Amish both reject mainstream definition of "best interest" as socio-economic advantage and limit access to education in English (although in different ways) as one means of instead focusing on "best interest" as inner salvation.
7. In the preceeding paragraph he talks about the "invidious connotations of tribalism". Whatever those connotations are, social scientists have "scrapped" the term *tribe* altogether, which for my purposes I regret since there is no more accurate way to discuss language problems and social organization in e.g. Somalia and Kurdistan.
8. Although it would be misleading to claim that structural–functional theory has given way to neo-Marxism. The leading research paradigm on bilingual education remains a structural–functional perspective (albeit with notable exceptions [see Paulston 1980, 1982]) which at times leads to infelicitous claims because the very nature of ethnic groups in contact frequently tends towards conflict, and so group conflict theory may hold greater insight. On the other hand, in situations marked by calm and basic good will, neo-Marxist theory can lead to misleading interpretations and mischief-making claims.
9. I am here only talking from a viewpoint of educational efficiency. There are many other strong arguments for mother tongue teaching of an affective nature (Gaarder, 1977; Pascual, 1976; Pialorsi, 1974; Sevilla-Casas *et al.*, 1973). There is

also the argument that languages are national resources which are being wasted without support in the educational systems (Fishman, 1972c).

10. That life may be after death, as in Jihad, Holy War.
11. All linguists know that we owe the original impetus for our discipline to Panini who more than 2000 years ago devised a way of describing the sound system of Sanskrit to keep people from changing the pronunciation.
12. Dell Hymes had coined the term communicative competence (1972) to include not only the linguistic forms of a language but also a knowledge of when, how and to whom it is appropriate to use these forms. Communicative competence includes the social meaning of the linguistic forms, and Hymes points out that were a man to stand on a street corner and utter all and only the grammatical sentences of English (Chomsky's definition of linguistic competence), he likely would be institutionalized.
13. The significance of symbols can change. During the Vietnamese war, to fly the flag in the United States meant that you supported the war, and flag-burning was common. During this time, the U.S. flag lost a great deal of its *national* symbolism, but this significance has been restored as was obvious during the last Olympics in Los Angeles.

Bibliography

AKZIN, B. 1964, *State and Nation*. London: Hutchinson.

ALATIS, J. E. 1978, *International Dimensions of Bilingual Education*. Washington, D.C.: Georgetown University Press.

ALBA, V. 1975, *Catalonia: A Profile*. New York: Praeger.

ALBERT, M. & OBLER, L. 1978, *The Bilingual Brain*. New York: Academic Press.

ALBO, X. 1970, Social Constraints on Cochabamba Quechua, Latin American Studies Program. Dissertation Series. Ithaca, NY: Cornell University.

ASMAH, HAJI O. 1979, *Language Planning for Unity and Efficiency*. Kuala Lumpur: Penerbit Universiti Malaya.

BARTH, F. 1969, *Ethnic Groups and Boundaries*. Boston, MA: Little, Brown & Co.

BARTON, A. H. & LAZARSFELD, P. F. 1961, Some functions of qualitative analysis in social research. In: S. M. LIPSET & N. J. SMELSER (eds), *Sociology: The progress of a decade*. Englewood Cliffs, New Jersey: Prentice Hall.

BAUMAN, J. J. 1980, *A Guide to Issues in Indian Language Retention*. Washington, DC: Center for Applied Linguistics.

BELL, W. & FREEMAN, W. E. (eds) 1974, *Ethnicity and National Building: Comparative, International and Historical Perspectives*. Beverly Hills: Sage.

BENNETT, J. W. 1975a, *The New Ethnicity: Perspectives from Ethnology*. St. Paul: West Publishing.

— 1975b, A Guide to the collection. In: J. W. BENNETT (ed.), *The New Ethnicity: Perspectives from ethnology*. St. Paul: West Publishing Co.

BOYD, S. 1984, Minoritets spraken ar borta om 25 ar? *Invandrare och Minoriteter*, 5–6, pp. 43–45.

BRESNAHAN, M. I. 1979, English in the Philippines. *Journal of Communication*, 29, 2: 64–71.

BRUDNER, L. 1972, The Maintenance of Bilingualism in Southern Austria, *Ethnology*, 11: 1, 39–54.

CARILLO, L. 1984, Reflections on Rodriguez' *Hunger of Memory*, *TESOL Newsletter*, 18: 5, 9–30.

CASINO, E. S. 1980, Ethnicity, Language Demands and National Development, *Ethnicity*, April 1: 65–72.

CENTER FOR APPLIED LINGUISTICS 1977a, *Bilingual Education: Current Perspectives*. Vol. 1, Social Science, Arlington, VA.

— 1977b, *Bilingual Education: Current Perspectives*. Vol. 2, Linguistics, Arlington, VA.

— 1977c, *Bilingual Education: Current Perspectives*. Vol. 3, Law, Arlington, VA.

— 1977d, *Bilingual Education: Current Perspectives*. Vol. 4, Education, Arlington, VA.

— 1977e, *Bilingual Education: Current Perspectives*. Vol. 5, Synthesis, Arlington, VA.

CHEUNG, Y-W. 1981, Effects of Parents on Ethnic Language Retention by Children: The Case of Chinese in Urban Canada. *Sociological Focus*, 14, 1: 33–48.

CHURCHILL, S. 1976, Recherches recentes sur le bilinguisme et l'education des francophones minoritaires au Canada: L'example ontarien. In: M. SWAIN (ed.), *Bilingualism in Canadian Education*, Yearbook. Canadian Society for the Study of Education.

COHEN, A. & SWAIN, M. 1976, Bilingual Education: The 'Immersion Model' in the North American Context. *TESOL Quarterly*, 10.1, 45–53.

COOPER, R. L. (ed.), A Framework for the Study of Language Spread, *Language Spread: Studies in Diffusion and Social Change*. Arlington, VA: Center for Applied Linguistics, and Bloomington, IN: Indiana University Press.

COTTAM, R. W. 1964, *Nationalism in Iran*. Pittsburgh: University of Pittsburgh Press.

COUNCIL OF EUROPE 1976, Factors which influence the integration of migrants' children into pre-school education in France. Strasbourg: Council for Cultural Cooperation.

CREWE, W. (ed.) 1977, *The English Language in Singapore*. Singapore: Eastern Universities Press.

CUMMINS, J. 1976, The Influence of Bilingualism on Cognitive Growth: A Synthesis of Research Findings and Explanatory Hypothesis. *Working papers on Bilingualism*. No. 9, 1–43.

DAS GUPTA, J. 1970, *Language Conflict and National Development: Group Politics and National Language Policy in India*. Berkeley, CA: University of California Press.

— 1974, Ethnicity, Language Demands and National Development, *Ethnicity*, April 1: 65–72.

DEUTSCH, K. W. 1953, *Nationalism and Social Communication: An Inquiry into the Foundations of Nationality*. Cambridge: MIT Press.

— 1966, *Nationalism and Social Communication*, 2nd ed. Cambridge, MA: MIT Press.

— 1968, The Trend of European Nationalism — the Language Aspect. In: J. A. FISHMAN (ed.), *Readings in the Sociology of Language*. The Hague: Mouton.

DEUTSCH, K. W. & FOLTZ, W. J. (eds) 1963, *Nation-building*. New York: Atherton Press.

DE VOS, G. & ROMANUCCI-ROSS, L. 1975, Ethnicity: Vessel of Meaning and Emblem of Contrast, *Ethnic Identity: Cultural Continuities and Change*. Palo Alto: Mayfield.

DE VRIES, J. 1977, Explorations in the Demography of Language: Estimation of Net Language Shift in Finland 1961–1970, *Acta Sociologica*, 20–2, 145–53.

DIL, A. S. (ed.) 1972, *Language in Sociolinguistic Change: Essays by J. A. Fishman*. Stanford, CA: Stanford University Press.

DORIAN, N. 1981, *Language Death: The Life Cycle of a Scottish Gaelic Dialect*. Philadelphia: University of Pennsylvania Press.

DOUHAN, B. 1982, The Walloons in Sweden, *American–Swedish Genealogical Review*, 2: 1–17.

DRESSLER, W. & WODAK-LEODOLTER, R. (eds) 1977, Language Death, Special Issue. *International Journal of the Sociology of Language*, No. 12.

DREYER, J. T. 1978, Language Planning for China's Ethnic Minorities. *Pacific Affairs* 5,1: 369–83.

EASTMAN, C. M. & REECE, T. C. 1981, Associated Language: How Language and Ethnic Identity are Related. *General Linguistics*, 21, 2: 109–16.

ECKERT, P. 1983, The Paradox of National Language Movements, *Journal of Multilingual and Multicultural Development*, 4: 4, 289–300.

ELAZAR, D. & FRIEDMAN, M. 1976, *Moving Up: Ethnic succession in America.* New York: Institute on Pluralism and Group Identity of the American Jewish Committee.

EMERSON, R. 1960, *From Empire to Nation: The Rise to Self-Assertion of Asian and African Peoples.* Cambridge: Harvard University Press.

ENGLE, P. L. 1975, *The Use of Vernacular Languages in Education*, Papers in Applied Linguistics. Bilingual Education Series No. 3. Arlington, VA: Center for Applied Linguistics.

ENLOE, C. 1970, *Multi-Ethnic Politics: The Case of Malaysia.* Berkeley, CA: University of California, Center for South and Southeast Asia Studies.

EPSTEIN, N. 1977, *Language, Ethnicity, and the Schools: Policy Alternatives for Bilingual–Bicultural Education.* Washington, DC: The George Washington University, Institute for Educational Leadership.

ERVIN-TRIPP, S. 1973, *Language Acquisition and Communicative Choice.* Stanford: Stanford University Press.

ESCOBAR, A. 1972a, *Lenguaje y discriminacion social en America Latina.* Lima: Milla Batres.

— (ed.) 1972b, *El reto del multilinguismo en el Peru*, Peru-Problema No. 9. Lima: Instituto de Estudios Peruanos.

FEINSTEIN, O. (ed.) 1971, *Ethnic Groups in the City.* Lexington, Mass.: Heath Lexington Books.

FERGUSON, C. A. 1959, Diglossia, *Word*, Vol. 15: 325–40; reprinted in P. P. GIGLIOLI, 1972, (ed.), *Language and Social Context*, pp. 232–51.

— 1962, The language factor in national development. In: F. A. RICE (ed.), *Study of the Role of Second Languages in Asia, Africa and Latin America*, pp. 8–14.

FISHMAN, J. A. 1966a, *Language Loyalty in the United States.* The Hague: Mouton and Co.

— 1966b, Language Maintenance and Language Shift: The American Immigrant Case, *Sociologus*, NS16: 19–39.

— 1968, Nationality–nationalism and nation–nationism. In: J. A. FISHMAN, C. A. FERGUSON & J. DAS GUPTA (eds), *Language Problems in Developing Nations.* New York: Wiley.

— 1971, National languages and languages of wider communication in the developing nations. In: W. H. W. WHITELEY (ed.), *Language Use and Social Change*, pp. 27–56.

— 1972a, *Advances in the Sociology of Language*, Vol. 1 and 2. The Hague: Mouton.

— 1972b, *Language and Nationalism: Two Integrative Essays.* Rowley, MA: Newbury House.

— 1972c, *Language in Sociocultural Change.* Stanford, CA: Stanford University Press.

—1973, Language modernization and planning in comparison with other types of national modernization and planning, *Language in Society*, Vol. 2, No. 1,

pp. 23–42.
— 1974, *Advances in Language Planning*. The Hague: Mouton.
— 1977a, Language, ethnicity, and race. In: SAVILLE-TROIKE (ed.), *Proceedings of the Georgetown University Roundtable on Language and Linguistics: Linguistics and Anthropology*. Washington: Georgetown University Press.
— 1977b, Language Maintenance, *Harvard Encyclopedia of American Ethnic Groups*. Cambridge: Harvard University Press.
— 1978, *Advances in the Study of Societal Multilingualism*. The Hague: Mouton.
— 1980, Minority Language Maintenance and the Ethnic Mother Tongue School. *Modern Language Journal*, 64, 2: 167–72.
FISHMAN, J. A., COOPER, R. & CONRAD, A. (eds) 1977, *The Spread of English*. Rowley, MA: Newbury House.
FISHMAN, J. A., FERGUSON, C. & DAS GUPTA, J. (eds) 1968, *Language Problems of Developing Nations*. New York: Wiley.
GAARDER, B. 1977, *Bilingual Schooling and the Survival of Spanish in the United States*. Rowley, MA: Newbury House.
GAL, S. 1979, *Language Shift: Social Determinants of Linguistic Change in Bilingual Austria*. New York: Academic Press.
GALLAGHER, C. F. 1963, Language, Culture and Ideology: The Arab World. In: K. H. SILVERT (ed.), *Nationalism and Development*. New York: Random House, 19–231.
GANS, H. J. 1979, Symbolic Ethnicity: the future of ethnic groups and cultures in America, *Ethnic and Racial Studies*, January, 2: 1, 1–20.
GENDRON, J. D. 1972, *The position of the French language in Quebec*. Quebec: L'editeur officiel de Quebec.
GIGLIOLI, P. P. 1972, *Language and Social Context*. Middlesex, England: Penguin Books.
GLAZER, N. 1983, *Ethnic Dilemmas*. Cambridge, MA: Harvard University Press.
— 1966, The process and problems of language maintenance: an integrative review, In: J. FISHMAN (ed.), *Language Loyalty in the United States*. The Hague: Mouton.
GLAZER, N. & MOYNIHAN, D. P. 1975, Introduction. *Ethnicity: Theory and experience*. Cambridge: Harvard University Press.
GRANDGUILLAUME, G. 1983, *Arabisation et politique linguistique au Maghreb*. Paris: Maisonneuve & Larose.
GREELY, A. 1974, *Ethnicity in the United States*. New York: Wiley.
GROSJEAN, F. 1982, *Life with Two Languages: An Introduction to Bilingualism*. Cambridge, MA: Harvard University Press.
GUMPERZ, J. 1971, *Language in Social Groups*. Stanford, CA: Stanford University Press.
HARTFORD, B., VALDMAN, A. & FOSTER, C. R. 1982, *Issues in International Bilingual Education*. New York: Plenum Press.
HAUGEN, E. 1966a, *Language conflict and language planning: The case of modern Norwegian*. Cambridge, MA: Harvard University Press.
— 1966b, Dialect, Language, Nation. *American Anthropologist*, 68: 4, 922–35.
— 1972, *The Ecology of Language*. Stanford, CA: Stanford University Press.
HEATH, S. B. 1972, *Telling Tongues: Language Policy in Mexico — Colony to Nation*. New York: Teachers College Press.
HORNBY, P. 1977, *Bilingualism: Psychological, Social, and Educational Implications*. New York: Academic Press.
HYMES, D. 1972, On Communicative Competence. In: J. B. PRIDE & J. HOLMES (eds), *Sociolinguistics*. Harmondsworth, England: Penguin.

INHASLY, B. 1977, Language and Religion in Conflict Between Ethnic Groups. *Internationales Asienforum*, 8, 3–4: 337–55.

ISAJIW, W. 1974, Definitions of ethnicity. *Ethnicity*, 1, 111–24.

JAKOBSON, R. 1968, The Beginning of National Self-Determination in Europe. In: J. A. FISHMAN (ed.), *Readings in the Sociology of Language*. The Hague: Mouton.

JARET, C. 1979, The Greek, Italian, and Jewish American Ethnic Press: A Comparative Analysis. *Journal of Ethnic Studies*, 7,2: 47–70.

JERNUDD, B. 1973, Language Planning as a type of Language Treatment. In: J. RUBIN & R. SHUY (eds), *Language Planning: Current Issues and Research*. Washington, D.C.: Georgetown University Press.

JERNUDD, B. & DAS GUPTA, J. 1971, Towards a theory of language planning. In: J. RUBIN & B. JERNUDD (eds), pp. 195–215.

JESPERSEN, O. 1946, *Mankind, Nation and Individual from a Linguistic Point of View*. London: G. Allen and Unwin, Ltd.

JONZ, JON G. 1978, Language and *LaAcademia*, If English works, por que se emplea Espagnol? *Journal of Ethnic Studies*, 5, 4: 65–79.

KABIR, M. 1985, Nationalistic Movements in Bangladesh. Unpublished doctoral dissertation, University of Pittsburgh.

KENNEDY, C. 1984, *Language Planning and Language Education*. London: Allen & Unwin.

KHLEIF, B. B. 1979, Language as Identity: Toward an Ethnography of Welsh Nationalism. *Ethnicity*, 6, 4: 346–57.

KHUBCHANDANI, L. M. 1979, Language planning processes for pluralistic societies, *Language Problems and Language Planning*, Vol. 2, No. 3, pp. 141–59.

KIRSCH, P. 1977, Review of B. Schlieben-Lange, *Okzitanisch und Catalanisch. Ein Beitrag zur Soziolinguistik zweier romanischen Sprachen. International Journal of the Sociology of Language*, Language Death. Vol. 12, 113–14.

KLOSS, H. & MCCONNELL, G. D. 1985, *Linguistic Composition of the Nations of the World: Europe and the USSR*. Quebec: University of Laval Press.

KOENIG, E. L. 1980, Ethnicity: Key variable in a Case Study of Language Maintenance and Language Shift. *Ethnicity*, 7, 1: 1–14.

KOHN, H. 1944, *The Idea of Nationalism: A Study of its Origins and Background*. New York: Macmillan.

— 1968, Nationalism. *1968, International Encyclopedia of the Social Sciences*, 11, 63–70.

KUHN, T. S. 1970, *The Structure of Scientific Revolutions*. Chicago: University of Chicago Press.

LAMBERT, W. E. 1972, *Language, Psychology, and Culture*. Stanford, CA: Stanford University Press.

LAMBERT, W. & TUCKER, R. 1972, *Bilingual Education of Children: The St. Lambert Experiment*. Rowley, MA: Newbury House.

LANGUE ET IDENTITE NATIONALE. 1977, *Recherches Sociologiques*, VIII: 1.

LEPAGE, R. S. 1964, *The National Language Question: Linguistic Problems of Newly Independent States*. London: Oxford University Press.

LEVY, S. B. 1975, Shifting Patterns of Ethnic Identification among the Hassidim. In: J. W. BENNETT (ed.), *The New Ethnicity: Perspectives from Ethnology*. St. Paul: West Publishing Co.

LEWIS, G., issue editor. 1977, *International Journal of the Sociology of Language. Bilingual Education*, Vol. 14.

LIEBERSON, S. 1981, *Language Diversity and Language Contact*. Stanford: Stanford

University Press.

LIEBERSON, S. & CURRY, T. J. 1971, Language Shift in the United States: Some Demographic Clues. *International Migration Review*, 5: 125–37.

LIEBERSON, S., DALTO, G. & JOHNSTON, M. E. 1975, The Course of Mother Tongue Diversity in Nations. *American Journal of Sociology*, 81: 1, 34–61.

LOPEZ, D. E. 1976, The Social Consesquences of Chicano Home/School Bilingualism, *Social Problems*, 24: 2, 234–46.

LOPEZ-ARANGUREN, E. 1981, Linguistic Consciousness in a Multilingual Society: The Case of Spain, *Language Problems and Language Planning*, 5: 3, 264–78.

MACDOUGALL, J. A. & FOON, C. S. 1976, English Language Competence and Occupational Mobility in Singapore, *Pacific Affairs*, 49: 2, 294–312.

MACKEY, W. 1976, *Bilinguisme et contact des langues*. Paris: Editions Klincksiek.

— 1979, Language and Policy and Language Planning. *Journal of Communication*, 29, 2: 48–53.

MACKEY, W. F. & ORNSTEIN, J. (eds) 1979, *Sociolinguistic Studies in Language Contact*. The Hague: Mouton.

MACKINNON, K. M. 1977, Language Shift and Education: Conversation of Ethnolinguistic Culture Amongst Schoolchildren of a Gaelic Community. *Linguistics*, 198: 31–55.

MANNHEIM, B. 1984, Una nacion acorrolada: Southern Peruvian Quechua language planning and politics in historical perspective, *Language in Society*, 13, 291–309.

MARJAMA, P. 1979, Bilingual, Multicultural Education: An Anglo-American Point of View. *Hispania*, 62, 1: 115–17.

MCKINNEY, J. C. 1954, Constructive typology: explication of a procedure. In: J. T. DOBY (ed.), *Introduction to Social Research*, Harrisburg, Pennsylvania: Stackpole.

— 1957, The polar view variables of type construction. *Social Forces*, 35, 300–306.

MIRACLE, A. (ed.) 1983, *Bilingualism*. Athens, GA: University of Georgia Press.

MOLDE, B. & SHARP, D. 1984, Second International Conference on Minority Languages (special issue). *Journal of Multilingual and Multicultural Development*, 5: 3–4.

MORRIS, H. S. 1968, Ethnic Groups, *International Encyclopedia of the Social Sciences*.

MYRDAL, G. 1974, The Case against Romantic Ethnicity, *Center Magazine*, 26–30.

NAHIR, M. 1984, Language Planning Goals: A Classification, *Language Problems and Language Planning*, 8: 3, pp. 294–327.

NELDE, P. H. 1980, *SprachKontakt und SprachKonflikt (Languages in Contact and Conflict)*. Wiesbaden: Franz Steiner Verlag.

NGUYEN, L. T. & HENKIN, A. B. 1982, Vietnamese Refugees in the United States: Adaptation and Transitional Status. *Journal of Ethnic Studies*, 9, 4: 101–16.

OHANNESSIAN, S., FERGUSON, G. & POLOME, E. (eds) 1975, *Language Surveys in Developing Nations*. Arlington, VA: Center for Applied Linguistics.

OKSAAR, E. 1972, Bilingualism. In: T. A. SEBEOK (ed.), *Current Trends in Linguistics*. The Hague: Mouton.

ORIOL, M. 1979, Identite produite, identite instituee, identite exprimee: confusions des theories de l'identite nationale et culturelle, *Cahiers internationeaux de Sociologie*, 6: 6, 19–28.

OSSENBERG, R. J. 1978, Colonialism, Language, and False Consciousness: the Mythology of Nationalism in Quebec. *Canadian Review of Sociology and Anthropology*, 15, 2: 145–47.

PAINTER, M. 1983, Aymara and Spanish in Southern Peru: The Relationship of Language to Economic Class and Social Identity. In: A. MIRACLE (ed.), *Bilingual-*

ism. Athens, GA: University of Georgia Press.

PANNU, R. S. & YOUNG, J. R. 1980, Ethnic Schools in Three Canadian Cities: A Study in Multiculturalism. *Alberta Journal of Educational Research* 26, 4: 247–61.

PASCUAL, H. W. 1976, La educacion bilingue: retorica y realidad. *Defensa* 4 and 5: 4–7.

PATCH, R. W. 1967, La Parada, Lima's Market. Serrano and Criollo, the Confusion of Race with Class, *AVFSR*, West Coast South America Series, XIV: 2, February, pp. 3–9.

PAULSTON, C. B. 1974a, *Implications of Language Learning Theory for Language Planning: Concerns in Bilingual Education.* Arlington, VA: Center for Applied Linguistics.

— 1974b, Linguistic and Communicative Competence. *TESOL Quarterly*, 8: 4.

— 1975, Ethnic Relations and Bilingual Education: Accounting for Contradictory Data. In: R. TROIKE & N. MODIANO (eds), *Proceedings of the First Inter-American Conference on Bilingual Education.* Arlington, VA: Center for Applied Linguistics.

— 1977a, Language and Ethnic Boundaries. In: T. SKUTNABB-KANGAS (ed.), *Papers from the First Nordic Conference on Bilingualism.* Helsinki: Helsingfors Universitet.

— 1977b, Language and ethnicity in bilingual education: Some further comments. *Conference Proceedings: Bilingual Education: Ethnic Perspectives.* Philadelphia: National Service Center and the Community College of Philadelphia.

— 1980, *Bilingual Education: Theories and Issues.* Rowley, MA: Newbury House.

— 1982, *Swedish Research and Debate about Bilingualism.* Stockholm: National Swedish Board of Education.

PAULSTON, R. G. 1970, Estratificacion social, poder y organizacion educacional: el caso peruano, *Aportes*, Vol. 16, pp. 92–11. Also in English version, Sociocultural constraints on Peruvian educational development, *Journal of Developing Areas*, Vol. 5, No. 3 (1971), pp. 401–15.

— 1977, Separate Education as an Ethnic Survival Strategy: The Findlandssvenska Case. *Anthropology and Education Quarterly*, VIII: 3.

PFAFF, C. W. 1981, Sociolingustic problems of immigrants: foreign workers and their children in Germany (a review article), *Language in Society*, 10: 155–88.

PHILIPS, S. 1970, Acquisition of Rules for Appropriate Speech Usage. In: J. ALATIS (ed.), *Bilingualism and Language Contact.* 21st Annual Roundtable, Georgetown University.

PIALORSI, F. 1974, *Teaching the Bilingual.* Tucson: University of Arizona Press.

POOL, J. 1972, National development and language diversity. In: J. FISHMAN (ed.), *Advances in the Sociology of Language*, Vol. 2, pp. 213–30.

RA'ANAN, U. & ROCHE, J. P. 1980, *Ethnic Resurgence in Modern Democratic States.* New York: Pergamon Press.

RAMOS, M. *et al.* 1967, *The Determination and Implementation of Language Policy.* Quezon City: Alemar-Phoenix.

RICE, F. A. (ed.) 1962, *Study of the Role of Second Languages in Asia, Africa, and Latin America.* Washington, D.C.: Center for Applied Linguistics.

RICHMOND, A. H. 1974, Language, ethnicity and the problem of identity in a Canadian metropolis. *Ethnicity*, 1, 175–206.

RODRIGUEZ, R. 1982, *Hunger of Memory.* Boston: Grodine.

ROSIER, P. & HOLM, W. 1980, *The Rock Point Experience: A Longitudinal Study of a Navajo School Program.* Washington, DC: Center for Applied Linguistics.

ROYAL INSTITUTE OF INTERNATIONAL AFFAIRS. 1939, Nationalism: A Report by a Study Group. London.

ROYCE, A. P. 1982, *Ethnic Identity: Strategies of Diversity.* Bloomington, IN: Indiana

University Press.
RUBIN, J. 1968, *National Bilingualism in Paraguay*. The Hague: Mouton.
RUBIN, J. & JERNUDD, B. 1972, *Can Language Be Planned?* Honolulu, HI: University of Hawaii Press.
RUBIN, J., JERNUDD, B., DAS, GUPTA, J., FISHMAN, J. A. & FERGUSON, C. (eds) 1977, *Language Planning Processes*. The Hague: Mouton.
SACHS, L. 1983, *Onda Ogat eller bakterier*. Stockholm: Liber.
SANDBERG, N. C. 1974, *Ethnic Identity and Assimilation*. New York: Praeger.
SAVARD, J. G. & VIGNEAULT, R. 1975, *Les Etats Multilingues: problemes et solutions*. Quebec: Universite Laval.
SCHERMERHORN, R. A. 1970, *Comparative Ethnic Relations*. New York: Random House.
— 1974, Ethnicity in the Perspective of the Sociology of Knowledge, *Ethnicity*, April 1: 1–14.
SCHLIEBEN-LANGE, B. 1977, The Language Situation in Southern France, *International Journal of the Sociology of Language*, 12: 101–108.
SCOTTON, C. M. 1972, *Choosing a Lingua Franca in an African Capital*. Edmonton, Canada and Champaign, IL: Linguistic Research Associates.
SEVILLA-CASAS *et al.* 1973, 'Addenda of Chicanos and Boricuas' to Declaration of Chicago, IX International Congress of Anthropological and Ethnological Sciences, September 7.
SHABAD, G. & GUNTHER, R. 1982, Language, Nationalism, and Political Conflict in Spain. *Comparative Politics*, 14, 4: 443–77.
— 1976, *Nationalism: Its Nature and Interpreters*. Washington, DC: American Historical Association.
SHAFER, B. C. 1972, *Faces of Nationalism*. New York: Harcourt, Brace, Jovanovich.
SHARARA, ABD AL-LATIF, 1962, The Idea of Nationalism. In: S. HAIM (ed.), *Arab Nationalism*. Berkeley: University of California Press.
SHILS, E. A. 1975, *Center and Periphery: Essays in Macrosociology*. Chicago: University of Chicago Press.
SIGUAN, M. (ed.) 1983, *Lenguas y Educacion en el Ambito del Estado Espanol*. Barcelona: Ediciones de la Universidad de Barcelona.
SITHOLE, N. 1960, *Obed Mutezo, the Mudzimu Christian Nationalist*. Nairobi.
SMITH, A. D. 1971, *Theories of Nationalism*. London: Harper & Row.
— 1979, *Nationalism in the Twentieth Century*. New York: New York University Press.
SMITH, R. P. & DENTON, J. J. 1980, The Effects of Dialect, Ethnicity, and an Orientation to Sociolinguistics on the Perceptions of Teaching Candidates. *Educational Research Quarterly*, 5, 1: 70–79.
SNYDER, L. L. 1954, *The Meaning of Nationalism*. New Brunswick, N.J.: Rutgers University Press.
— (ed.) 1964, *The Dynamics of Nationalism*. Princeton, N.J.: Van Nostrand.
— 1968, *The New Nationalism*. Ithaca: Cornell University Press.
— 1976, *Varieties of Nationalism: A Comparative Study*. Hillsdale, Ill.: Dryden Press.
SORENSEN, A. P., Jr. 1972, Multilingualism in the Northwest Amazon. In: J. B. PRIDE & J. HOLMES (eds), *Sociolinguistics*. Harmondsworth, England: Penguin Books.
SOTOMAYOR, M. 1977, Language, Culture and Ethnicity in Developing Self-concept. *Social Casework*, 58, 4: 195–203.
SPOLSKY, B. (ed.) 1972, *The Language Education of Minority Children*. Rowley, MA: Newbury House.
— 1977, American Indian Bilingual Education. *International Journal of the Sociology*

of Language, Vol. 14.

SPOLSKY, B. & COOPER, R. (eds) 1977, *Frontiers in Bilingual Education*. Rowley, MA: Newbury House.

— (eds) 1978, *Case Studies in Bilingual Education*. Rowley, MA: Newbury House.

STEIN, W. 1972, *Mestizo Cultural Patterns: Culture and Social Structure in the Peruvian Andes*. Buffalo, NY: New York State University Press.

STEINBERG, S. 1977, Ethnicity in the United States: A Sociological Perspective. *International Journal of Group Tensions*, 7: 3, 5, 130–44.

STRUBBS, M. 1980, *Language and Literacy*. London: Routledge & Kegan Paul.

SWAIN, M. (ed.) 1976, Bilingualism in Canadian Education: Issues and Research. Yearbook. Canadian Society for the Study of Education.

SWAIN, M. & LAPKIN, S. 1982, *Evaluating Bilingual Education: A Canadian Case Study*. Clevedon: Multilingual Matters, Ltd.

SWING, E. S. 1982, Education for Separatism: The Belgian Experience. In: P. HARTFORD *et al.* (eds), *Issues in International Education*. New York: Plenum.

THOMASON, S. & KAUFMAN, T. Forthcoming, *Language Contact, Creolization, and Genetic Linguistics*.

THOMPSON, R. M. 1974, Mexican American Language Loyalty and the Validity of the 1970 Census. *International Journal of the Sociology of Language*, 2, 6–18.

TIRYAKIAN, E. A. 1968, Typologies. *International Encyclopedia of the Social Sciencies*, 16, 177–86.

TIVEY, L. (ed.) 1981, *The Nation-State*. New York: St. Martin's.

TOSI, A. 1984, *Immigration and Bilingual Education: A case study of movement of population, language change and education within the EEC*. Oxford: Pergamon Press.

UNESCO 1984, Mother tongue and educational attainment. *Prospects*, XIV: 1.

VAN DER BERGHE, P. L. 1970, *Race and Ethnicity: Essays in Comparative Sociology*. New York: Basic Books.

VAN DEN BERGHE, P. L. 1968, Language and 'Nationalism' in South Africa. In: J. A. FISHMAN, C. A. FERGUSON & J. DAS GUPTA, (eds), *Language Problems in Developing Nations*. New York: Wiley.

VELTMAN, C. 1983, *Language Shift in the United States*. The Hague: Mouton.

VERDOODT, A. 1972, The Differential Impact of Immigrant French Speakers on Indigenous German Speakers: A Case Study in the Light of Two Theories. In: J. A. FISHMAN (ed.), *Advances in the Sociology of Language*. Part II. The Hague: Mouton.

— (ed.) 1978, Belgium, *International Journal of the Sociology of Language*, Vol. 15.

WALLACE, A. 1966, Revitalization movements. American Anthropologist 59.

WEINREICH, U. 1968, *Languages in Contact*. The Hague: Mouton.

WEINSTEIN, B. 1983, *The Civic Tongue: Political Consequences of Language Choices*. New York: Longmans.

WHITELEY, W. 1969, *Swahili — the Rise of a National Language*. London: Methuen.

WHITELEY, W. H. W. (ed.) 1971, *Language Use and Social Change*. London: Oxford University Press.

YOUNG, C. 1976, *Politics of Cultural Pluralism*. Madison: University of Wisconsin Press.

10 Who wants to change what and why — conflicting paradigms in minority education research[1]

TOVE SKUTNABB-KANGAS

Research is the new god in many secularized Western countries. Many of these countries claim that educational decisions are guided by or based on research results. With the computerized flow of information the same research results are or could be accessible in most Western countries. Still there are conflicting interpretations of the same results. Both researchers themselves and politicians/administrators can come to diametrically opposing conclusions on the basis of the same research results.

This state of affairs is not unique to research into minority education, but in this field the debates and the constant struggle have been more emotional and fierce than in many other educational fields. Both in Sweden and in the USA there have been major controversies over the last decade. If the debates were only squirmishes inside the academic community, like many research debates are, they might not be of any interest outside Academia. But as one might expect in a field of considerably practical-political importance, arguments from the research debates have been used to support or counteract differing positions and views in the implementation of educational decisions also.

The two sides in these debates can roughly be characterized as *proponents* (hereafter PROPS) and *opponents* (OPS) of mother tongue medium maintenance education for minority children. The *practical recommendations* made by PROPS and OPS are different. Both parties claim that their recommendations are *based on research*. Both present research results to support their claims. *None accepts the research evidence presented by the other party*, but for different reasons. The positions of the two sides seem to be immovable — there is no real dialogue. It seems that the parties are speaking completely different languages: they do not seem to share even the most elementary views on what research is all about and how it should be conducted. OPS seem to be more monolingual than PROPS, i.e. less able to understand what the other party says. The debates seem very similar across countries, and therefore it is instructive to compare them.

The purpose of this chapter is to analyse some of the controversies in terms of several background factors, most importantly *different research paradigms*. The chapter presupposes that some of the controversial views, presented in several reports and articles, are well known[2] and only short summaries will be presented here. The chapter starts by discussing the role of the minority mother tongues in the recommendations by OPS and PROPS, seen in relation to official policy towards the minorities, and shows that there is little difference in the official assimilationist goals in Sweden and the USA, despite superficial dissimilarity in the rhetoric. But while US PROPS are forced to use a defensive argumentation for mother tongue medium education (showing that it leads to better proficiency in the majority language) Scandinavian PROPS can use a more offensive argumentation, speaking of mother tongue medium educations as a basic linguistic human right. Next some of the reasons for rejecting the research evidence of the other party are presented and discussed. This leads to an examination of the group membership of OPS and PROPS, of the types of question each asks, and of their openness about their own biases. The OPS are shown to use more deficit-based explanations for minority children's problems at school, while the PROPS are moving towards enrichment-based explanations and demands. OPS blame the minority child, while PROPS want to change the schools and the societies. Finally, it is shown that most of the controversies which are made to look like controversies about acceptable scientific methods can be deduced from OPS and PROPS following different philosophy of science paradigms and having different world views. The conclusion is that methodological controversies cannot be analysed in a vacuum — methods must be seen as integral parts of philosophical and political ideologies, if we want to understand the debates in minority education.

The role of the minority mother tongue

The *practical recommendations* of the two sides (which both claim to follow from research evidence) are very different. Table 1 summarizes them. Since it is claimed that decisions on minority education are based on research results, the practical recommendations have to be backed up by research. Often major debates have been triggered off by the publication of a summary of current research, ordered by the government or the Ministry of Education, or a government report which draws heavily on research (e.g. the Baker & de Kanter report 1981 in the USA, or the Bratt Paulston report (ordered by the Swedish National Board of Education) 1982 and the Ulvhammar report (a governmental report by the Commission on Migrant Languages and Cultural Heritages in School and Adult Education, 1983, in Sweden)). In all these reports the assimilationist goals are evident at different levels, as will be shown in the next section. If governments want assimilation for the minorities, they obviously support both financially and otherwise research which tries to show that measures leading to assimilation are good for the minority child and for society as a whole. Research is not conducted in a sociocultural or political vacuum, out of a pure academic interest. Somebody pays for research and not out of charity. Those who pay want to get a return on their investment, so they also determine what has to be done. The steering of research can be more or less direct or discreet. It seems to be more direct in the USA and more discreet in Sweden, but the results of the steering are equally visible. In the following sections we examine the roles of the minority language and majority language in some of the reports and in the writings of the OPS and PROPS in the USA and Sweden in relation to the extent to which they support linguistic assimilation.

TABLE 1 *Recommendations by* OPS *and* PROPS *for minority education*

	PROPS	OPS
Medium of Education	— MiL-medium at least during the first 6 years, ideally longer	— Most or all MaL-medium
Role of the other language	— MaL as a second language throughout schooling	— MiL may be used (if at all) orally for necessary explanations, or even as a medium part of the time initially
Transition	— Late or no transition to MaL-medium education	— As fast a transition to MaL-medium education as possible
Criteria for efficient programmes	— Promote both languages in addition to affective and social factors; never evaluated in terms of test results only	— Promote MaL-proficiency, even when they lead to poor proficiency in MiL; test results the only reliable results
Goal	— High levels of bilingualism	— High levels of proficiency in MaL

MiL = Minority Language. MaL = Majority Language.

The concentration on the majority language and the active denigration of the mother tongue are more brutal and blatant in the US than in Sweden, and more openly assimilationist terms are used. Baker & de Kanter put it like this (1982a: 5):

". . . the basic Federal policy concerns . . . recognize the need to prepare language-minority children to function successfully *in an English-speaking nation*. A programme that produces mediocre English performance while maintaining the home language skills will be judged a worse program than one that produces better second language performance while *ignoring home language skills*. The justification for this viewpoint is that in the United States any successful education program must prepare the students to *participate in an English-speaking society*. Therefore, *the overriding concern in evaluating* instruction for bilingual students is *how well they learn English*." (My emphases.)

The *goal* is thus *high levels of proficiency in the majority language*. To achieve this, something they call "structured immersion",[3] "shows promise" and should get more attention (Baker & de Kanter, 1982a: 24). Structured immersion amounts to the old submersion,[4] except the teachers should try harder to adapt the language of instruction, which is English only, to the students' level. It is also symptomatic that the Baker & de Kanter reports *do not even mention mother tongue medium maintenance programmes as a possibility*, not even in their large research summary which is supposed to cover most of the research evidence in the world about education for language minority students. There is thus no possibility to counteract the assimilationist policy by suggesting alternative measures because all the programmes for minority children accepted to be examined in the reports are assimilationist. It is just a question of choosing the "best" way for minority children to be assimilated. This is in marked contrast with Sweden, where the policy does *not* officially advocate assimilation.

When the Swedish parliament proclaimed its immigrant and minority policy goals, *equality, freedom of choice and partnership*, in 1975 (Prop., 1975: 26), it also decreed that Swedish society has a responsibility to *promote and stimulate active bilingualism* among immigrants and minority children. *All national unions for immigrant organizations in every Scandinavian country unanimously want mother tongue medium maintenance educations to achieve the goal of active bilingualism*. There is thus no possibility in democratic Sweden to deny the importance of minority mother tongues officially. (We (= the minority organizations) have been able to force Sweden (but not Denmark or Norway) to organize mother tongue medium education for a small fraction of the minorities. But there is constant struggle around these mother tongue medium classes. And even if the authorities have been forced to concede more and more, there is vocal opposition among many administrators and their researchers.

The responsibility of the school in promoting bilingualism was recently formulated by Birgitta Ulvhammar, the former General Director of the Swedish National Board of Education, in a report by the Commission on Migrants' Languages and Culture in School and Adult Education (SKU), in a way which is typical for the soft and diplomatic Swedish educational minority policy:

> "To summarize, SKU considers that active bilingualism in the teaching should mean that pupils with a home language other than Swedish should acquire *basic knowledge* so as to attain functional bilingualism. By functional bilingualism SKU understands the capacity to *understand* two languages and in speech and writing to *live and operate* in two cultures. This means being able to *make use of* both languages in *various situations* where they are *required* and *desired*, with a *natural functional differentiation* between the languages." (SKU, 1983: 57, 220, my translation and emphases).

Compared to the US Federal policy this sounds pluralistic. The report also contains passages about the importance of multicultural and inter-cultural education for all, about respect for all cultures etc. But when the practical suggestions come, they resemble the American suggestions much more than one could expect from the divergent principal declarations of goals. Even if transitional bilingual education is grudgingly accepted, learning the mother tongue is still not a *right* for minority children.

The pluralistic official policies in Sweden may to a large extent be the empty phrases of well-meaning bureaucrats. This might explain why the action they lead to does not necessarily differ much from more directly assimilationist policies. The official policy in Sweden is just more subtle in both promoting and achieving its assimilationist goals.

Sometimes it comes through in as racist a way as in the US. It is to me amazing that the US can be called "an English-speaking nation" (see Baker & de Kanter above) when one knows that over 30 million people have other mother tongues. But the Swedish Minister for Immigrant Affairs, Anita Gradin, in pluralistic and multilingual/multicultural Sweden said in January 1984 (Stockholmstidningen 29.1.1984): "Sweden is Swedish. Sweden can never become bilingual. Swedish is the common language of all of us." When one recalls *that* at one point a third of Stockholm's inhabitants were Germans, *that* there have always been Sámi- and Finnish-speaking indigenous minorities in Sweden, *that* Finnish was to a large extent used as lingua franca in the Northern Calotte region (Aikio, 1984) and *that* one Swede in eight has at least one parent who immigrated to Sweden, the Minister's claims look peculiar. They reveal more about Swedish attitudes of forced assimilation than reality. And when one goes back to the declarations of the Swedish parliamentary report, it is easy to notice that its formulations are at best ambiguous and allow for very different interpretations, some of which are as assimilationist and as degrading vis-à-vis the minority mother tongues as the formulations of the OPS in the US. What is meant by "basic knowledge" in L1 — it could be 200 words or age-appropriate native competence? "Required" and "desired" by whom? Swedish society certainly does not require or even desire the minority children's mother tongue for anything, and the minority organizations' requirements and desires about more mother tongue education and use are at present not being met. Is a "natural functional differentiation" one where L1 is only used at home and has no rights outside, where everything official quite "naturally" takes place in Swedish? Etc., etc.

And when we go from government reports to the formulations by administrations researchers, many of the pluralistic phrases disappear in the writings of the Swedish OPS. Christina Bratt Paulston (who in other contexts has come with more PROPS-oriented opinions) advocates in a report written on the request of the Swedish National Board of Education that "migrant children . . . by being allowed to assimilate and incorporate . . . will with time become good Swedes" (1982: 65). The transitional and minor role accorded to the minority mother tongues and the dominant role for the majority language which resembles the US OPS attitudes, come blatantly through in the writings of Lars Henric Ekstrand, one of the most eager Swedish OPS. He thinks that balanced bilingualism is "impossible" (1978a: 8), "demands too much work from the individual" (1979), that "the instruction should aim at bilingualism with Swedish as the dominant language" (1979), that "the sooner the switch (from L1 to L2) is made, the better are the prospects of the second language becoming the best" (1978c: 72) and that "for some immigrant children, the optimum (in L1) might well be to keep the level a bit above the risk level for complete decay" (1978b: 11).

From the OPS views on the role of both languages we move on to examine what roles the PROPS would like to accord to them. The *proponents* of mother tongue medium maintenance education for minorities want L1 to be the main medium of education, with the majority language as a second language, at least during the first six years, but preferably for longer. There is often no theoretical need to make a transition to majority language medium at all. The OPS claim that students in mainly L1-medium classes do not learn L2, but this is explicitly counteracted by the PROPS. For instance Cummins (1983: 76) claims that there are few constraints in terms of the amount of instructional time devoted to the heritage language (a Canadian term for minority mother tongues) nor in terms of the duration of the programme, when the outcome of the programmes is assessed in terms of student achievement in the majority language. He shows that programmes which last from K (= Kindergarten) to the 12th grade with 50–80% of the instruction through L1, give good results in L2, English. In addition, they lead to good results in L1. It is appreciated by the PROPS that learning L2 to a native or near-native level takes a long time. The children in programme evaluations are not expected to reach native L2-proficiency during the first few years of mother tongue medium education. This makes all evaluations of L2-proficiency during the first few years, at least up to grades 4–5, invalid as measures of the efficiency of mother tongue medium programmes vis-à-vis L2. But the PROPS are certain about good results in both languages at a later stage, towards the end of obligatory education, when the transfer effect from having been able to develop the common underlying proficiency for both languages starts to show (Cummins, 1980a & b). This is of course also borne out by the results of the education given to powerful indigenous minorities, like the Swedish-speaking minority in Finland, for whom mother tongue medium education throughout the educational system has always been self-evident (Allardt, 1984; Knubb-Manninen, 1982, 1983), or to those immigrant children in Sweden who have had most of their education through the medium of their L1, for instance Finnish children in Botkyrka and Upplands Väsby (Skutnabb-Kangas, in press).

For both North American and Scandinavian *PROPS high levels of bilingualism is the goal*. The North American PROPS are forced to use a *defensive* strategy in their argumentation. They have to stress that mother tongue medium education leads to results in L2 which are as good as or mostly better (as Cummins argues above) than the L2 proficiency reached in other types of education. They are in other words forced to argue on the terms of those who think that results in L2 are the only important results. We Scandinavian PROPS use a more *offensive* strategy in arguing for mother tongue medium education. Even if we also think L2-proficiency is of the utmost importance, we regard the higher proficiency in L2 reached by mother tongue medium education as a positive biproduct, not as the main reason for mother tongue medium education. We claim that mother tongue medium education is also a *basic linguistic human right* for a child:

"The declaration of a child's linguistic human rights:
— Every child should have the right to positively identify with the

mother tongue(s) and have her identification accepted and respected by others
— Every child should have the right to learn the mother tongue(s) fully
— Every child should have the right to choose when s/he wants to use the mother tongue(s) in all official situations" (Skutnabb-Kangas, 1984a: 40).

Mother tongue is in this declaration defined in terms of origins. It is the language first learned, as opposed to "best known" (definition of competence), "most used" (definition of function) or "identified with" (definition of identification) (on definitions of mother tongue and bilingualism see the chapters on definitions in Skutnabb-Kangas, 1984b). The declaration also includes the situation where a child in a bilingual family has *two* mother tongues.

In addition, affective and social results are stressed by Scandinavian (and also US) PROPS, while the OPS either do not mention them at all, or explicitly deny their importance, for instance claiming that emotional factors show no correlation with language learning, like Ekstrand does.

Thus, OPS stress proficiency in the majority language as the most important outcome, and evaluate programmes in terms of test results in majority language mainly. The PROPS stress both bilingualism and affective and social outcomes.

Research evidence rejected

Both parties claim that their practical recommendations are *based on research*. None, however, accepts the research evidence presented by the other, but for different reasons. In this section we will examine the reasons by both parties for not accepting the evidence presented by the other party.

The PROPS have two main reasons for not accepting the evidence and arguments presented by the OPS against mother tongue medium education. One is that the OPS only address themselves to a tiny fraction of the issues which are relevant for educational outcomes, and ask the wrong questions in evaluating different programmes. The second is that they make untenable generalizations.

The PROPS claim that the OPS do laboratory-like research where only a few cognitive and linguistic outcomes are measured but where neither social nor affective outcomes are described or evaluated. They focus on the majority language only and disregard the mother tongue. This "narrow emphasis on English-only learning — is culturally genocidal and socially destructive", according to the PROPS (Hernández-Chávez, Llanes, Alvarez & Arvizu, 1981: 11). The OPS use test results only in their evaluation of the efficiency of bilingual programmes. The test results are chosen according to what OPS call "standard methodological criteria" (Baker & de Kanter, 1981: 5) without mentioning (or maybe even knowing) whose standards are being followed (i.e. without knowing that there are other equally valid methods — many OPS seem to live in a world where (they think) there is *one* method only). And only those test results are chosen which suit the argument, as Hernández-Chávez *et al.* show has been done by Baker & de Kanter. This is comfortable because it allows OPS to "dismiss contradictory data with claims upon the canons of quantitative methodology" as Christina Bratt Paulston claims that Ekstrand does (1981: 29), when he is "defending his own view of the world . . . he sees issues of research methodology as the best defense. It is convenient in that it assures that any data, not of his choosing, is not acceptable" (1981: 29).

The PROPS claim that it is impossible to understand or evaluate bilingual education properly without also discussing the political and philosophical arguments and the whole societal context of it (Hernández-Chávez *et al.*, 1981; Skutnabb-Kangas, 1984b). The PROPS also claim that many of the positive effects of mother tongue medium education cannot yet be tested with the help of quantitative measures, in the way positivists demand — the methods are still too crude. But qualitative data should not be dismissed just because we do not yet have reliable ways of measuring them. Accepting quantitative data only destroys the picture and prevents us from finding the "truth". What OPS do when accepting quantitative data only because it is easy to get, is, according to PROPS, like looking for a lost coin under the street light where it is easier to look rather than looking in the darker place where it was lost.

Secondly, the OPS also make inappropriate generalizations, incorrectly assuming validity for findings which come from different contexts.

Some of these generalize:

— from *majority children* to *minority children* (Ekstrand, Baker & de Kanter)
— from *foreign language learning* to *second language learning* (Ekstrand, Baker & de Kanter)
— from *additive* to *subtractive L2-learning situations*, i.e. from *immersion* to *submersion* (Ekstrand, Baker & de Kanter)
— from *learning a foreign language at school* to *learning a minority mother tongue* (Ekstrand)

— from *the situation of elite bilinguals* (e.g. children of linguists etc.) to *the situation of working class minority children* (Ekstrand, Oksaar)

— from *transitional bilingual education* to *mother tongue medium maintenance education* (Baker & de Kanter, Ekstrand).

All these distinctions are according to the PROPS necessary. The PROPS, in summary, claim that the OPS do insufficient and biased research, while pretending to be objective. Some of the OPS research is psychometrically sound, but it is to a large extent irrelevant for the education of minority children because it asks the wrong questions.

The OPS also have two main reasons for not accepting PROPS evidence and arguments. They claim that the PROPS base their recommendations on poor quality research which does not satisfy "standard methodological criteria" (i.e. positivistic criteria on quantitative data). Secondly, they claim that the PROPS are not objective because they are committed in what they are doing. They are accused by the OPS of doing emotional political propaganda under the guise of research.

The strategies used by some OPS to try to show that the PROPS do poor research are sometimes both sad and amusing. Baker & de Kanter reject Skutnabb-Kangas & Toukomaa study (1976) partly on the grounds of claiming that there is a severe attrition of data, with "almost 80% of the data missing" (1982a: 16) and are worried because "the authors give no consideration to this problem". The key analysis in the English language report is based on only 150 students, while the whole study covers 687 students. Obviously Baker & de Kanter like many other speakers of "languages of wider communication" have difficulties in imagining that results about the education of minority children published in minority languages (in this case Finnish and Swedish) really do exist . . . . Something to be remembered for us minority language speakers: if we do not publish in English, maybe we do not exist either, just like the "missing data". A new, exciting existential dilemma . . .

The following table lists some of the characterizations some OPS use when describing their own work and that of some PROPS (the list with the explanations and references comes from Skutnabb-Kangas 1983, the OPS here are Lars Henric Ekstrand and Sven Öhman, while the PROPS are Hanson and Skutnabb-Kangas & Toukomaa).

It is almost embarrasing to point out that some of the OPS also sometimes come with unsupported claims or claims which the existing evidence counteracts (for instance Bratt Paulston and Edwards) or use sheer lies

TABLE 2

OPS characterize themselves	OPS' characterizations of PROPS
— A pluralistic approach	— An extreme mother tongue ideology
— All serious researchers	— Whoever can make people believe that he or she is a researcher (and the definition of this concept seems to become ever wider each year)
— Competent researchers	— If these "revelations" are delivered by "researchers", interest is especially great
— In my capacity as a university professor and linguist	— Contributions on a very low level of competence
— An academically minded researcher	— "Chock reports" . . . which were very soon identified by competent researchers as extraordinarily poorly grounded purely empirically and based on a very crude and unsophisticated linguistic theory
— The more securely tenured wing of researchers who can afford a greater dose of moderation and reflection	— Some contributions to the immigration and semilingualism debate have had the character of political agitation disguised as assumed science
— Science in a more intellectual sense	— The more agitational "research reports"
— This kind of analysis is much more laborious and time-consuming	— Has a clear political agitation goal
— Scientifically qualified studies	— The question of whether these "research results" serve a definite political function
— How language should be properly studied	— The agitation is done so to say in the name of science, i.e. where the speaker gives himself/herself the appearance of being a researcher
	— A habit of speaking in the name of science
	— Has burning pathos for her/his cause
	— Plays . . . to full house

(Ekstrand).[5] Even if one does not agree with another researcher, it should be possible to give an honest presentation of her or his results and claims.

The OPS claim as the list also shows that the PROPS let themselves be guided by research-external ideologies when interpreting data. This is of course both true and unavoidable. But the troubling factor is that the OPS themselves claim to be immune to such influences, which is of course sheer rubbish, as even the strongest proponents of hardcore positivism in the philosophy of science now admit. It becomes difficult for our OPS to analyse their biases and expose them to open criticism (like most PROPS do) if they firmly and incorrectly believe that they have not got any biases. This leads us to the next phase: examining the biases of each side.

On whose side is the researcher?

Many of the reasons why OPS do not accept the evidence presented by the PROPS have been phrased in terms of methodology, *how* research should be done. But *how* is subsumed under broader questions in the steering of research. When the steering is done by financial means, so that some research gets funded while other types of research do not get funded, *what* and *who* questions are asked before *how* questions. *What* research gets done, i.e. what kind of research questions are asked? *Who* does the research?

The researcher's own group membership is important. In 1981 we founded a Nordic Association of Immigrant and Minority researchers. One of the association's aims is to support research done by us minority members ourselves to study questions posed by the minorities, and to do it from a minority perspective. We feel that this is an important addition to the research done, paid for and controlled by the majority representatives, especially by those who want us to assimilate. Robert Petersen, himself Inuit, the leader of Inuit Institute in Nuuk, Greenland, former professor of Eskimology in Copenhagen talks in several of his papers about the need for minorities to develop alternative expertise of their own (also instead of the well-meaning "alternative cultural imperialists", for instance all the ESL and EFL-experts in Third World countries, selling the English language — see Pattanayak, this volume, Chapter 2 and Skutnabb-Kangas & Phillipson, 1985). Without wanting to question the good will, the attempts for objectivity or the attempts to understand which majority members exhibit, Robert Petersen claims that it is impossible in certain situations for a majority group member to be objective or to pose the right questions about the minority group, especially in conflict situations. And the education of minority children has always been a situation with potential conflicts. According to Petersen, minorities must to a much greater extent take care of their own research and develop it so that they ask questions, develop concepts and define reality from the minority's own point of view. Then the minority does not need to use majority experts as its own experts, a common situation now. And a prerequisite for equal co-operation where none of the parties dictates the rules is that both parties have their own experts, both are allowed to define themselves, and both can get their own definition of *their* reality accepted by the other party (Skutnabb-Kangas, 1983: 34). If we want to have research which starts from the needs and the definitions of reality that the minorities themselves have, then we must do that research ourselves.

Majority researchers can of course do good research both on the minorities and about questions important for the minorities also. But majority researchers do not do the same type of research into minority questions as the minority members themselves, according to a study by Markku Peura & Taisto Hujanen (1983).

It seems to me that in both Scandinavia and the US many (but not all) PROPS come from the minority groups themselves. Many of the PROPS *ask research questions which are important from the minorities' own point of view,* and *are also active in supporting the minority organizations in their fight to try to achieve equity and justice.* This necessarily means that many of the PROPS also include among the criteria for efficient programmes that these should help the minority to achieve equity. They are *openly on the minority's side,* and expose their value judgements to open criticism. They define the future of the minority in terms of a clear wish for the minority itself to be able to decide to what extent it wants to continue its existence as a minority. And since it is decisive for most minorities to keep and develop their own languages (see Smolicz, 1979 for language as a cultural core value) and since this presupposes that the language is given a wide range of meaningful functions, they also see it as natural to promote educational programmes which develop the minority language and political programmes which want to assure the minority language at least a semi-official status.

By contrast, many of the OPS (but not all) come from the majority groups. Often they do not even know the language of the minority they are studying. They *ask research questions which are important for the majority society and its administrators* (i.e. for the ones who pay them) *for controlling the minorities.* But instead of admitting this many of the OPS *claim to be neutral,* on nobody's side. Usually they do not co-operate with the minority organizations (even if they may co-operate with individual minority members). Instead they co-operate with the administrators. And since most administrators either officially (USA) or at least unofficially (Sweden) support assimilation (which they suppose is both possible and less divisive for the nation than facilitating the establishment of permanent minorities), this is reflected in the research goals of the administration researchers, the OPS, too. And as has been said earlier, if the administrators want assimilation for the minorities, they support (both financially and otherwise) research which shows that measures leading to assimilation are "good" for both the individual child and the minority group. That also leads to the attitude which these opponents have toward the two languages: since assimi-

TABLE 3

Reason for Problems	Measure	Goal
DEFICIT THEORIES		
1 *Linguistic L2-related handicap, learning deficit* (the child does not master L2 well enough)	*More teaching of majority language* (auxiliary teaching, ESL, introductory classes etc.); *compensatory*	*Minority is to become majority language-speaking as fast as possible*
2 *Social handicap, socially linked learning deficit* (the child's parents come from lowest social classes)	*More social and pedagogical help* (aids, tutors, psychologists, social workers, career advisors etc.); in addition to measure 1; *compensatory*	Same as 1
3 *Cultural handicap, culturally linked deficit* (the child has a "different" cultural background; the child has low self-confidence; the child is discriminated against)	*Inform* minority children *about* majority culture/about their own culture; inform all children about minority cultures/start multicultural/intercultural educational programmes; eliminate discrimination/racism in teaching materials; attitudinal courses for teachers; in addition to measures 1–2; *compensatory*	*Minority language in the family 1–2 generations*; minority-children need help to appreciate minority culture (until they become majority language-speaking)
4 *Linguistic L1-related handicap, learning deficit because of L1 deprivation* (the child does not know her own L properly and	*Teaching of L1 as subject; elementary education through the medium of L1 with as fast a transition to L2-medium as possible.*	Same as 3

lation is seen as the inevitable and desirable goal, the focus in evaluating programmes is on the majority language. The minority language which is supposed to disappear in the course of a few generations anyway should be privatized: stay inside the family, and not get much attention (for instance Bullivant, 1984; Edwards, 1984b).

Different problem definitions

Within these competing frameworks the PROPS and OPS also *define the problems which minority children have at school* in completely different ways. A useful typology here is one I have assembled and modified from different tables in Stacy Churchill's report for OECD on minority education (1983, 1986), Table 3.

TABLE 3 *(continued)*

Reason for Problems	Measure	Goal
has therefore poor grounding for the learning of L2 *CALP*) (the child loses content while learning L2)	Minority language has no intrinsic value, it is thera-peutic, *compensatory* (more self confidence, better co-operation with home, gives better basis for minority language learning, functions as bridge for transmission of content during L2-learning); in addition to measures 1–3	

ENRICHMENT THEORIES

5 *High levels of bilingua-lism beneficial for the individual but difficult to attain*, demands much work and energy. The primary goal is to learn majority language prop-erly; it is a prerequisite for equal opportunity	*Teaching through the medium of minority language for several years inside majority-school; obligatory teaching of majority language; transi-tion to majority language medium teaching after elementary education*	*Minority language is allowed to be maintained for private use;* bilingualism necessary; *minority language is allowed to exist* (in a diglossic situation) as long as demographic basis exists
6 *Bilingualism enhances development*. If problems arise, the causes are simi-lar to those of mono-lingual children; some problems may be caused by racism/discrimination	*Separate, equal school systems for minority and majority children, L1 is medium for both and L2 obligatory (or possible to study) for both.* Positive discrimination of the minority economically (smaller units allowed)	*Existence of minorities is enriching for the whole society. Minority language has (at least some) official status and its use is en-couraged also for majority language children*

The first four phases in the typology (which can be seen as forming a historical development on which different countries can be placed) build on *deficiency-related explanations* for difficulties minority children have at school: there is *something wrong with the child or her group*, and this causes the problems. In all the deficiency phases the societal goal for the minority is assimilation. In the first two phases the assimilation should ideally be as fast as possible. In the last two the minority language is supposed (and allowed) to be used inside the family for some generations. The measures taken at the different stages correspond to the specific deficiency the child is supposed to suffer from and they try to *compensate* for the deficiency:

— if the main problem is defined as lacking proficiency in the majority language, an *L2 handicap*, then the measures consist of compensatory L2-teaching, for instance all the English as a second language programmes,

— if the problem is defined as a *social handicap* (= the child has working class parents), different types of special education and guidance is used,

— if the problem is defined as a *cultural handicap* where the minority child's cultural background is "different", where the child has low levels of self-confidence, or where it may even be admitted that the child is discriminated against by majority children, the measures consist of informing the minority child about the majority culture; about the child's own culture (Black studies, ethnic studies etc.); informing *all* children about minority cultures; so-called multicultural and intercultural education. Teaching materials are examined for racist stereotypes, teacher attitudes are scrutinized,

— if the problem is defined as an *L1 handicap, mother tongue deprivation* and therefore also a poor basis for developing proficiency in the intellectually more demanding academic aspects of L2, teaching in the mother tongue is introduced, and in a later phase also transitional bilingual education (TBE). It is important to note, though, that even TBE still builds on a deficiency hypothesis: the mother tongue is only accorded instrumental value in that it is used only so as to prevent a cognitive lag vis-à-vis subject matter while L2 is being learned, or to support L2 development. It is *not* used because of its intrinsic value, or because it would be considered a human right for every child to learn her mother tongue fully. These arguments come only in the last two phases, which look at bilingualism as an enrichment, firstly for the individual concerned and secondly for the whole society.

Most OPS seem to hold views which correspond to the first three deficiency phases, while most PROPS start off with the last deficiency stage, mother tongue deprivation, and move on to seeing bilingualism as a possible enrichment, and to seeing mother tongue education as a natural right of a child, and as a good way of achieving high levels of bilingualism. Policy and practice in this field seem to have evolved with varying speed and with varying focus in different countries.

One of the central factors seems to be what most strikingly distinguishes the majority and the largest minority groups. The Swedish discussions centred from the very beginning around the language deficits, partly because the main difference between the Swedes and the largest minority

group, us Finns, is linguistic and not so much cultural or social. Many of the
large minority groups in the UK were speakers of English or English-based
creoles, and the proportion of middle class people among the minorities was
considerably higher than in Sweden, West Germany or France. Therefore it
is understandable that British discussions have focused on cultural differences, and explanations based on cultural "deficits". Despite large cultural
differences between West Germans and the largest minority group, the
Turks, the focus has been on explanations stressing the social handicap of
the Turks. But the most important factor determining how far different
countries have come in their policy development is the power status that the
minority has. It is, therefore, logical that for instance the Swedish-speaking
minority in Finland, a former power-majority representing the former
colonizers, reached the final stage long ago: we have our own Swedish-
medium day care centres, schools, universities etc., and it is accepted that
the existence of the Swedish-speaking minority is an enrichment for the
whole country. Even so, there are every now and then debates where some
Finnish-speakers question the right of the Swedish-speakers to the status
and constitutional rights which we have. Likewise it is understandable that
the Finnish-speaking mainly immigrant minority in Sweden, which seems to
me to be the best organized and best legally protected labour migrant
minority in the world just now, has moved at least to the fifth stage in its own
consciousness development, and has almost succeeded in forcing the official
Swedish policy to make the move from 4 (and 3 which the government report
— see SOU, 1983 — tried to introduce as the new big thing) to 5 also. It is
also predictable that the minorities in the USA have not as yet succeeded in
pushing the official policy much beyond the first stage, even if there are
many separate measures belonging to the 2nd, 3rd and even 4th stages too. It
also seems to me that the relative number of OPS is larger in USA than in
Europe. If the minorities in the US were united and strong, they could
obviously make all the changes they wanted immediately. The question then
is if they want a change, and in case they do, what they want to change. Here
the differences between the PROPS and the OPS in conceptualizing the
reasons for the problems which minority children experience at school seem
to me to reflect a more general theorizing about what should be changed
when some children do not get much out of schools. The issue of working or
lower class children in the middle class school and different solutions proposed show many parallels with solutions proposed for minority children.

Who wants to change what?

We know from many studies that "the educational and cultural system
is an exceptionally important element in the maintenance of existing relations of domination and exploitation" (Apple, 1980). We also acknow-

ledge "the important role schools — and the overt and covert knowledge within them — play in reproducing a stratified social order that remains strikingly unequal by class, gender and race" (Apple, 1980). The different phases in the development of problem definitions can also be looked upon as indicators of *how much each of them blames (and wants to change) the child* (and her parents, her group and its culture) *or the school.* If one only wants to change the child to fit the school, then one at least implicitly accepts the role of the school in maintaining and reproducing inequality and exploitation. If one also wants to change the school, it might mean some kind of protest against the existing stratified social order. It seems that the OPS want to change the child, while the PROPS want to change the majority middle class school, so as to make it a better fitted place for the minority child. But if one does not go further than to try to change the school so that minority children get a fairer opportunity to cope and achieve, the next problems arises. In an American book called "Who Gets Ahead?" (1979) Jencks *et al.* "document the fact that not only are economic returns from schooling twice as great for individuals who are economically advantaged to begin with, but for, say, black students, even finishing high school will probably not bring any significant benefits. Thus, even if we could alter the school to equalize achievement, the evidence suggests that it might not make a significant difference in the larger framework in which schools exist" (Apple, 1980).

A pessimistic diagnosis might be that minority children do not get as much out of schools as majority children do, and even if they did (for instance by participating in mother tongue medium maintenance education when the school has changed) it might not help them to get good jobs anyway, as long as our societies are the way they are. Three possible conclusions seem to offer themselves:

Apathy: Why bother, since one cannot change anything anyway?
Radical pessimism: As long as the society is the way it is, it is no use trying to do anything with the schools. Instead, try to change the society, and after that the schools will change. While you do that, try to help individual minority children to cope (= add to their repertoire), by supporting them so that they get some of the qualifications needed for competing on the labour market (a bit of optimism). Or: you cannot help the individual children anyway while the society is the way it is, so concentrate on the society.
Radical optimism: Try to change the society. At the same time, try to change the school, not only for minority children (mother tongue medium maintenance education) but also for majority children (immersion programmes, anti-racist education). At the

same time, try to help individual minority children to cope, by giving them extra support so that they get some of the qualifications needed for competing on the labour market even before the schools and the societies have changed. *Most PROPS belong to this group of radical optimists.*

An *idealistic liberal* on the other hand might come with a completely different diagnosis. Many of the idealistic liberals have the same type of attitude as the PROPS to minority language and cultures: they are good and enriching for the societies. They also share with the PROPS the belief that it is the school that should change, not the child. The idealistic liberals strongly oppose any attempts to change the minority child: the child, her language and her culture are perfect, and should be accepted by the school as they are. There is nothing wrong with the child's linguistic or communicative or cultural competence, and those who claim that the child might need something else too are labelled as deficit theorists, regardless of whether they think the child should have something else *instead of what she has* (like the OPS do) or *in addition to what she has* (like the PROPS and the radical pessimists do). Most idealistic liberals do not include any kind of analysis of the power relations in their diagnosis, and do not necessarily see schools as reproducers of inequality. Discrimination for them becomes a question of morals, not power. Thus their recommendations for changes in schools mostly have to do with pleas for more just attitudes: once the majority children and adults are informed that minority children's languages and cultures are just as good, discrimination disappears, schools change and everybody is enriched. It seems to me that this attitude is very common among American progressive researchers, but in practice it serves to support the OPS. On this scale of who or what should be changed (see Table 4), the OPS only seem to want to change the minority child — that is where the blame is placed. The school need not change, the minority child should fit in to the "normal school curriculum" (V. Edwards, 1984: 59), "normal" being majority language medium. The minority child's culture and language should have no (or almost no) place in schools, because "matters of ethnicity are best left to those directly concerned" (J. Edwards, 1984b: 299), "the symbolic value of language is essentially a private ethnic marker" (p. 289), and public institutions, like schools, should not "promote private ethnicity" (p. 300), also because "language support is of dubious worth and, indeed, it may do some harm" (p. 289). (Obviously it does not do any harm to promote the majority language or the majority children's private ethnicity in schools — maybe they are so strong that they can take this "harm"). But the minority children should not be segregated from the majority either, according to the OPS, because the majority children may get used to minority children and see them as "quite normal classmates" after a while, i.e. the presence of minorities may be potentially enriching for majority children in the intercultural era.

Table 4 summarizes who wants to change what.

TABLE 4 *Who wants to change what in minority education?*

Wish to change	Society	School for the Minority	Majority	Minority child herself
Apathetics	−	−	−	−
Opponents	−	−	add	+
Idealistic Liberals	−	+	add	−
Radical Pessimists	+	−	−	add
Radical Optimists (PROPS)	+	+	+	add

The whole question of what one wants to change and why, is strictly speaking not an intradisciplinary question. It has to do with our political ideology of what needs to be changed and what can be changed. Some researchers, among them most OPS, think that this type of question does not belong to the domain of research at all. Many researchers, among them most PROPS, think that more narrow questions in bilingual education as well as the debates are impossible to analyse scientifically without openly discussing the political ideology of the researchers and the research traditions. Whether or not one includes questions of the political ideology and political consequences of research in the research framework in turn depends on the philosophical ideology that guides the researcher's thinking. And the methodological questions discussed at the beginning of this chapter can, it seems to me, be deduced from the conflicting political and philosophical ideologies that different researchers adhere to.

I see many of the debates and conflicts in bilingual education research as results of the fact that some researchers, mainly the OPS, do not know or do not admit that many of the conflicting views about for instance the effectiveness of mother tongue medium education are methodological conflicts, which can be traced back to the researchers following different scientific traditions, different paradigms, which in turn can be traced back to or connected to researchers having different ideologies, both philosophical and political. Many of the researchers who do not admit or do not know that it is a question of methodological, paradigmatic and ideological conflicts, are unable to see the causal relationship and even the correlation between the methods researchers use and the paradigm and the ideology. Instead they try to make it look as if there was just *one* canonized right way to do research in a scientific and sound way, and as if all the conflicts were caused by the fact that *some* researchers — namely they themselves and others inside the same paradigm — are better researchers, and *some* researchers — namely those who represent another paradigm — are bad researchers, not methodologically sound, or that they maybe are not even real researchers but are only making emotional and biased political propaganda.

There are many ways of discussing the ideological, paradigmatic (in Kuhn's sense) and methodological issues concerned. Christina Bratt Paulston, building on Rolland Paulston's typologies, has analysed bilingual education paradigms in a superb way (for instance Bratt Paulston, 1977, 1981, building on especially Paulston, 1976). In Table 5 where I have polarized the different views (in addition to trying to squeeze something that should at least be a tripartite division [see Habermas, 1971] to a real polarization) I have tried to describe the views which I see closely connected with the PROPS (the left side) and the OPS (the right side of the Table).

To summarize so far, I claim that we as researchers have different political and philosophical ideologies. We have in our training as scholars learned how to work inside a certain scientific tradition, a paradigm. Even if we know something about other paradigms, many of us, especially at the beginning of our careers, when trying to establish our identity as researchers,

TABLE 5

Socialist political ideology	Liberal/conservative political ideology
is often combined with	
Materialistic/phenomenological-existentialistic philosophical ideology	Idealistic/logical-analytical philosophical ideology
is often connected with	
Critical/hermeneutic paradigm of science	Positivistic paradigm of science
which often leads to use of	
Theoretical-scientific thinking, based on developing scientific concepts, which describe the essence of phenomena and try to explain, understand and criticize	Empirical thinking, based on developing empirical everyday concepts, which describe the appearance of phenomena and try to explain apparent, superficial correlations only
and which mostly uses	
Qualitative methods, often combined with quantitative methods	Quantitative methods only

From Skutnabb-Kangas, 1983.

may very naively see our own paradigm as the only scientific way to do research. Discussions of the connections and relationships between our political and philosophical ideology and our paradigm are often not included in our training, at least not so that they would be specifically related to current theories in our own field. We have also in our training learned certain methodological procedures and concepts, a proficiency which gives us a certain security, reliability and trustworthiness in the eyes of others, and maybe also in our own eyes. For many researchers it seems to take an incredibly long time to understand and/or admit *that* our methods are connected with our philosophy of life, our ideology, and our paradigms, and especially *in which ways* they are connected.

When reading about the last 100 years of discussions in the philosophy of science and more recently the sociology of knowledge, one sees that almost every argument used in our debates has been aired before. They are almost nothing more than classic examples of conflicts between different scientific paradigms, where the OPS seem to represent a hard positivistic paradigm, while PROPS range from critical to hermeneutic. But what makes the debates so sad and depressing is that most OPS do not seem to be able to conceptualize the controversies in terms of different paradigms and ideologies. It seems incredible that it should still be possible — in the 1980s — to claim, for instance, that there is a "standard methodology" (Baker & de Kanter), or that researchers can be objective, neutral and value-free, and get away with that. But it shows that it is possible to be very sophisticated at one level in the polarized scheme (for instance methodologically, as is often the case with people with a thorough positivistic training) and very "elementary" in one's development at the other levels, barely conscious of their existence. In the worst case researchers can be barely conscious of the fact that their views have a name and that there are alternatives — and this seems to be all too common with some of the OPS. This also means that it is impossible to solve some of the problems in the methodological debates in bilingual education, unless methods are examined as logical parts of a larger complex. Methods are not a separate collection of neutral recipes which you can learn in your training, out of context, and then apply to any problem. All methods are integral parts of or at least related to specific paradigms and specific philosophical and political ideologies, and controversies about methods have to be seen in this context.

When some of the recent debates in bilingual education are analysed in this way (see my analysis of the Loman/Hansegård & Öhman, Ekstrand/ Hanson, Hernández-Chávez *et al.*, Toukomaa & Skutnabb-Kangas and Baker & de Kanter/Cummins & Skutnabb-Kangas & Toukomaa controversies, in Skutnabb-Kangas, 1983 forthcoming), it becomes clear that most OPS are more monolingual than most PROPS, i.e. seem to have less possibility of understanding that there are alternative paradigms, and, in fact, that they themselves represent a paradigm (monolingual naivety, thinking that there is one way only to look at the world, one language only). It also becomes clear that there are not only scientific reasons behind defending the assimilationist world view, but also very solid economic reasons.

I do not intend to discuss economics and world view here. Instead I shall point out just one consequence it would have for many of the OPS if they accepted that other methodologies are equally valid, or maybe better for studying minority education. As long as quantitative data only are accepted as data, researchers who represent the majority group (without in-depth knowledge of the languages and cultures of the minorities) can do research. But as soon as there are requirements of qualitative data also, majority researchers become incompetent. It is simply impossible for them to get valid and rich qualitative data, because they cannot come close to their subjects, they do not understand them. In its extreme form this means that if criteria for good methodology in minority studies were changed so as to make quantitative data alone invalid, and so as to have objectivity criteria which do not build on intersubjectivity but on exposing one's value judgements to criticism, most of the OPS would lose their jobs. They would simply be declared incompetent for doing minority research. But as long as most minorities have almost no say in the criteria applied when studying them, and as long as the majority researchers deliver results which show that what majorities are doing to minorities, even educationally, is good for the minorities (which can be done by ignoring those outcomes of the treatment which show bad results from the minority's point of view), the criteria for good methods in minority research are not likely to change. Unless we minorities organize and get more power. Also we minority researchers. It is important for us to analyse all the reasons why we should do our own research, and how we should do it.

I think the image of researchers as cooks is helpful as a last image. The debates are about what ingredients (what data) are acceptable for a cookery book (a scientific undertaking): what methods (recipes) should be followed; whether or not the cook can be interested in food (be partisan) and whether the cook should be allowed to eat the food herself (come from the minority). And, most importantly, the PROPS and OPS cooks come from different cooking schools, and especially the OPS do not admit that the cookery books used in the PROPS cooking contain real recipes at all — they do not perceive them as fulfilling the "standard methodological criteria" for what real recipes should look like. The PROPS have mostly attended both the cooking school where the OPS have had their training and another one, and they therefore say that the OPS recipes are good for *some* cooking, but insufficient for cooking for minority children — where other types of recipes are needed. It is like meat-eaters and vegetarians where the meat-eaters usually know next to nothing about human physiology and global ecology and dismiss greens as emotional fanatics, while the vegetarians in the West are often reformed meat-eaters and know more even about meat than the meat-eaters do. And while the OPS think that scientific results of meat-eating should be analysed in terms of the amount of animal protein the child gets in one meal, the PROPS insist on analysing both the difference between animal and plant protein and the consequences for global ecology and economy and world peace in eating or not eating meat, and propose that this is scientific and valid.

Notes to Chapter 10

1. I would like to thank Göte Hanson, Eduardo Hernández-Chávez, Sunil Loona, Christina and Rolland Paulston, Arturo Tosi, Pertti Toukomaa, Georgios Tsiakalos and Birgitta Ulvhammar for inspiring discussions on the topics of this chapter, Jim Cummins and Merrill Swain for both discussions and an opportunity to present some of the philosophy of science underpinning of them (a topic for a forthcoming paper) at OISE, Toronto, and John Edwards for persisting and constructive opposition. Hartmut Haberland, Markku Peura, Robert Phillipson and Ulf Teleman have commented on an earlier version and showed me how impossibly difficult the topic is, especially for a short chapter. I couldn't agree more. But I am not solely responsible for having to write about it — part of the responsibility lies with those hundreds of PROP-parents, teachers and students who call, write or come, saying: now X has written this and this again, and our headmaster/director says that Y. What should we do?

2. For some of the OPS views see Baker & de Kanter, 1981, 1982a, 1982b; Bullivant, 1984; Drake, 1984; Edwards 1984a, b; Ekstrand, 1978a, b, c, 1979, 1983; Bratt Paulston, 1982; Öhman, 1981 a, b.

3. For some of the PROPS views see Cummins 1976, 1977, 1979, 1980a, b, 1981, 1983, 1984a, b; Dutcher, 1982; Hanson 1982a, b; Hernández-Chávez *et al.*, 1981; Keskitalo, 1984; Bratt Paulston 1976, 1977, 1981; Bratt Paulston & Paulston, 1977; Skutnabb-Kangas, 1984b; Skutnabb-Kangas & Toukomaa, 1976; Smolicz, 1979, 1984; Tingbjörn, 1982, forthcoming; Tosi, 1984; Toukomaa & Skutnabb-Kangas, 1977; Troike, 1979.

4. "An *immersion* programme is a programme where majority children with a high status mother tongue voluntarily choose to be instructed through the medium of a (foreign) minority language, in classes with majority children only, where the language of instruction is foreign to all of them, where the teacher is bilingual so that the children can communicate all their needs to the teacher and to each other at the beginning in their own language, and where their own mother tongue is in no danger of not developing or of being replaced by the language of instruction: an

additive language learning situation" (from Skutnabb-Kangas, 1982a). Already from the definition it can be seen that immersion per definition cannot be used with minority children.

4. "A *submersion* programme is a programme where minority children with a low status mother tongue are forced to accept instruction through the medium of the foreign majority language (with high status), in classes where some children are native speakers of the language of instruction, where the teacher does not understand the mother tongue of the minority children, and where the majority language constitutes a threat to their mother tongue — a subtractive language learning situation" (Skutnabb-Kangas, 1982a).

5. Examples: Bratt Paulston claims in her report that Finns in Sweden have "little aspiration for upward social mobility" (p. 45) — all the studies where questions about this have been asked show the opposite: Finnish parents want their children to get as much education as possible. She says in the same report that "Finnish culture is said to be low in verbal output (although the Finns I know talk nonstop), and it is possible that there is less verbal input for language learning in a Finnish family than say a Spanish family". In the next sentence the low verbal input is treated as a fact, as a causal factor in explaining Finnish children's poor school achievement in Sweden. There are no studies comparing the verbal input in Finnish and Spanish or Finnish and Swedish families — the only proof offered is a racist stereotype about Finns (see also Skutnabb-Kangas, 1984c).

Edwards claims (1984a: 14) that "we know, however that communicative language retention is *not* a feature of most settled minorities", or that "the desire for cultural pluralism is in many cases an ideal of the élite, and not in accord with the desires and ideology of the masses of ethnics" (cited in Drake, 1984: 146). In the same book where these claims are put forth, the very strong support for cultural pluralism, minority language maintenance and a desire for mother tongue education is reported on in several articles (Cummins, 1984b; Skutnabb-Kangas, 1984d).

Ekstrand has in many of his articles (for instance 1978a, 1983) had a wealth of claims about other researchers' work which are incorrect (some of them are presented in Skutnabb-Kangas, 1982b). Göte Hanson, Pirjo Pöllänen, Gunnar Tingbjörn etc. have pointed out some of them, but since it does not seem to have any effect on Ekstrand, many Scandinavian researchers do not want to waste their time on corrections (personal communication with the ones mentioned above).

References

AIKIO, M. 1984, Some Issues in the Study of Language Shift in the Northern Calotte. Paper presented at the 7th World Congress of Applied Linguistics, Brussels, August 5–10, 1984.

ALLARDT, E. 1984, The Ecology of Multilingualism. Paper presented at the 4th Nordic Symposium on Bilingualism, Uppsala, June 5–7, 1984.

APPLE, M. 1980, Reproduction, Contestation and Curriculum. Occasional Papers 8. University of New York at Buffalo, Faculty of Educational Studies.

BAKER, K. & DE KANTER, A. 1981, Effectiveness of Bilingual Education. A Review of the Literature, Final Draft Report, Washington D.C: Office of Technical and Analytic Systems, U.S. Department of Education, September 25.

— 1982a, Federal Policy and the Effectiveness of Bilingual Education, revised draft manuscript for J. CUMMINS & T. SKUTNABB-KANGAS (eds), *Education of Linguistic Minority Children*. Clevedon, Avon: Multilingual Matters.

— 1982b, Recent Federal Policy Changes and Research in the United States, draft manuscript for J. CUMMINS & T. SKUTNABB-KANGAS (eds), *Education of Lingusitic Minority Children*. Clevedon, Avon: Multilingual Matters.

BULLIVANT, B. M. 1984, Ethnolinguistic Minorities and Multicultural Policy in Australia. In: J. EDWARDS (ed.), *Linguistic Minorities, Policies and Pluralism*, pp. 107–40.

CHURCHILL, S. 1983, *The Education of Linguistic and Cultural Minorities in OECD Countries*. Paris: OECD, Centre for Educational Research and Innovation.

— 1986, *The Education of Linguistic and Cultural Minorities in the OECD Countries*. Clevedon, Avon: Multilingual Matters.

CUMMINS, J. 1976, The Influence of Bilingualism on Cognitive Growth: A Synthesis of Research Findings and Explanatory Hypotheses. *Working Papers on Bilingualism*, 9, 1–43.

— 1977, Psycholinguistic Evidence, in Bilingual Education: Current Perspectives, Vol. 4, Education. Arlington, Virginia: Center for Applied Linguistics, 78–79.

— 1979, Linguistic Interdependence and the Educational Development of Bilingual Children. *Review of Educational Research*, 49, 222–51.

— 1980a, The Entry and Exit Fallacy in Bilingual Education. *NABE Journal*, IV: 3, 25–60.

— 1980b, The Cross-lingual Dimensions of Language Proficiency: Implications for Bilingual Education and the Optimal Age Question. *TESOL Quarterly*, 14.

— 1981, The Role of Primary Language Development in Promoting Educational Success for Language Minority Students, in Schooling and Language Minority Students. A Theoretical Framework. Sacramento, California: Office of Bilingual Bicultural Education, Department of Education, 3–49.

— 1983, Heritage Language Education. A Literature Review: Ontario Institute for Studies, in Education, in press.

— 1984a, *Bilingualism and Special Education: Issues in Assessment and Pedagogy*. Clevedon, Avon: Multilingual Matters.

— 1984b, Linguistic Minorities and Multicultural Policy in Canada. In: J. EDWARDS (ed.), *Linguistic Minorities, Policies and Pluralism*, pp. 81–105.

DRAKE, G. F. 1984, Problems of Language Planning in the United States. In: J. EDWARDS (ed.), *Linguistic Minorities, Policies and Pluralism*, pp. 141–49.

DUTCHER, N. 1982, The Use of First and Second Languages in Primary Education: Selected Case Studies. Washington D.C.: World Bank Staff Working Papers No. 504.

EDWARDS, J. 1984a, Introduction. In: J. EDWARDS (ed.), *Linguistic Minorities, Policies and Pluralism*, pp. 1–16.

— 1984b, Language, Diversity and Identity. In: J. EDWARDS (ed.), *Linguistic Minorities, Policies and Pluralism*, pp. 277–310.

— (ed.) 1984c, *Linguistic Minorities, Policies and Pluralism*. London: Academic Press.

EDWARDS, V. 1984, Language Policy in Multicultural Britain. In: J. EDWARDS (ed.), *Linguistic Minorities, Policies and Pluralism*, pp. 49–80.

EKSTRAND, L. H. 1978a, Fakta och fiktion i invandrardebatten. Exempel på faktorer som har samband med invandrarbarns språkinlärning. Malmö: Lärarhögskolan. Särtryck och småtryck nr 249.

— 1978b, Bilingual and Bicultural Adaptation. Doctoral Dissertation. University of Stockholm.

— 1978c, Migrant adaptation — a cross-cultural problem. In: R. FREUDENSTEIN (ed.), *Teaching the children of immigrants*. Bruxelles: AIMAV, Didier.

— 1979 (titel otydlig). Förslag och rekommendationer. Malmö 20.1.1979; stencil, 4 pp.

— 1983, Maintenance or transition — or both? A Review of Swedish Ideologies and Empirical Research. In: T. HUSÉN & S. OPPER (eds), *Multicultural and Multilingual Education in Immigrant Countries*. Oxford: Pergamon Press, 141–59.

HABERMAS, J. 1971, *Knkowledge and human interest*. Boston: Beacon Press.

HANSON, G. 1982a, The Position of the Second Generation of Finnish Immigrants in Sweden. In I. MUNICIO (ed.), SPLIT-Report, Vol. 1, Bilingualism. Models of Education and Migration Policies. *Commission for Immigration Research Report*, No. 1: 1. Stockholm: 129–141.

— 1982b, *Integration and Participation*. Paper presented at the 5th International School Psychology Colloquium. Stockholm: August 1–6.

HERNÁNDEZ-CHÁVEZ, E., LLANES, J., ALVAREZ, R. & ARVIZU, S. 1981, The Federal Policy toward Language and Education: Pendulum or Progress. A Response to the de Kanter/Baker Review. Sacramento: Cross Cultural Resource Center. Monograph No. 12, California State University.

JENCKS, C. *et al.*, 1979, *Who gets ahead?* New York: Basic Books.

KESKITALO, J. H. 1984, Samisk eller norsk? På søking etter forhold som påvirker språktilhørighet og skoletilbud i et språklig sammensatt miljø. Oslo: Statens spesiallaererhøgskole.

KNUBB-MANNINEN, G. 1982, Språksituationen bland eleverna i de svenskspråkiga grundskolorna. Reports from the Institute for Educational Research, University of Jyväskylä, 326.

— 1983, Elevernas språkprofil och syn på undervisningen i finska vid inträdet i mellanstadiet. Reports from the Institute for Educational Research, University of Jyväskylä, 340.

ÖHMAN, S. 1981a, Halvspråkighet som kastmärke. In Att leva med mångfalden. Stockholm: Liber Förlag, 193–204.

— 1981b, Vetenskap och populärvetenskap inom invandrarforskningen — en meditativ betraktelse. In: E. M. HAMBERG & T. HAMMAR (eds), *Invandringen och framtiden*. Stockhkolm: Liber Förlag, 189–97.

PAULSTON, C. B. 1976, Bilingual Education and its Evaluation: A Reaction Paper. In: *Bilingual Education: Current Perspectives*, Vol. Linguistics. Arlington, Virginia: Center for Applied Linguistics, 87–151.

1977, Theoretical Perspectives on Bilingual Education Programs. *Working Papers on Bilingualism*, 13, 130–77.

— 1981, Recent Developments in research on bilingual education in the United States. In: E. EJERHED & I. HENRYSSON (eds), *Tvåspråkighet*. Föredrag från tredje Nordiska Tvåspråkighetssymposiet 4–5 juni 1980. Acta Universitatis Umensis. Umeå Studies in Humanities 36. Umeå, 24–38.

— 1982, A Critical Review of the Swedish Research and Debate about Bilingualism and Bilingual Education in Sweden from an International Perspective. A Report to the National Swedish Board of Education, October 1982.

PAULSTON, C. B. & PAULSTON, R. 1977, Language and Ethnic Boundaries. In: T. SKUTNABB-KANGAS (ed.), *Papers from the First Scandinavian Conference on Bilingualism*. Department of Nordic Languages. University of Helsinki. Series B No. 2.

PAULSTON, R. 1976, *Conflicting theories of social and educational change: A Typographic Review*. University of Pittsburgh: University Center for International Studies Publications.

PETERSEN, R. 1978, *A Greenlandic Problem of lack of Intermediate Persons*. Paper prepared for Symposium Indigenous Anthropology in non-Western Countries, July 15–24. 1978, New York: Wenner-Gren Foundation for Anthropological research.

— 1981, On the Possibility of Minority Group to Use "Alternative Expertise". In: N. DITTMAR & P. KÖNIGER (eds), *Proceedings of the Second Scandinavian–German Symposium on the Language of Immigrant Workers and their Children*. Berlin: Freie Universität Berlin, Linguistische Arbeiten und Berichte, 19—29.

PEURA, M. & HUJANEN, T. 1983, Rapport om nordisk invandrarforskning. In: M. PEURA (ed.), *Invandrarminoriteter och demokratisk forskning*. Stockholm: Riksförbundet Finska Föreningar i Sverige, 148–215.

SKU 1983: 57, Olika ursprung, gemenskap i Sverige. Utbildning för språklig och kulturell mångfald. Huvudbetänkande av språk- och kulturarvsutredningen (SKU). Statens offentliga utredningar 1983: 57, Stockholm.

SKUTNABB-KANGAS, T. 1982a, Some prerequisites for learning the majority language — a comparison between different conditions. In: *Handlungsorienterung in Zweitspracherwerb von Arbeitsmigranten*. Hrsg. F. Januschek & W. Stölting. Osnabrücker Beiträge zur Sprachtheorie, 22, 63–95.

— 1982b, Bilingualism as an Unrealistic Goal in Minority Education. In: I. MUNICIO (ed.), *Bilingualism, Models of Education and Migration Policies*. Commission for Immigration Research, Sweden. SPLIT-Report Vol. 1, Stockholm: Liber Förlag, 56–82.

— 1983, Om metodologier, paradigm och ideologier i minoritetsutbildningsforskningen. In: M. PEURA (ed.), *Invandrarminoriteter och demokratisk forskning*. Stockholm: Riskförbundet Finska Föreninger i Sverige, 29–79.

— 1984a, Barns mänskliga språkliga rättigheter. Om finsk frigörelsekamp på den svenska skolfronten. Kritisk Psykologi 1–2, 1984, 38–46.

— 1984b *Bilingualism or Not — The Education of Minorities*. Clevedon, Avon: Multilingual Matters.

— 1984c, Vart försvann rasismen? *Invandrare och Minoriteter*, 1, 23–27.

— 1984d, Children of Guest Workers and Immigrants: Linguistic and Educational Issues. In: J. EDWARDS (ed.), *Linguistic Minorities, Policies and Pluralism*. London: Academic Press, pp. 17–48.

— in press, *Minoriteter, skola, språk*. Lund: Liber Förlag.

— forthcoming, Article in: T. SKUTNABB-KANGAS & J. CUMMINS (eds), *Education of Linguistic Minority Children*.

SKUTNABB-KANGAS, T. & PHILLIPSON, R. 1985, Cultilinguistic imperialism — what can Scandinavia learn from the Second and Third Worlds? In: T. SKUTNABB-KANGAS & R. PHILLIPSON (eds), *Educational Strategies in Multilingual Contexts*. ROLIG 35. Roskilde University Centre.

SKUTNABB-KANGAS, T. & TOUKOMAA, P. 1976, *Teaching Migrant Children's Mother Tongue and Learning the Language of the Host Country in the Context of the Socio-cultural Situation of the Migrant Family*. A Report prepared for Unesco, Tampere, Department of Sociology and Social Psychology, University of Tampere, Research Reports 15.

SMOLICZ, J. J. 1979, *Culture and Education in a Plural Society*. Canberra: Curriculum Development Centre, University of Adelaide.

— 1984, Education for a Cultural Democracy. A Summary, Report of The Task Force to Investigate Multiculturalism and Education. Report to the Minister of Education, June 1984, Adelaide, Australia (chairperson: J. J. Smolicz).

TINGBJÖRN, G. 1982, Immigrant Children and Bilingualism. In: I. MUNICIO (ed.), SPLIT-Report Vol. 1. Bilingualism. Models of Education and Migration Policies. Stockholm, Commission for Immigration Research, Report No. 1: 1, 105–25.

— forthcoming, Active Bilingualism — the Swedish goal for immigrant children's language instruction, manuscript for T. SKUTNABB-KANGAS & J. CUMMINS (eds), Education of Linguistic Minority Children. Clevedon, Avon: Multilingual Matters.

TOSI, A. 1984, Immigration and Bilingual Education. A case study of movement of population, language change and education within the EEC. Oxford: Pergamon Press.

TOUKOMAA, P. & SKUTNABB-KANGAS, T. 1977, The Intensive Teaching of the Mother Tongue to Migrant Children at Pre-school Age. A report prepared for Unesco, Tampere, Department of Sociology and Social Psychology, University of Tampere, Research Reports 26.

TROIKE, R. 1979, Research Findings Demonstrate the Effectiveness of Bilingual Education. Paper presented at the NABE meeting in Seattle, 1979.

11 Overcoming language barriers to education in a multilingual world

BERNARD SPOLSKY

One of the marks of modernism (perhaps its main feature) has been the enormous growth of cities and urban populations throughout the world, a phenomenon that has been even more marked over the last few decades. In 1950, demographers tell us, there were only seven urban centres with more than 5 million population: now there are 34, and by the year 2025, there could be over 90, 80 of them in emerging nations. In this chapter, I will focus on one seemingly small but in fact critical aspect of this process, the educational consequence of the linguistic patterning of large modern urban developments and its growing influence on smaller towns, as the city and its ways invade the countryside.

Look at the kind of changes that are occurring. London was once known as the centre from which standard English spread: now, it is estimated that fewer than 20% of the children coming to school there do so with any control over standard English. Toronto and Melbourne were not so many years ago considered the acme of homogeneity and monolingualism: now each is a vibrant example of complex multilingualism, and Melbourne boasts of being the largest Maltese speaking city in the world, and one of the largest for Greek, Italian and several other languages. When the educational authorities of the city of Chicago set out to start dealing with the problems of linguistic minorities, they developed a questionnaire that named 98 languages, using the 99th code for any others (and you may be sure there were others). But this complexity should not surprise: in a sociolinguistic survey we have been carrying out within the walls of the Old City of Jerusalem we have so far found speakers of over 30 different languages!

The first generalization that we can make then is that large cities tend to be linguistically complex. Cities are by their nature places where people from diverse backgrounds gather, bringing with them the language and culture and behaviour of the multitude of places from which they come; the wider the sources of origin, the more complex the current pattern is likely to be. A second force for maintaining diversity is within the city itself: its very complexity requires that its residents live in separate neighbourhoods, and the fact that so many of its inhabitants come from different backgrounds makes it natural that in their first settlement in the city at least they should seek to live in a neighbourhood with others with similar background and language. In addition to these driving forces for diversity, there are other factors: the complexity of occupational roles, the necessity for specialization, and the consequent development of socially and economic distinct groups each tending to spend its non-working life among its peers lead naturally to the development of socially distinct language varieties as well as socially distinct ways of behaviour. Finally, the differential need for education and for control of the educationally-valued variety of language means that the population of a city is divided in the values it attaches to the autonomous style of verbalization associated with school.

These four dimensions work individually and in combination to produce a potential language barrier to education for sections of the population: unless this barrier can be overcome, there can be no equality of opportunity or equity in education, and excellence is likely to be restricted to an elite and denied to the majority. Let me first look at each of the kinds of linguistic difference that we find in cities, and note the special problems it poses to those who are responsible for education.

The barrier of different languages

The first kind of difference is the simplest to recognize, for it is marked by the fact that each variety is a distinct language, with a recognized name. Thus, it is easy to recognize that cities like Brussels and Montreal will need to allow for two different languages in their educational programme, for each city is known to be bilingual with distinct populations using the two languages. Similarily, a city with a large number of immigrants will recognize that the immigrant children have a potential linguistic problem. When the growing school system of the new Jewish population in Eretz Israel decided to use Hebrew as the language of instruction, it recognized that for many children learning of the language would start in school; and as the State of Israel has worked to assimilate its huge numbers of immigrants, the need to teach Hebrew has been in the forefront of attention.

Knowing that the problem is there is not enough, but it is a good starting point, as the sad fate of many children treated as mentally retarded because they do not speak the language of the school attests. There are various approaches, ranging from the malign neglect of submersion programmes through the full care of maintenance bilingual programmes. All assume as a primary goal the learning of the language (or occasionally, languages) selected by the school system as the medium of teaching.

How should this school-selected language be characterized? It is marked generally by certain distinctive features, which even if they do not actually exist, are inevitably assumed to be present. First, it has all the properties of what sociolinguistics characterize as a standard language (Fishman, 1974: 1639): fundamental is a widespread belief that there exists a "standard" or "correct" version of the language, hopefully the version recorded in the dictionaries and grammar books used by the school, and theoretically reflecting the usage of the best writers and thinkers of the present and past. I say hopefully and theoretically, for as anyone who has studied normativism knows, it is rare that there will be agreement even among the experts as to what constitutes this standard variety. It is not uncommon that a situation develops, as it has with modern Hebrew, where while the general public agrees with the self-proclaimed purists that there is a correct grammar, no one can show where or what it is; rather, there are a large number of idiosyncratically decreed shibboleths. (Rabin, 1983). A second critical feature of a school language is that, like a standard language, it is believed to be independent, autonomous, not a modified version dependent on some other language; it is not in other words a dialect. (Fishman, 1974: 1639). This reminds one of the definition of a language as a dialect with an army and a flag behind it. As long as the immigrants in South Africa thought they were speaking a dialect of Dutch, they were restrained from teaching their own variety; once they knew they spoke Afrikaans, they could proclaim its value as a school language. Similar difficulties face many new nations in their choice of a language for school. Of course a school system may choose to use a language from elsewhere, but it is reluctant to teach what it considers a dialect: witness the resistance to anything but standard British or American varieties of English in foreign teaching of the language.

Thirdly, a school language, like a standard language, has historicity: a sense that it it associated with some Great Tradition, whether national or religious or intellectual: it is believed, in other words, to be the language of a culture of major importance, although the culture need not be the one that is most widespread among the population from which the school draws its pupils (Fishman, 1974: 1640).

The fourth characteristic of a standard language is vitality, the existence of native speakers, of people who grow up speaking it and learn it from their parents. (Fishman, 1974: 1640). In fact, this is not usually the case with school languages: it is indeed my argument in this chapter that such a state of affairs is quite rare, that it is the exceptional case for a child to come to school having learned at home the specific language, regional and class variety, and kind of language that the school favours.

The barrier of different dialects

When the language of home and school are clearly distinct, as when new immigrants to Israel come to schools that teach in Hebrew, the problem should be clear to all involved. But it is much less clear in the second kind of situation, when the language of the home is considered to be a dialect of the standard language used in school. Dialects are generally reflections of geographical differences, but they may also mark religious, ethnic or social variety. I will consider this last kind of variety separately, and concentrate for the moment on the first set. By its nature, the city gathers into it people from various parts of a country: when they arrive they bring with them a marked way of speaking that can cause at least two kinds of problem. The first arises out of actual differences between the varieties: real phonological differences, different lexical items, different semantic systems, and even more, different pragmatic rules, can all lead to real misunderstandings. (Labov, 1966; Milroy, 1984). But in fact the major redundancies built into natural language mean that such misunderstanding is usually no more than a source of momentary confusion and has its main function in jokes. More serious are the potential attitudinal effects of dialect differences, where stereotypes determine treatment of people from certain parts of the country (Edwards & Giles, 1984).

A particularly challenging situation is set up where there is the kind of dialect situation that Ferguson (1959) called diglossia: the existence side by side of two related versions of a language, one not usually spoken natively but accepted for public and intellectual functions, and the other used in most daily life activities. The classical case of this is Arabic, where local varieties (however educated and prestigious their speakers may be) all take a second place to the Classical language required to be used for higher functions including writing. A good way to appreciate this is to look at the face of a speaker of Arabic who is asked to write down a sentence he has used in normal spoken Arabic. Typically, these diglossic situations lead to an educational pattern in which only the H or classical variety is taught in school, although the teaching naturally takes place in the L or local dialect.

The barrier of social class dialects

The third kind of difference is similar to the second, for social dialects function much like regional ones: they create not so much linguistic misunderstanding as social judgements. Studies in the US and in Europe have shown us the existence of these socially distinct varieties within cities. We see that not only do people tend to talk like the members of their social class, but that in many situations they tend to talk like the people with whom they deal: thus one classic study has shown that department store staff used language that reflected the social class of their customers (Labov, 1966) and another has documented a case of a travel agent whose pronunciation varies according to the customer (Coupland, 1984).

What is most critical in this phenomenon is the attribution of value to social variety: in spite of the structural linguist's rather naive claim that all languages are equal, it is generally the case that all varieties are differentially valued. Bell (1984) in a recent paper has elegantly demonstrated that individual stylistic variation is a reflex of community social variation, proposing that stylistic variation can be characterized as audience design: a speaker changes his way of speaking according to a present (or absent but significant) audience, in accordance with the values he places on converging with or diverging from this audience. From the educator's point of view, the critical issue is once again one of attitude: the self fulfilling prophecy of those who will categorize students by their accents as bright or stupid.

The barrier of preferred style of verbalization

The fourth dimension of difference is one that is less easy to characterize, for it does not seem to have the clear linguistic marks of the variety differences I have been talking about so far: it does not show up in phonology or grammar or even pragmatics, but rather in the highest level of discourse. I am referring to a culturally and socially determined preference for what I am most comfortable calling, in Kay's terms, autonomous verbalization. It is a phenomenon that has been most deeply and controversially studied by Basil Bernstein, who, I am sure would be the first to admit, shares in difficulties of naming the phenomenon. Let me try to explain the issue in my own words.

Language starts, as Elizabeth Bates (1976) has pointed out, unspecialized as to channel: young children start off using physical gestures and oral signals equally, but are usually encouraged to develop their verbal rather than their gestural skills for the main task of communication. Spoken language continues however to make considerable use of non-verbal means, whether in gesture or intonation. Because language is a social phenomenon, the efficiency of communication depends on what is shared between speaker and listener. One obvious thing that is shared is the grammar and the lexicon. A second is the pragmatic system, rules for language use which help explain how we understand that what looks like a statement like "The salt is at your end of the table." is a request. A third is a physical context. A fourth is a shared knowledge of the world. Without any of these, communication is difficult. Conversely, the more that is shared, the simpler communication is.

The phenomenon that Bernstein has drawn to our attention is a socially valued (and, as he has argued, transmitted) tendency to prefer communication with maximum or minimum extra-linguistic support, ranging along a continuum from a breakfast table grunt asking a child to pass the butter to let us say a history book. Consider the differences on the criteria I have mentioned: because the father has just taken a piece of toast and is pointing with his knife at the butter plate (physical context including gesture, and shared knowledge of the fact that one puts butter on the toast), the verbal load can be minimal. The historian on the other hand is writing, without shared physical context, for strangers whose general knowledge he will find difficult to guess at. Thus, he deliberately cultivates a style which puts maximum emphasis on verbal communication.

What Bernstein has pointed out to us is the relationship of social facts to this pattern; he has further demonstrated that there are social structures that favour each kind of verbalization, producing in certain cases that he has studied a social class associated differentiation in verbal style. Further, he has pointed out that modern Westernized education with its emphasis on reading and writing is heavily biased towards autonomous verbalization, producing thus particular problems for children from certain classes.

I do not have time in this short chapter to do justice to this fascinating idea, nor to consider its basic complexity. That it is oversimplified does not detract from its importance, nor does the fact that it needs to be balanced and refined by considering the implications of other kinds of literacy and education than the general modern Western tradition (I think of the very different model inherent in Yeshiva learning, based on the mediated literacy of traditional Judaism). What is important for us is that there will commonly exist a major gap between the style of verbalization encouraged by the home and that demanded by the school, adding one more to the language barriers faced by children coming to school.

Misdiagnosing language problems

There are then these four potential language barriers that can face children coming to school, and that will most commonly block the access to equal education for children in the growing cities of the world: first, that their language is not the same as the language of the school; second, that their regional or religous or ethnic dialect is not that of the school; third, that their social dialect is different from that favoured by the school; and fourth, that their socially or culturally determined preference for verbal style is different from that cultivated by the school. Even more seriously, the existence of these four separate causes, each with potentially different treatments, can be confounded and lead to an early mislabelling of pupils as uneducable. For it is one of the special features of modern mass education that it encourages the belief that it has the last word not just on how to do things but on what should be done: that it believes that only the language it wants to teach exists; that it acts as though only its style of verbalization is possible.

For we must distinguish between what I would characterize as a healthy additive approach to language education and a damaging replacive approach. We have ample evidence of the possibilities and value of additive approaches: I mention the successful French immersion programmes for anglophone Canadians, the traditional teaching of Loshn Koydesh to Yiddish speakers in Eastern European communities, the addition of High German to the linguistic repertoire of Swiss Germans or of English to the linguistic repertoire of Scandinavians. But replacive language teaching, an approach that assumes there is something wrong with the language brought to school by the child, is a much different matter. Learning a second language is not easy at the best of times, for it requires not just time and effort but a willingness to be open to completely new ways of thinking about and even perceiving things that are intimately tied up with one's personality; being forced to learn a second language that is intended to replace one's first language is a direct assault on identity.

The solution to the problems set up by the language barriers to education is far from easy, for it involves dealing with some of the most basic issues in school and in the wider society it serves. For by its nature, language is a core factor in any education, for education depends on communication and verbal coding of human knowledge. Nor can dealing with language issues alone solve social problems. But until the existence of the language barriers to education have been recognized and their working carefully analyzed, there is no chance of successful steps to overcome the barriers and provide equal educational opportunities for all.

Towards a responsible and feasible language education policy

In arriving at a responsible and feasible policy for language and education, there are two basic principles, often competing in their application, that must be taken into account. The first concerns the rights of individual members of a society to equality of educational opportunity; the second concerns the rights of individuals and groups in a multilingual community to maintain, if they choose, their own linguistic varieties. I will look at each in turn, and then consider conflicts.

Equality of educational opportunity has two complementary parts to it. The first is the right, wherever feasible, to be educated in the variety of language one learned at home, or at a basic minimum when this is not feasible, to be educated in a school that shows full respect for that variety and its strengths and potentials. Such a principle then supports either mother tongue education (wherever it is reasonably achievable) or some form of additive (not replacive) bilingual education. The second is the right to learn in the best way feasible the standard or official language or languages of wider communication selected for the society as a whole. A mother tongue education programme which denies access to the standard language (as seems to be the aim with some European guest worker programmes, and as is a common source of fear of bilingual education) is no more acceptable than a submersion programme that rejects the mother tongue. Note that in some cases there may be more than one official language, adding further educational burdens to the curriculum just like those that are provided by the need for other additional foreign languages.

When there is more than one official language, we have a degree of social recognition of the significance of the multilingual setting, but language education policy does not always follow from this. There would be good grounds to argue that social ends are best served by setting as the main second educational language any other major offical language: thus, in Israel one would expect Arabic rather than English to be the major second language taught, and in New Zealand Maori rather than French. But in many cases, pragmatic needs or educational traditions are in fact stronger than these social values.

The second major principle recognizes the right of the individual or the group to do whatever is possible to preserve or strengthen varieties of language that have important ethnic, traditional, cultural, or religious values for them. The application of this principle will of course vary, according to the value assigned by individuals and groups to the variety and according to the value assigned by society as a whole to the acceptance of multiculturalism. Thus, we may have an individual immigrant in an otherwise homogenously monolingual society (or one with those values at least) who considers his immigrant language sufficiently important to continue to speak it at home; the social responsibility under the equity principle then calls for a language education policy that will teach the standard language without destroying the basis for this home policy. A group of immigrants, an ethnic or a religious group, may band together to provide at their own expense and in their free-time education in an ethnic or religious language for their own community. A society valuing heterogeneity and multiculturalism will be prepared to provide support for such initiative within the framework of the school curriculum. At its very least, this principle rejects outright governmental action against such programmes, as for instance the present Soviet persecution of Hebrew language teachers and teaching.

These two straightforward principles, because of the complexity of situations in which they apply and because of the complexity of factors that come to affect them (see Spolsky, 1978), can lead in actual fact to a large number of possible policies, but at the same time (and this I believe is their real importance) they make clear the irresponsibility of other policies that flout them. They help us in other words to judge how well a policy meets the challenges of the various language barriers, provide a basic measure of the fitness and justice of a particular language education policy, and show how we might avoid some of the worst effects of linguistic insensitivity. They underly the various positions that have been presented in this volume; the disagreements that have appeared often result from different weight given to the two principles rather than fundamental differences in analysis. While it is clear that scientific analysis is seldom sufficient to deal with real life problems, it is a necessary first step.

References

BATES, E. 1976, *Language and context: the acquisition of pragmatics*. New York: Academic Press.

BELL, A. 1984, Language style as audience design. *Language in Society*, 13, 2, 145–205.

BERNSTEIN, B. 1971, *Classes, codes, and control*. Volume 1. London: Routledge and Kegan Paul.

COUPLAND, N. 1984, Accommodation at work: some phonological data and their implications. *International Journal of the Sociology of Language*, 46, 49–70.

EDWARDS, J. & GILES, H. 1984, Applications of the social psychology of language: sociolinguistics and education. In: P. TRUDGILL (ed.), *Applied Sociolinguistics*. London: Academic Press.

FERGUSON, C. A. 1959, Diglossia. *Word*, 15, 325–40.

FISHMAN, J. A. 1974, The Sociology of Language. In: T. A. SEBEOK *et al. (eds), Current Trends in Linguistics*. The Hauge: Mouton, pp. 1629–1784.

KAY, P. 1977, Language education and speech style. In: B. BLOUNT & M. SANCHEZ (eds), *Sociocultural dimensions of language change*. New York: Academic Press.

LABOV, W. 1966, *The social stratification of New York English*. Washington, DC: Center for Applied Linguistics.

MILROY, L. 1984, Comprehension and context: successful communication and communication breakdown. In: P. TRUDGILL (ed.), *Applied Sociolinguistics.* London: Academic Press.

RABIN, C. 1983, The sociology of normativism in Israeli Hebrew. *International Journal of the Sociology of Language.* 41, 41–56.

SPOLSKY, B. 1978, A model for the evaluation of bilingual education. *International Review of Education*, 3, 347–60.

Notes on Contributors

Hugh Africa teaches in the University of Zambia.

Richard A. Benton is Head of the Maori Language Unit of the New Zealand Council for Educational Research; his publications include *The Flight of the Amokura: Oceanic languages and formal education in the South Pacific.*

M. N. Guboglo is a researcher in the Institute of Ethnography of the Soviet Academy of Sciences.

Barry McLaughlin teaches in the Department of Psychology of the University of California-Santa Cruz.

Melanie Mikes carries out research in linguistics and teaches postgraduate students at the University of Novi Sad, Yugoslavia.

D. P. Pattanayak is Jawaharlal Nehru Fellow and Director of the Central Institute of Indian Languages, Mysore, President of the Indian Council of Communication Research and Training, and member of the Indian Council of Social Science Research. His publications include *Multilingualism and Mother Tongue Education.*

Christina Bratt Paulston is Professor and Chairman of General and Applied Linguistics at the University of Pittsburgh. She has recently published *Swedish Research and debate about bilingualism.*

Robert Phillipson is Associate Professor of English and Languages Pedagogy at Roskilde University Center, Denmark, and author of *Learner language and language learning.*

Tove Skutnabb-Kangas is guest researcher at Roskilde University Center, Denmark, and co-chair of the AILA Scientific Commission on Language and Education in Multilingual Settings and her published works include *Bilingualism or not: the education of minorities.*

J. J. Smolicz teaches in the Department of Education in the University of Adelaide, Australia.

Bernard Spolsky is Professor of English at Bar-Ilan University, Israel and co-chair of the AILA Scientific Commission on Language and Education in Multilingual Settings. His published works include *Frontiers of Bilingual Education*.

Index

194